W9-ATU-539

By taking a reflexive engagement approach to the study of organizational change, the authors show why conventional organization development orientations are limited and provide new breakthrough insights about how to lead systemic change and development in today's environment.

Abraham B. Shani, Professor, California Polytechnic State University, USA

This book provides a powerful systems approach to formulate and implement strategic change. The authors develop a practical framework that makes it possible to break down and evaluate the complex aspects of strategic choice in large organizations operating in a chaotic world. As CEO of Philadelphia Insurers I have used the framework several times, including the decision to take the company public and, later on, when considering Tokio Marine's acquisition offer. The framework was extremely helpful in both occasions.

James Maguire, Founder of Philadelphia Insurers, USA

ORGANIZATIONAL CHANGE AND STRATEGY

Organizations change, usually driven by strategies, yet strategic management and organizational change are generally understood as separate domains in the business world. This book integrates the behavioural dynamics of learning, change and strategy at and across individual, team, interdepartmental, group and organizational levels.

This new edition emphasizes what can be done in organizations to enable strategy to be effective and to help organizations to change and learn. Central to the book is a reflexive engagement approach through inviting the readers to apply concepts to their own organizational situations and via reflective exercises. The authors also offer cases from a wide range of organizations, from universities to steel and digital businesses.

This practical book addresses managers, consultants, students and researchers and provides specific orientation to assist each readership group to learn from its own perspective.

David Coghlan is Professor Emeritus of Organisation Development at the Trinity Business School Dublin, Ireland.

Nicholas S. Rashford President Emeritus and University Professor of Management at Saint Joseph's University, Philadelphia, USA.

João Neiva de Figueiredo is Associate Professor of Management at Saint Joseph's University, Philadelphia, USA and Senior Fellow at the University of Pennsylvania's Wharton School, USA.

ORGANIZATIONAL CHANGE AND STRATEGY

An interlevel dynamics approach

Second edition

David Coghlan, Nicholas S. Rashford and
João Neiva de Figueiredo

LONDON AND NEW YORK

Second edition published 2016
by Routledge
2 Park Square, Milton Park, Abingdon, Oxon OX14 4RN

and by Routledge
711 Third Avenue, New York, NY 10017

Routledge is an imprint of the Taylor & Francis Group, an informa business

© 2016 David Coghlan, Nicholas S. Rashford and João Neiva de Figueiredo

The right of David Coghlan, Nicholas S. Rashford and João Neiva de Figueiredo
to be identified as authors of this work has been asserted by them in accordance
with sections 77 and 78 of the Copyright, Designs and Patents Act 1988.

British Library Cataloguing in Publication Data
A catalogue record for this book is available from the British Library

Library of Congress Cataloging in Publication Data
Coghlan, David, author.
  Organizational change and strategy : an interlevel dynamics approach / David
Coghlan, Nicholas S. Rashford and João Neiva de Figueiredo. – 2nd edition.
    pages cm
  Includes bibliographical references and index.
  1. Organizational change. 2. Communication in organizations. I. Rashford,
Nicholas S., author. II. Figueiredo, João Neiva de, author. III. Title.
    HD58.8.C6 2016
    658.4'06–dc23
          2015029625

ISBN: 978-1-138-91168-0 (hbk)
ISBN: 978-1-138-91169-7 (pbk)
ISBN: 978-1-315-69248-7 (ebk)

Typeset in Bembo
by Taylor & Francis Books

CONTENTS

FIGURES

TABLES

PREFACE TO THE SECOND EDITION

As in the first edition, this second edition book brings together three typically distinct and separated fields: organizational behaviour and organization development (OD), strategy formulation and implementation, and organizational learning. The broad framework for the book's set-up derives from understanding organizations as adaptive complex learning systems and from viewing the process of organizing through intentional strategic action as necessarily encompassing several layers of subsystems. There recently has been an evolution in the management literature on strategy formulation, implementation, organizational learning and change. One reason for this evolution is the ever-changing conditions in which organizations find themselves in the modern complex global environment. Another reason is the self-understanding of organizations that has developed in recent decades. New approaches to planning view organizations as complex adaptive learning systems and increasingly draw on biology and complexity theory, particularly theories of self-organization, therefore going beyond the more mechanistic approaches which had dominated strategic thinking in the latter decades of the twentieth century.

A particular thrust of this second edition is the emphasis on what we are calling 'reflexive engagement' whereby we ground engagement with the three fields of organizational behaviour and organization development (OD), strategy formulation and implementation, and organizational learning in a process of critical examination based on the action learning work of Reginald Revans and the clinical inquiry approach of Edgar Schein. As in the first edition we invite readers to question the material in the light of their experience of an organization with which they are familiar and, by means of exercises at the end of each chapter, to extend their learning beyond theoretical understanding to learning-in-action.

The book targets four specific audiences. First, company leaders (CEOs, presidents, general managers) with final budgetary responsibility who are struggling to make informed decisions as they manage scarce resources in the face of an ever-changing external context. Second, organizational members (i.e. those not in senior management positions), whose careers benefit not only from understanding the organization's strategic direction, but also from participating to the extent possible (both directly and indirectly) in the strategy formulation and implementation process. Third, organization development consultants who are called in to help senior organization leaders understand trends, develop learning organizations, and effect meaningful change. Finally, the book also targets students, especially those who undertake their studies in conjunction with working in an organization, either in full-time employment or on placement and who can bring their experience to dialogue with the material in this book. We invite each of these audiences to engage with the theory and practice contained in these pages from within their own context and perspective.

CONTRIBUTORS

David Coghlan is Fellow and Professor Emeritus of Trinity Business School, Trinity College Dublin, Ireland. He specializes in organization development and action research and is active in both communities internationally. He has published over 100 articles and book chapters. Recent co-authored books include: *Doing Action Research in Your Own Organization* (Sage, 4th edn, 2014) and *Collaborative Strategic Improvement through Network Action Learning* (Edward Elgar, 2011). He is co-editor of the *SAGE Encyclopedia of Action Research* (2014), the four volume set, *Fundamentals of Organization Development* (Sage, 2010), and the proposed four volume set, *Action Research in Business and Management* (Sage, 2016). He is currently on the editorial boards of: *Journal of Applied Behavioral Science*, *Action Research*, *Action Learning: Research and Practice* and *Systemic Practice and Action Research*, among others.

Nicholas Rashford is University Professor Emeritus of Management at Saint Joseph's University, Philadelphia and was President and CEO from 1986 to 2003. He was formerly Dean of the School of Management at Rockhurst University, Kansas City. He holds a B.S. degree in Urban Sociology and an M.A. in Theology from Saint Louis University. He also holds an S.M. from MIT's Sloan School of Management and a Sc.D. in Behavioral Science from Johns Hopkins University. He was Visiting Professor of Management at Universidad Alberto Hurtado in Santiago, Chile and Visiting Professor at Trinity College in Dublin, Ireland. He is a former Chairman of the Delaware River Port Authority and a Commissioner of the Philadelphia Regional Port Authority. He has consulting experiences with companies such as AT&T, Butler Manufacturing, Blue Cross Blue Shield, Equitable Trust, and The Philadelphia Insurance Company.

João Neiva de Figueiredo is Associate Professor in the Department of Management at Saint Joseph's University's Haub School of Business and has been a Senior

Fellow at the University of Pennsylvania's Wharton School since 2009. His research and teaching focus on business strategy and organizational sustainability and he has published extensively in these areas. In addition, he co-edited the books *Green Products: Perspectives on Innovation and Adoption* and *Green Power: Perspectives on Sustainable Electricity Generation*. With over 20 years' experience in international business prior to his academic career, Dr. Neiva was a consultant at McKinsey & Company, a Vice President at Goldman Sachs, and a partner at JPMorgan Partners. Dr. Neiva holds Electrical and Systems Engineering degrees from Rio de Janeiro's PUC, an M.SC. in Systems Engineering from the Federal University of Rio de Janeiro, an MBA with high distinction (*Baker Scholar*) from the Harvard Business School, and an M.A. in Economics and a Ph.D. in Business Economics from Harvard University's Graduate School of Arts and Sciences.

ACKNOWLEDGEMENT

We are grateful to colleagues, friends, clients and participants on our courses with whom we have discussed our ideas and who supported and challenged them. David thanks Rami Shani and Paul Coughlan for their friendship and colleagueship.

We are very grateful to the groups with which we have worked and who contributed to testing the frameworks as they reflected on their own experience and worked enacting change in organizations. Nicholas and João thank the graduate students in the Saint Joseph's University who over the years have participated in countless live cases and have taught us more than we taught them. We also want to thank the entrepreneurs and business people cited throughout the book, whose openness allowed us to teach from their challenges as well as their successes. This book would be weaker without the illustrations they generously provided. In addition to all the gratitude we have for those who were acknowledged in the first edition, we would like to mention a few people without whom the second edition would not have been finalized. Anthony Hayek provided invaluable help with graphics: his professionalism, good cheer, and willingness to go the extra mile are sincerely appreciated. Jeannine Kinney provided unwavering logistical support throughout and we are very grateful for her ever-positive attitude. Nicholas would like to acknowledge Michael Magree, who was an inspiration throughout the difficult process of academic writing.

We thank Bill Torbert for permission to draw on his work and Christian Haub for his generosity and willingness to present the A&P case.

David and Nicholas owe a deep debt to their intellectual mentors, Ed Schein and the late Dick Beckhard and Chris Argyris who formed a sense of process and a spirit of inquiry in us that has transformed both our lives.

We acknowledge the invaluable help and support of the Routledge editorial and production teams, especially Terry Clague, Sinead Waldron and Ruth Bradley.

PART I

Setting up

Reflexive engagement, levels and interlevels

In Part I, comprising four chapters, we provide foundations for the approach to learning and to studying organizing which we use throughout. First we propose a reflexive approach to engaging with this book in which you are invited to confront what you read with your day-to-day experience, to discern possibilities, and to test hypotheses through action which will lead to learning and to new experiences. Chapter 2 provides some templates which help you benefit the most from the experience of reading this book. Chapter 3 introduces the framework of organizational levels as four modes of behaviour in the process of organizing. These four levels are: the individual, the team, the interdepartmental group and the organization. We present the four organizational levels as essential for understanding the dynamic inter-relationship between individuals, teams, aggregations of teams and an organization's strategic endeavours in a complex world of discontinuous change. Finally, in Chapter 4 we go on to show how the four organizational levels are implicitly interconnected. Each level is linked to each of the others. We argue that an understanding of this interconnectedness is essential for the manager or consultant in assessing the workings of each level and in preparing and implementing interventions.

1

AN INVITATION TO REFLEXIVE ENGAGEMENT

> There can be no learning without action and no (sober and deliberate) action without learning. Those unable to change themselves cannot change those around them.
>
> *Reginald Revans (2011)*

This chapter introduces you to the learning approaches that underpin this book. We are taking a reflexive engagement approach to this book whereby we invite you, the reader, to reflect on your own situation in light of the concepts and case situations presented and see how they inform your own assessment of what is going on in your organizational setting and what action you might plan to take. The methodological framework under which you may be doing this may have different titles, for example: action research (Coghlan and Brannick, 2014), action learning (Revans, 2011), clinical inquiry (Schein, 1987), developmental action inquiry (Torbert, 2004), experiential learning (Kolb, 1984), reflexive inquiry (Oliver, 2005), to name a few. While we are using the term, reflexive engagement, we are using it inclusively to cover the many applications of reflexive, action-oriented approaches that exist.

By taking a reflexive engagement approach in this book we mean that we invite you the reader, whether you are a senior manager, a non-executive organizational member, an external OD consultant or a student not only to understand the concepts developed in this book, but to question what is going on around you, both inside and outside the organization. This questioning is supported by the concepts which help you make sense of your experience and then engage in action, evaluate outcomes, reflect on learning and develop knowledge. We recommend that you not do this on your own or keep your reflections private, but that you engage relevant others in conversations and shared reflections.

Inquiry can be focused outward (e.g. what is going on in the organization, in the team, etc.) or inward (e.g. what is going on in you). Throughout the book we outline some conceptual frameworks that provide a basis for understanding organizational processes, which then are utilized for outward-focused inquiry and reflection. The reflexive engagement activities at the end of many of the chapters enable you to reflect on an organization with which you are familiar. Indeed, we invite you, wherever and whenever possible, to engage in these reflective activities on the same organization throughout the book so as to build up your analytic skills. If you are external to the organization, either as an OD consultant or a student, then your reflections are in collaboration with colleagues or with local managers. The vignettes within chapters and the cases at the end of chapters provide illustrations and aim to provoke further reflection and discussion.

Reflexive engagement is grounded in the inquiry-reflection process. Schon's (1983) notion of the 'reflective practitioner' captures the essentials of knowing-in-action and reflection-in-action. Knowing-in-action is tacit and opens up questions that fall within the boundaries of what you have learned to treat as normal. Reflection-in-action occurs when you are in the middle of an action and you ask questions about what you are doing and what is happening around you. The outcome is immediate as it leads to an on-the-spot adjustment of your thinking and of your action. As Kahneman (2011) demonstrates, catching how your mind works is an exciting adventure.

Reflexive engagement

At the heart of this book is Revans' famous learning formula, $L=P+Q$ (Revans, 2011). L stands for learning, P for programmed knowledge (i.e. current knowledge in use, already known, that which is codified in books, and that which prescribes solutions) and Q for questioning insight. The concept of *programmed knowledge* relates to technical expertise, functional specialism and the fruits of research and instruction. P typically includes a basis for the analysis of a problem in terms of what was done before. This book contains a lot of P in the theories of behaviour, change and strategy. However, to follow the guidance of P in an unquestioning way may be foolhardy. For Revans, P is insufficient for learning. Questioning insight (Q) involves asking fresh questions, unfreezing underlying assumptions, and creating new connections and mental models. Q challenges both the usefulness of programmed knowledge (P) to the current situation and the ignorance of the participants. Questioning others both admits to lack of knowledge and increases the scope of the search for solutions. It also carries the potential for new insight into the current state.

Underpinning this approach to learning is a distinction between and among different kinds of issues. Revans distinguished between puzzles and problems. *Puzzles* are those difficulties for which a correct solution exists and which are amenable to specialist and expert advice. *Problems*, on the other hand, are difficulties where no single solution can possibly exist. Most complex organizational issues of behaviour, change and strategy fall into the category of a problem, as there is no single solution while there are likely to be many opinions as to what the preferred course of action might be. For Revans, puzzles were difficulties from which escapes were thought to be known and, therefore, amenable to solution by programmed knowledge. If the task is to solve a puzzle, then $L=P$. The experts solve it! However, if the task is to solve or ameliorate a problem, then, for Revans, $L=P+Q$ and learning always begins with Q.

In inviting you to engage your learning in terms of $L=P+Q$, we lay the foundations in this opening chapter by first introducing the notion of taking a clinical perspective that works to make sense of what is going on in an organization. Second, we describe the process of knowing and learning and thereby introduce a method (reflexive engagement) that you can use throughout the book. Third, we relate learning to three practices: engaging in self-learning (first person), working collaboratively with others (second person), and being able to generalize one's learning for an impersonal audience (third person). Reflexive engagement helps you to understand our intentions, to enhance your capacity to plan and develop strategies that reflect your aspirations, to reflect on the skills of your implementation, and to see the impact of your actions.

Taking the clinical perspective

Edgar Schein (1987) writes about taking what he calls a 'clinical perspective'. This he describes as six activities, which we are adopting to engage with the behavioural, change and strategic issues we explore throughout the book (Schein, 1997):

1. In-depth observation of crucial cases of learning and change. Here you are invited to think about what you understand as critical incidents and study what happened, why and to what effect.
2. Studying the effects of interventions. Here you observe what happens when individuals and groups (especially management) do something, i.e. you frame a new strategic direction or introduce new procedures for dealing with customers.
3. Focusing on pathologies and post-mortems as a way of building a theory of health. Here you can look back on incidents and ask critical questions as to how these incidents inhibit the organization from functioning effectively.
4. Focusing on problems and anomalies that are difficult to explain. What puzzles you?
5. Building theory and empirical knowledge through developing concepts which capture the real dynamics of the organization. Here you link your experience and understanding to your reading and to relevant theory that helps you explain what is happening.
6. Focusing on the characteristic of systems and systemic dynamics. In your study of organizations you learn to go beyond blaming individuals and develop insight into how an organization works as a system.

This clinical approach gives focus to the learning formula, $L=P+Q$ as it sharpens the questioning when confronting problems, and engages that questioning with knowledge of organizational behaviour, change and strategy so as to generate learning and change.

Knowing and learning

The structure of human knowing is a three-step heuristic process: experience, understanding and judgement (Lonergan, 1992; Coghlan, 2012). First, we attend to our experience. Then we ask questions about our experience and receive an insight (understanding) and we follow that up by reflecting and weighing up the evidence to determine whether our insight fits the evidence or not (judgement). The pattern of these three operations is invariant in that it applies to all settings of cognitional activity, whether solving a crossword clue, addressing an everyday problem or engaging in scientific research.

Experiencing

Experience is an interaction of inner and outer events, or data of sense and data of consciousness. You can not only see, hear, smell, taste and touch, imagine, remember, feel and think but you can also experience yourself as seeing, hearing, thinking, feeling, remembering and imagining. In the context of being a manager, a non-executive organizational member, an OD consultant or a student, you experience events in the organization and you experience yourself having thoughts and feelings about these events and about your thoughts about having these thoughts.

Understanding

Experiences evoke questioning. What was that noise? What did it mean? What is going on? When you ask questions you receive answers (though not necessarily immediately). We are calling these answers insights. An insight is an act of understanding that grasps the intelligible connections between things that previously have appeared disparate. An insight goes beyond descriptive experience to an explanatory organization of the experience's possible meaning.

Judging, or exercising judgement

While insights are common; they are not always accurate or true. The question then is, does the insight fit the evidence? This opens up a question for reflection. Is it so? Yes or no? Maybe. You don't know. You need more evidence to be sure. The shift in attention turns to a verification-oriented inquiry for possible accuracy, sureness and certainty of understanding. So you move to a new level of the cognitional process, where you marshal and weigh evidence and assess its sufficiency. You set the judgement up conditionally; if the conditions have been fulfilled, then it must be true or accurate. There may be conflicting judgements and you may have to weigh the evidence and choose between them. If you do not think that you have sufficient evidence to assert that your insight fits the data then you can postpone judgement or make a provisional judgement and correct it later when you have more or other evidence.

Human knowing is not any of these three operations on their own. All knowing involves experiencing, understanding and judging.

Knowing in the physical world may be straightforward enough. You may be able to verify easily that your experience of your head getting wet means that it is indeed raining. But when you try to know the world of human behaviour and organizational engagement, it is more difficult because this world is carried by meaning. Meaning goes beyond experiencing, as what is meant is not only experienced but is also something you seek to understand and to affirm. There is the task of seeking to understand the many meanings that constitute organizations and social structures, in language, in symbols and in actions (Schein, 2009; Argyris, 2010). Accordingly, you may inquire into how values, behaviour and assumptions are socially constructed and embedded in meaning, and what you seek to know comes through emergent inquiry that attends to purposes and framing, that works actively with issues of power and multiple ways of knowing. There is also the meaning of the world you make, through your enactment of the intentions, plans, actions and outcomes.

You may learn to construct your respective world by giving meaning to data that continuously impinge on you from within yourself as well as from without. But as we all know, it is not all that simple. There are, of course, such things as stupidity, obtuseness, confusion, divergent views, lack of attention and a general lack of intelligence. Understanding may not spontaneously flow from experience. Many insights may be wrong. Your interpretations of data may be superficial, inaccurate or biased. Your judgements may be flawed. Being careless about these operations has consequences. If you're careless about being attentive then your understanding is flawed. If you're careless about your understanding then your judgements are untrustworthy. You can gain insight into these negative manifestations of knowing by the same threefold process of knowing: experience, understanding and judgement.

Valuing, deciding and taking action

You are not merely a knower; you also weigh options, make decisions and take action. Deciding to take action is based on making a judgement of value, i.e. a judgement that something is good or worthwhile. So you may ask questions, like 'What will I do?' 'Is it worth my while?' The process of judging value and deciding is a similar process to that of knowing. You experience a situation. Using sensitivity, imagination and intelligence you may seek to answer the question for understanding as to what possible courses of action there might be. At this level you may ask what courses of action are open to you and you may review options, weigh choices and decide. You may reflect on the possible value judgements as to what is the best option and you may decide to follow through the best value judgement and you may take responsibility for consistency between your knowing and your doing.

To conclude this section, these four processes of experiencing, understanding, judging, deciding/taking action operate as a cycle where one cycle sets up another cycle of experiencing and so on. Learning becomes a continuous cycle through life. Figure 1.1 depicts this process in graphical terms.

You need to develop skills at each activity: be able to experience directly, be able to stand back and ask questions, be able to conceptualize answers to your questions, and be able to take risks and experiment in similar or new situations. We now consolidate this process in an empirical method which will act as the foundation for inquiring into organizational processes of behaviour, change and strategy throughout the book.

General empirical method for reflexive engagement

The operations of experience, understanding, judgement and decision/action form a general empirical method, which requires attention to observable data, envisaging possible explanations of that data, preferring as probable or certain the explanations which provide the best account for the data, and deliberating and choosing between alternative actions and taking action. These require the dispositions to perform the operations of attentiveness, intelligence, reasonableness and responsibility. Accordingly, the general empirical method is:

- be attentive (to data)
- be intelligent (in forming understanding)
- be reasonable (in making judgements)
- be responsible (for your actions)

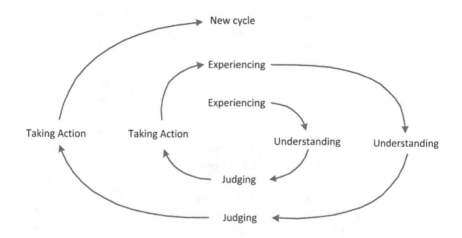

FIGURE 1.1 Sequence of continuous learning cycle

We want you to understand the relationship between questioning and answering. The general empirical method is a framework for collaborative creativity that deals with different kinds of questions, each with its own objective. So questions for understanding of specific data (What is happening here?) have a different focus from questions for reflection (Does this fit?) or questions of responsibility (What might I do?). As you engage in the material of this book we invite you to apply this method of being attentive, being intelligent, being reasonable and being responsible.

First, second and third person practice

A third foundation for engaging with the material in this book is the framework of first, second and third person practice that has been articulated by Torbert (2004; Fisher et al., 2000).

First person practice is typically characterized as a form of inquiry and practice that is about you and your self-learning. If you are an executive it may involve learning your personality profile, career anchor, values, learning style and how you influence others by the way you act (Boyatzis et al., 2006; Schein and Van Maanen, 2013). If you are a non-executive organizational member, you may learn about how you respond to motivational stimuli by managers, how you engage in teams and so on. If you are an OD consultant, it may involve learning how to engage with clients in a mode that is helpful to them (Schein, 1999). If you are a student, your personal learning may come about through your engagement with your classroom peers. In your engagement with the material in this book we are inviting you to bring the general empirical method to bear on yourself, as a manager, a non-executive organizational member, an OD consultant or a student by attending to what and how you learn about yourself and how you think (Kahneman, 2011).

Second person practice occurs through engagement with others in face-to-face collaboration. Here the challenge and the skills are to create, build and sustain collaborative relationships with relevant others through working on significant projects that are of corporate and mutual interest and concern. If you are a manager, your second person practice is paramount to fulfilling your role in building collaborative working relations with individuals and teams through, for example, executive management practices, project teams, change teams and the like. This second person practice is essential for long-term success as you work with your individuals and teams within the organization and customers outside of it (Boyatzis, 2009). If you are an OD consultant, second person practice is at the centre of building collaborative relationships with clients (Schein, 1999). If you are engaging in a classroom setting, then second person practice finds expression in working collaboratively in learning teams.

Third person takes practice from the immediate and directly relational and brings it to a broader, impersonal context where there has been no direct involvement and where an audience has not been engaged in the direct experience and is seeking to draw learning from it from a more removed perspective. At this level, issues of the generalizability or transportability to other projects/settings, of the identification of competencies and learning mechanisms, and of sustainability pertain. Third person is impersonal and is actualized through dissemination by reporting, publishing and extrapolating from the concrete to the general. This is particularly important for students who produce assignments that seek to encapsulate learning for a third party, such as a professor or an examiner, or for researchers who seek to publish their findings.

The framework of first, second and third person practice forms an integrated framework that encompasses personal learning, effective collaboration, and actionable knowledge generation. In our view, second person practice is primary. It is through working with others through collaborative processes of managing, changing, strategizing, assisting and learning that individual (first person) learning takes place and from that second and first experience and learning that actionable knowledge for a third person audience emerges.

Conclusions

In this chapter we have introduced reflexive engagement as the philosophy of learning that permeates our approach to this book. The core insight is that this is not a book to be read in a detached manner in the way you might approach most books. By taking a reflexive engagement approach in this book we mean that we are inviting you the reader, in whatever role you have, not only to understand the concepts developed in this book, but also, informed by the book, to engage in reflexive engagement by inquiring into what is going on around you and in you. We are inviting you to a reflexive engagement in $L=P+Q$, to adopt a clinical perspective, to attend to how your mind works as you strive to be attentive, intelligent, reasonable, and responsible to what is happening in you and in the organizations that you are studying, to engage in inquiring conversations with relevant others and to build your knowledge of organizational behaviour, change and strategy.

The reflexive engagement activities at the end of many of the chapters enable you to reflect on an organization with which you are familiar. Indeed, we invite you, where possible, to engage in these reflexive engagement activities on the same organization throughout the book so as to build up your analytic skills. If you are external to the organization, either as an OD consultant, a student or as a researcher in the mode of collaborative management research (Shani et al., 2008), then your reflections are in collaboration with the local managers. The vignettes within chapters and the cases at the end of chapters provide illustrations and aim to provoke further reflection and discussion. Chapter 2 introduces some templates around which we can structure reflexive engagement.

References

Argyris, C. (2010) *Organizational Traps*. New York: Oxford University Press.

Boyatzis, R. (2009) Creating sustainable, desired change in teams through application of intentional change and complexity theories. In P. Docherty, M. Kira and A.B. Shani (Rami) (eds), *Creating Sustainable Work Systems*. London: Routledge, pp. 103–116.

Boyatzis, R., Smith, M. and Blaize, N. (2006) Developing sustainable leaders through coaching and compassion. *Academy of Management Learning and Education*, 5(1), 8–24.

Coghlan, D. (2012) Understanding insight in the context of Q. *Action Learning: Research and Practice*, 9(3), 247–258.

Coghlan, D. and Brannick, T. (2014) *Doing Action Research in Your Own Organization*. 4th edn. London: Sage.

Fisher, D., Rooke, D. and Torbert, W.R. (2000) *Personal and Organizational Transformations through Action Inquiry*. Boston, MA: Edge/Work Press.

Kahneman, D. (2011) *Thinking Fast and Slow*. New York: Penguin.

Kolb, D.A. (1984) *Experiential Learning*. Englewood Cliffs, NJ: Prentice-Hall.

Lonergan, B.J. (1992) *Insight: An Essay in Human Understanding. The Collected Works of Bernard Lonergan*, Vol. 3, F. Crowe and R. Doran (eds). Toronto: University of Toronto Press (original publication 1957).

Oliver, C. (2005) *Reflexive Inquiry*. London: Karnac.

Revans, R. (2011) *ABC of Action Learning*. Farnham: Gower.

Schein, E.H. (1987) *The Clinical Perspective in Fieldwork*. Thousand Oaks, CA: Sage.

Schein, E.H. (1997) Organizational learning: What is new? In M.A. Rahim, R.T. Golembiewski and L.E. Pate (eds), *Current Topics in Management, Vol. 2*. Greenwich, CT: JAI Press, pp. 11–26.

Schein, E.H. (1999) *Process Consultation Revisited: Building the Helping Relationship*. Reading, MA: Addison-Wesley.

Schein, E.H. (2009) *The Corporate Culture Survival Guide*. 2nd edn. San Francisco, CA: Jossey-Bass.

Schein, E.H. and Van Maanen, J. (2013) *Career Anchors: The Changing Nature of Careers*. New York: Wiley.

Schon, D.A. (1983) *The Reflective Practitioner*. New York: Basic Books.

Shani, A.B. (Rami), Mohrman, S.A., Pasmore, W.A., Stymne, B. and Adler, N. (2008) *The Handbook of Collaborative Management Research*. Thousand Oaks, CA, Sage.

Torbert, W.R. and Associates (2004) *Action Inquiry*. San Francisco, CA: Berrett-Koehler.

2

CONTEXT AND TEMPLATES FOR REFLEXIVE ENGAGEMENT

In Chapter 1 we introduced the central approach of this book which we framed as reflexive engagement. By reflexive engagement we meant that the learning formula, $L=P+Q$, whereby we learn (L) by subjecting programmed learning (P), i.e. the theories and frameworks from research and in books, to questioning in the light of experience (Q) and that we approach the questioning of organizational processes in a clinical mindset. In this chapter we introduce some templates that we suggest you use to enable you to apply your reflexive engagement in the various elements of P (behaviour, learning, change and strategy) that we explore in the following chapters. This chapter suggests conceptual tools which we have found useful as simplifying templates to sharpen the context of reflexive engagement.

Organizations as social constructions and moral enterprises

Organizations are social constructions (Campbell, 2000). They are artefacts created by human beings to serve their ends. They follow processes that are shaped and affected by human purposes and actions and they do not exist outside of human minds and actions. They are systems of human action in which means and ends are guided by values and intended outcomes. Organizations are held together by common fields of experience, common modes of understanding, common measures of judgement and common consent. There are many carriers of meaning: statements of mission and strategy, plans, structures, actions, language and symbols, to cite some of the more important ones.

In the field of organizational studies, taking 'organizing' as the focus trying to understand organizations provides a more dynamic perspective than the more static notion of organization (Weick, 1979). Organizing focuses on the experiences, understandings, judgements and actions of organizational actors and others. The experiences are shared but the understandings may differ as different actors may understand causal links and systemic processes differently. Accordingly, judgements of value differ and different courses of action may be proposed and enacted. Understanding organizational actions requires inquiry into the constructions of meaning that individuals make about themselves, their situation and the world, and how their actions may be driven by assumptions and compulsions as well as by values. So we can say that the process of organizing hangs on meaning, formed by acts of meaning.

Systems thinking

A particular meaning that helps us understand the complexities of organizing is the notion of organizations as systems. Systems thinking is a social construction that provides a framework for seeing wholes rather than individual parts, for seeing patterns of inter-relationships rather than static snapshots. A system is a group of interacting, inter-related, and interdependent elements that form a complex whole and which shows how a configuration of parts is connected and joined together by a web of relationships. Systems thinking means that the whole is different from, and greater than, the sum of its parts. Systems are all around us. Biological systems include single-celled organisms, plants and animals. Social systems include the family, communities, organizations and institutions. Physical systems include natural systems such as the planetary system as well as man-made systems such as a chemical plant with a continuous flow process. This book is focused on one particular type of social system, the organization.

Organizations are open systems in constant interaction with their environment as they take in inputs, transform them and produce outputs in the form of products or services which then feed into further inputs (Williams and Hummelbrunner, 2013). The different parts of an organization may exist in different environments through their technology, markets and socio-political circumstances. By open system, we mean that organizations have multiple interfaces with the environment as they transform inputs (resources needed) and use processes (transformation of those resources) into outputs (outcomes obtained). It is possible to represent virtually any phenomenon in systemic language through these three elements, allowing us to sharpen our analysis to focus on the most relevant aspects given specific objectives.

Because social systems are in constant interaction with their contextual environment, events that disturb their equilibrium are often non-linear (that is, they do not necessarily follow from what previously occurred) and are not predictable from what happened before (Forrester, 1971). Besides their predictive uncertainty, these systems are also adaptive in that their components collectively adjust to changing contextual conditions in the way perceived as most appropriate for the system's continued operation. Organizations change both from the top down and from the bottom up. The former is a result of deliberate strategic change in which the leader explicitly articulates and follows a formulated strategy that is communicated throughout and intentionally implemented within the organization. The latter is the result of the bottom–up organic action of each individual reacting to changes in the external environment, which results in an emergent strategy (Mintzberg and Waters, 1985; Powell et al., 2011). The organization and its subsystems are continuously adapting to an environment of limited predictability, i.e. a chaotic world. In the midst of this continuous adaptation, the leader *organizes* based on an intentional strategy. In Parts II and III we discuss systemic change and strategic change arising from leader's intentionality.

Systems that exhibit non-linear and unpredictable behaviour are complex systems (Miller and Page, 2007; Holland, 2014). Organizations are complex systems as is the society within which they operate. Complex systems have several attributes, all of which are observed in large organizations. The first is the existence of what can be referred to as emergent properties leading to the impossibility of making completely accurate predictions based on the behaviour of system components or subsystems. The second is the self-organizing, or adaptable nature of complex systems as they consume energy to attempt to improve their internal structure given information received from the environment. This is observed not only in social systems, but also in biological systems such as cells and bee or ant colonies. The third is the existence of unexpected bifurcation properties as certain events can lead to outcomes which would be completely unpredictable by linear methods (the emergence of a set of completely unexpected actions leading to vastly different outcomes, a new path). Unpredictable behaviours may ensue when subsystems fail, as exemplified by internal component changes or outside forces causing cancerous cell malfunctions and threatening the broader systems, namely the organs and organisms. Social systems in general, and organizations in particular, are complex adaptive learning systems (some use the word organisms) which exist and operate in an environment of limited predictability, i.e. in a chaotic world.

An important characteristic of systems, especially for our objectives, is the existence of subsystems which execute or represent a subset of the processes, and therefore are components of a broader system. Most systems are composed of subsystems and at the same time are also components of broader systems. The subsystems of an organization may be functional departments, business units, subsidiary plants or offices of a large organization. These units may be experienced and studied as systems in their own right while also being a subsystem of a parent system. In turn, each functional department, business unit, and subsidiary plant or office, while components of a larger system, also have their own subsystems as they organize in sub-departments, divisions and production teams to execute specific tasks. Again, in turn, each of these is a system in its own right.

Organizing involves multiple interdependencies among several layers of systems and subsystems which may be fluid and may change depending on a task at hand. Throughout this book we chart interdependencies in terms of four levels: the individual within the organization, the team, the interdepartmental group and the organization with its environment. Each of these levels is both a system with component subsystems and a subsystem (component) of a larger system. Furthermore, each of these levels exhibit complex adaptive learning system characteristics in how they are open to the volatility and discontinuity of forces for change. We introduce these levels in the next couple of chapters and bring them to the challenges of changing and strategizing. The perspective of 'organizing' opens up seeing it as an intentional moral project. In the organizing process, individuals and teams are linked in common acts of meaning that lead to patterns of action that are grounded in the moral obligations that are attached to roles within the organization and to the organization's role in society.

Template for diagnosis and action

Our first template is one for assessing issues and for taking action. Fifty years ago Blake and Mouton (1964) taught us that it is not enough to concentrate on the tasks we have to do, but that we also need to have an eye on the relationships which are needed to complete the task, whether these be interpersonal in a team, inter-team or inter-organizational. Gittell (2009) has introduced the notion of relational coordination which she defines as 'the coordination of work through the relationships of shared goals, shared knowledge and mutual respect' (p. 13). So we note that actions that need to be taken to complete tasks successfully also need to include actions to build and maintain relationships on which completing the tasks depend. (Table 2.1).

After over 60 years of OD we are well attuned to the distinction between content and process (Schein, 1999). Content refers to *what* is done, while process refers to *how* it is done. Content and process apply to both task and relational issues. So we can usefully identify *task content* which refers to what the organization, interdepartmental group, team or individual is intending to do: its mission, the task to be done, the problems arising around clarity of mission, assignment of functions to meet tasks, and analysis of information. We can note how *task process* points us to how the organization, interdepartmental group, team or individual engages in defining mission, setting goals, completing tasks, reviewing progress, etc. These issues require attention if the tasks are to be completed satisfactorily.

Relational content refers to the particular roles members of an organization play with regard to other members. *Relational process*, which overlaps somewhat with interpersonal content, focuses more on what is happening in the team, interdepartmental group, or organization, and how they function in relation to the members: how people listen or don't listen to each other, how they agree or

	TASK	RELATIONAL
Content		
Process		
Culture		

TABLE 2.1 Template for assessment and action

disagree over specific issues, and how they support each other or support some people more than others.

Yet what we see and hear is not the whole picture on content and process issues. Much of what goes on in organizations is grounded in collective assumptions that constitute the organization's culture. They become embedded in the organization and in the different teams and interdepartmental groups that make up the organization. As Schein (2009) has shown, these assumptions become taken for granted and accordingly disappear from consciousness. They are passed on to new members and in effect become a structured way of thinking and behaving. Culture is the DNA of an organization. It pertains to the organization's survival in the external environment and, therefore, focuses on the issues of mission, goal setting, task accomplishment, and problem-solving. So within task issues there is *task culture* which points to the basic assumptions that have formed around critical task issues. Similarly, *relational culture* points to how authority and peer relationships are defined and how sub-cultures within functional areas and occupational communities relate to one another. Argyris (2010) illustrates how defensive routines, which serve to save face and to protect people from embarrassment, abound in organizations and become undiscussable and embedded in how the organization functions. Uncovering the embedded taken-for-granted patterns of behaviour that enable or inhibit the organization's change efforts while an organization is creating and implementing strategy is essential for managers and OD consultants.

Territories of experience

In order to engage in accurate and meaningful analysis of a complex system, it is necessary to understand what the system does, how it does it, why it behaves in a certain way, what will be the outcomes if that behaviour continues, and what the system should attempt to do, i.e. have a moral compass.

There are different arenas of experience, called the four territories of experience (Fisher et al., 2000; Torbert and Associates, 2004), which capture how behaviour and intentions lead to outcomes:

- *Intentionality*: This is the territory of purpose, goals, aims and vision.
- *Planning*: This is the territory of plans, strategy, tactics, ploys and schemes.
- *Action:* This is the territory of action, behaviour, implementation, skills and performance.
- *Outcomes*: This is the territory of results, outcomes, consequences and effects.

The parallel equivalent for organizing is visioning, strategizing, performing and assessing. A core reflexive engagement process is to develop your awareness, understanding and skills in each of these territories. Reflexive engagement helps you to understand your intentions, to develop your capacity to plan and develop strategies that reflect your aspirations, to reflect on the skills of your implementation and to see the impact of your actions. Reflexive engagement can also take you through how each of the territories is linked (Figure 2.1). A first or single inquiry loop can begin from outcomes and inquire into how you acted to produce those outcomes. A second or double inquiry loop can take you from outcomes to action to what you planned. A third or triple inquiry loop can take you from outcomes, through action, through strategy to ask questions about your intentions, aspirations and values. Throughout the book we adopt this three-level inquiry approach and invite you to connect outcomes with action, with strategies and with intentions.

This book's main focus is organizing, i.e. intentional change implementation, and because this implementation depends on an agent (a change sponsor for lack of a better expression) who might be a senior executive or another person within the organization, it is necessary for this agent not only to be aware of the degree of change sought (whether single, double, or triple loop change) but also to be constantly on the lookout for signs that any original assessment of the degree of change involved could, in fact, be incorrect and need adjustments.

Perspectives

We invite you to engage in reflexive engagement from four perspectives: leader, organizational member, OD consultant and outcomes because there is significant commonality and difference in each of these points of view. By this we mean two things. The first is that by taking a reflexive engagement in this book we mean that we invite you the reader, whether you are a senior manager, a non-executive

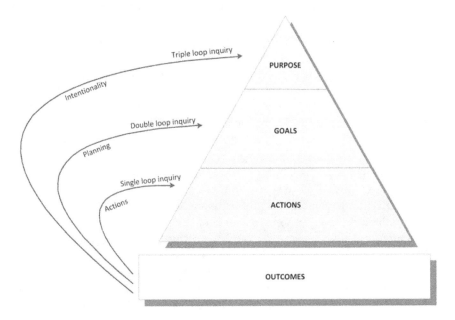

FIGURE 2.1 Single, double and triple loop inquiry
Source: Adapted from the work of Bill Torbert with permission.

organizational member, an external OD consultant or a student, not only to understand the concepts developed in this book, but also to engage in reflexive engagement by inquiring into the processes of organizing. We recommend that you not do this on your own and keep your reflections private, but that you engage others in conversations of shared reflections. Second, we invite you to work to understand the three perspectives other than your own.

First, consider the perspective of the senior executive who leads an organization with specific goals in mind. The task content is the set of organizational objectives to achieve the desired end, the direction that is pursued by the senior executive, i.e. the formulated strategy. The task process refers to the manner in which the objectives are reached (or will be reached, if aspirational), i.e. how implementation of the formulated strategy will occur. The task culture refers to the ability (or lack thereof) of the organization to adapt quickly to environmental shifts within the context of the desired organizational direction. These task elements could be either expectations of the senior executive (if the systems are already in place) or aspirations (if systems still need to be put in place to achieve the desired effect). From the leader's perspective, relational content is the ability for each actor involved (individual or team) to have true ownership of the desired goals and an understanding of his/her role and stake in helping the organization achieve those objectives. Relational process is 'how' the leader will help implement and provide reinforcement to widespread individual ownership in interactions among members throughout the organization. The relational culture relates to the implicit degree of acceptance of intentional leadership-driven change in the organization.

The perspective of a non-executive is somewhat different from that of the leader. The task content is the set of actions that the member knows he/she must accomplish within his/her own job and role to contribute to further the organization's goals. The task process relates to how the actions will be accomplished through job description. The task culture dimension refers to the organization's culture as it translates into assumptions that underpin getting the job done. Relational content refers to the roles the member plays and how these roles contribute to his/her motivation and sense of engagement with the organization and its goals. Relational process represents how organizational roles are enacted and how they facilitate the individual member's sense of belonging and commitment to the organization. Finally, relational culture from the point of view of the non-executive member refers to the implicit codes of behaviour and embedded relationships that allow or inhibit the member to have a sense of belonging and commitment to the organization.

The organization development (OD) consultant's perspective is that of one who has been invited to provide process help. This third perspective is different from the previous two in that usually the consultant has been brought in with a mandate to be helpful with regard to some issue, whether clearly outlined or not. The task content for the OD consultant is the mandate to be executed. The task process is the set of steps necessary for successful execution of the mandate. The task culture represents the impact of the mandate on the culture of the organization. The relational content from the OD consultant's perspective is the buy-in that the OD consultant feels relative to the mandate and consequent shared ownership with the organization's management. The relational process is the how, i.e. the manner in which the OD consultant is able to create effective working interactions with the requisite members of the organization, therefore allowing for successful execution of the stated mandate. Lastly, the relational culture is the set of unwritten and perhaps unspoken norms within the organization which facilitate or inhibit adaptation and change and therefore allow the OD consultant's mandate to be performed successfully.

We have added a fourth perspective, namely that of outcome. The desired outcome of the work of senior managers, members and OD consultants is that there be congruence or harmony between task content, task process, task culture, relational content, relational process and relational culture as a system where each affects each of the other and the equilibrium of the system depends on each being in place and working effectively.

References

Argyris, C. (2010) *Organizational Traps*. New York: Oxford University Press.

Blake, R. and Mouton, J. (1964) *The Managerial Grid*. Houston, TX: Gulf.

Campbell, D. (2000) *The Socially Constructed Organization*. London: Karnac.

Fisher, D., Rooke, D. and Torbert, W.R. (2000) *Personal and Organizational Transformations through Action Inquiry*. Boston, MA: Edge/Work Press.

Forrester, J.W. (1971) Counterintuitive behavior of social systems. *Technology Review*, 73(3), 52–68.

Gittell, J.H. (2009) *High Performance Healthcare*. New York: McGraw-Hill.

Holland, J.H. (2014) *Signals and Boundaries: Building Blocks for Complex Adaptive Systems*. Cambridge, MA: MIT Press.

Miller, J.H. and Page, S.E. (2007) *Complex Adaptive Systems: An Introduction to Computational Models of Social Life*. Princeton, NJ: Princeton University Press.

Mintzberg, H. and Waters, J.A. (1985) Of strategies, deliberate and emergent. *Strategic Management Journal*, 6(3), 257–272

Powell, T.C., Lovallo, D. and Fox, C.R. (2011) Behavioral strategy. *Strategic Management Journal*, 32(13), 1369–1386.

Schein, E.H. (1999) *Process Consultation Revisited: Building the Helping Relationship*. Reading, MA: Addison-Wesley.

Schein, E.H. (2009) *The Corporate Culture Survival Guide*. 2nd edn. San Francisco, CA: Jossey-Bass.

Torbert, W.R. and Associates (2004) *Action Inquiry*. San Francisco, CA: Berrett-Koehler.

Weick, K. (1979) *The Social Psychology of Organizing*. 2nd edn. Reading, MA: Addison-Wesley.

Williams, B. and Hummelbrunner, R. (2013) *Systems Concepts in Action*. Stanford, CA: Stanford University Press.

3

ORGANIZATIONAL LEVELS

Theory and practice

Conceptual foundations

When we think in terms of levels in organizing, we need to not only distinguish between hierarchy/echelon and complexity, but also focus on complexity as a more fruitful way to understand and engage with organizational learning, changing and strategizing. Several essential points need to be clarified about the concept and usage of the term 'organizational levels'. The notion of levels must be distinguished from that of echelon or hierarchy (Rousseau, 1985). Echelon refers to position on a chain of command in an organization, such as worker, supervisor, middle manager, etc. Levels of complexity – individual, group, inter-group, total organizational – are frequently used as frameworks for understanding organizational processes (Stapley, 2006).

Levels of organizational behaviour however, describe levels of complexity, as, for instance, described by Miller (1978) with regard to biological systems. He identifies seven levels: cell, organ, organism, group, organization, society and supernatural. They are hierarchical in that each system is composed of inter-related subsystems in a hierarchical order, i.e. organs are composed of cells, organisms composed of organs, etc. The hierarchical nature of the system also means that if any of its subsystems ceases to carry out its function, the system would cease to exist. Accordingly, a cancerous cell affects the functioning of the organ, affects the life of the individual person and has an impact on that person's family and friends. Therefore, a dynamic notion of levels of complexity is needed to more fully understand, appreciate and manage behaviour in a complex organizational system. The subsystems, which make up an organization as a living system, are: the individual, the face-to-face working team, the interdepartmental group of teams, and the organization. Clearly the notion of levels extends beyond the individual organization. An industry sector, such as financial services, healthcare, telecommunications, education, etc. where the participating organizations are governed by common regulatory laws, faces common challenges and at times may present a common front in order to negotiate with regulatory bodies, may be considered to be a fifth level. In this book we are focusing primarily on four levels, drawing on this fifth level when appropriate.

The construct or framework of organizational levels, therefore, is a) a point of view so one can look at organizing from whichever level one chooses; b) a platform for analysis; and c) an entry point for learning and change. Because it focuses on complexity, rather than hierarchy, it enriches the perspective of organizations as living systems and of organizing as a dynamic process. The construct thus accounts for the multiple patterns of complexity and unpredictability of participation in organizing.

Four levels of organization behaviour

We are presenting levels in terms of how people participate in organizing. Moreover, we will discuss how linking levels to one another provides an additional useful tool and core skills for managers and OD consultants. This framework describes four levels of participation – individual, face-to-face team, interdepartmental group, and organization. These four levels can be viewed as degrees or types of involvement, subsystems, or as degrees of complexity. It depends on your perspective.

Within each level there are tasks. These tasks are doubled-sided. There is the task from the viewpoint within each level, such as the individual's task to be an individual or the team's task to function well, and there is the task from the outside viewpoint at each level, such as management's requirement that an individual belong or that a team be effective. These dual tasks coexist at each level and create a tension between them as organizational levels can be viewed through the many lenses through which people's participation in organizations can be viewed (Bolman and Deal, 2013).

Each organizational level can be viewed from four different perspectives – manager, organizational member, OD consultant and outcomes. From the point of view of the individual, the least complex approach to participation is the membership which the individual has with the organization in order to meet personal life goals (Level I). The more complex approach exists in establishing effective working relationships in a face-to-face team, while also maintaining personal integrity (Level II). An even more complex involvement exists in terms of the interdepartmental group or divisional type of interface where the work of teams must be coordinated in their efforts in order to achieve complex tasks and maintain a balance of power among competing functional political interest groups (Level III). A further complexity from the point of view of the individual is the relationship of the total organization to its external environment, in which other organizations are individual competitors, competing for scarce resources to produce similar products or services. The key task for any organization is its ability to adapt to environmental forces driving for change (Level IV). When one approaches the question from the point of view of the individual member who is not in a senior executive position, the key issue is involvement in the organization (Table 3.1).

Leaders, CEOs and other senior managers grapple with issues of content and process as they attempt to integrate their use of power, knowledge and trust (Zand, 1997). So when one views organizational levels from the point of view of senior management the key issues are how different forms of participation in the organization are achieved (Table 3.2). From senior management's perspective (the output perspective in systems terms), the core issue is one of involvement. The most basic form of involvement is to get a person committed to the goals, values and culture of the organization. The second level of involvement is to establish good, working face-to-face relationships in functional teams. The third level of involvement is the group or divisional level in which complex information and data systems are used to extend the knowledge and to coordinate the functions of the total working group, made up of multiple face-to-face teams. Finally, the most complex of all is the unified effort of all participants in an organization towards the goal of making the organization profitable, growth-oriented, and functional in its external environment. This set of complex behaviours, then, is separated into a cognitive map – a mental construct of different types of participation and involvement – by the use of the concept of levels.

OD consultants view the four levels in terms of how they fit systemically with one another in relation to the successful management of change (Table 3.3). The 'matching' process between individuals and the organization is key to attitudes to the change process and how the attitudes influence action. Team effectiveness is critical to the change process, whether in formal statutory teams or in task forces or project teams set up to assist the change. Inter-team coordination and minimal conflict is also critical to the change process. Ultimately the change process is aimed to achieve better adaptation to a changing environment, with possible collaboration with other organizations.

The outcomes of the successful achievements of the tasks at each level describe the four tasks at each of the four organizational levels (Table 3.4). The four key tasks of *matching needs, creating a functioning, working team which is productive, coordination* and *adaptation* form a complex pattern.

It is in the working out of these tensions and the completion of the relevant tasks that participation at each level is most successful. For example, at Level II a team can work through its internal dynamics and create a cohesive, functioning unit, while at the same time, meet the organization's demands to be effective in terms measured by others outside the team.

Interventions

An intervention is a set of sequenced and planned actions or events intended to help the organization increase its effectiveness. The levels framework provides important insights into the types of intervention which are desirable in any given

TABLE 3.1 Individual members' tasks at each of the four organizational levels

Level	Task
I Individual	Membership and participation
II Face-to-face team	Creating effective working relationships
III Interdepartmental group	Coordinating joint effort
IV Organization	Adapting

TABLE 3.2 Leadership tasks at each of the four organizational levels

Level	Task
I Individual	Involvement
II Face-to-face team	Productive team functioning
III Interdepartmental group	Coordination of effective output
IV Organization	Competitive advantage

TABLE 3.3 OD consultants' perspectives at each of the four organizational levels

Level	Task
I Individual	Matching needs
II Face-to-face team	Productive team functioning
III Interdepartmental group	Coordination
IV Organization	Adapting to changing environment

TABLE 3.4 Outcomes at each of the four organizational levels

Level	Task
I Individual	Matching needs
II Face-to-face team	Creating a functioning team
III Interdepartmental group	Coordination
IV Organization	Adaptation

organization development and change programme. Each level demands its own most appropriate or 'key' intervention in terms of helping to fulfil the primary task of that level and also suggests the most relevant interventions to help link the tasks of the levels to one another. In our view, some interventions are more useful than others in resolving the core issues which define each level. An OD consultant utilizes interventions according to the joint assessment by consultant and client as to what is needed in a given situation (Schein, 1999). Our notion of key intervention does not attempt to predetermine or limit a consultant's ability to intervene effectively in the concrete situation of any given consultation.

Level I – Individual

Individuals within organizations have life-tasks, needs and wishes which extend far beyond their participation in any given work setting. Each individual struggles to find unique and personalized satisfactions in this regard. Management's perspective at the same point, however, is that individuals somehow belong to the organization in an appropriate formal and psychological contract. When the tasks at this level are reasonably and adequately met, individuals can allow the organization and its goals to be a source of personal goal motivation. Individuals will still retain their own individuality while 'belonging' to the organization. In contrast, the awareness and utilization of motivational techniques are the basic functions of management towards each individual in the organization in the hope that they will enhance growth and effectiveness. Therefore, management's ideal goal is to create a matching process in which people are able and encouraged to become involved, and find that the work situation develops them as human beings while the organization benefits from such an involvement (Schein, 1978, 1995). Not all individuals relate to management's goal in this regard, and some prefer to define the relationship with the organization in political and adversarial terms around issues of power and control (Bolman and Deal, 2013).

There is an inevitable serious tension in this matching process. Individuals attempt to be themselves and bring unique aspects of themselves to the organization while at the same time adapting to organizational norms. One common difficulty here is that the plurality of views and theories-in-use of how people are motivated produces contradictory approaches and undermines the growth process (McGregor, 1960). The manager who thinks that motivation is external and applied by force is in sharp contrast to the manager or subordinate who thinks that motivation comes from within the person. The point becomes even more critical if

TABLE 3.5 Perspectives at individual level

Perspective	
Leader	How do we create the conditions for high motivation and commitment to attain and maintain high performance?
Member	How does working in this organization meet my needs and enhance my development?
OD consultant	What effects does management behaviour have on members' motivation and commitment to the goals of the organization? Does employee behaviour reinforce management behaviour?
Outcome	How are organizational and individual members' goals matched?

in unexamined behaviour, a manager proposes one point of view in speech and acts in a contradictory manner (Argyris, 2010). The critical need is for managers to reflect on how different people might be motivated in diverse and changing situations. The more ownership and awareness that individuals have of their lives, the more capable they are of contributing their unique aspects which are so necessary for organizations to change and develop.

The key intervention on this level is the *career interview* in which the dynamics of the life-cycle, the work-cycle and the family-cycle are located and placed in juxtaposition so that the individual can locate his/her career in the context of his/her life (Schein, 1978). Through the person–centred nature of the interview, the individual can be facilitated to take ownership of his/her life and career, and adopt positive coping responses to the tasks facing him/her. It can empower individuals to initiate and promote change in the organization. At the same time, managers can utilize the process to reflect on and restructure managerial assumptions and behaviour. A technique such as the career anchor exercise, based on the individual's work experience, needs and values, is of great significance (Schein and Van Maanen, 2013). In the career anchor, that aspect of work which produces a sense of identity and self-concept in work is located by the individual and can be used in the setting of the contract between the individual and the organization for his/her contribution to the corporate endeavour and the organization's response.

> An electrical engineer in a high-tech company was promoted to a managerial position. After some time on the job, he reported to his superior that he was unhappy in this role and that he preferred to be back in the technical area of product design where he felt at home in the field of technological research. Because his superior knew and understood him, this request was granted. This recognition by the superior that he was happier as an engineer than as a manager (which in career anchor terms means that his career anchor was technical functional, rather than managerial), enabled the organization and the individual to reconfigure the relationship between them so as to achieve a better match of the individual's desires, skills and motivations with the organization's needs.

Level I applies throughout an organization. It works differently at different points on the chain of command. An administrator's or worker's commitment to the organization is typically different from that of the leader. If a Level I dysfunction from the individual's side occurs at senior management its consequences are different than if a similar problem were occurring for the warehouse clerk. If the dysfunction emanates from management policy, the effects can vary throughout the organization. A Level I dysfunction means that because of assumptions, attitudes or behaviours of either the individual or the organization's management, the Level I task of matching needs is frustrated with consequential negative results for working relationships, inter-team collaboration and ultimately the functioning of the organization.

In conclusion, the issues at the individual level are usefully viewed through the four perspectives (Table 3.5). Senior managers view them in terms of attaining and maintaining performance. Organizational members view them in terms of their own career and development. OD consultants view them in terms of the effect of managerial behaviour on members and their reciprocal response. The outcome is appropriate matching needs.

Level II – Face-to-face team

From the individual's perspective, entry into the work activity involves interfacing with other individuals in clearly defined units. Face-to-face teams are typically formal groups and defined in terms of:

1. Face-to-face interaction
2. Common objectives
3. Psychological awareness of other members, and
4. Self-definition as a team with member/non-member boundaries clearly defined

Level II is a more complex level than Level I because of the increased number of participants and interactions. Teams form part of a wider system in organizations and some of the dysfunctional issues which arise within the team may originate beyond the team in its technological and political interface with other teams. Problems which arise between teams are considered at Level III.

From the managerial perspective, any individual's task within the face-to-face team is to contribute to the collective ventures of the team. Management requires the team to be efficient, flexible and cooperative in its output towards the overall organizational tasks (Wheelan, 2015). Effective team functioning requires the team to be successful in accomplishing its tasks and skilled in learning from its experience in building and maintaining working relationships. While we are focusing primarily on the team as a face-to-face working unit, these process issues apply to what is termed 'virtual teams' or teams which utilize information technology as primary communication mechanisms.

The team's process, then, focuses on becoming a functioning work unit to build on success and learn from mistakes. It is critical for face-to-face teams to develop the appropriate skills of self-reflection and correct their own dysfunctions. Such skills typically constitute the definition of successful teams. Level II dysfunctions occur when assumptions, attitudes and behaviour of team members towards one another and the team's effort frustrate the team's performance. Generally the discovery of negative information is not valued in many organizations as people then tend to confront one another. This results from the learned patterns of inference, attribution and the placing of blame. Behaviours such as blaming, withholding

TABLE 3.6 Perspectives on tasks at team level

Perspective	Setting goals	Allocating and implementing work	Team process	Interpersonal relations
Leader	How much do I set the goals and invite opinions?	Who is responsible for what? Who does what? Who manages what? How do I allocate…?	What processes do we need to make the team work – meetings, communication mechanisms…? Does the team have the ability to change membership and be flexible to subdivide the work and add people for specific tasks? How do I deal with team dysfunction? What extra resources do I need?	How can interpersonal relations assist the work and not inhibit it? Can it relate to other teams?
Member	What is expected of me? Can I respond to other tasks if required?	Are my goals and tasks clear? Have I the competence and resources to complete my tasks? How will I be evaluated?	How do we communicate? Can I be critical? What happens if we have conflicts? Will I be listened to and heard?	Can I work with people I don't like or who have different approaches to me?
OD consultant	Are the goals clear? Are they agreed upon?	Is there a match between goals and roles? Is talent optimized? Is it flexible to reconfigure membership for other tasks?	How does the team work – communicate, give feedback, solve problems, make decisions, manage conflict…? What hidden norms are operative?	Do the different personalities, styles, etc. work together? Do they appreciate difference?
Outcome	Clear and agreed goals	Effective implementing of goals	Effective team working and achievement of goals in multiple situations and tasks	Effective interpersonal relations appropriate to goal achievement

information, inappropriate team leader style, misplaced competition, sexism, racism, and lack of trust can negatively affect the team members' capacity to work well together and also inhibit team development. Furthermore, within any given team the interaction skills of task achievement and relational function may not be equally developed. In most organizations, performance is not measured on the team level. Subsequently, rewards may be divisive in teams, break up teams through the transfer of successful individual members, and impose restrictive norms and practices. The team dynamics described above are relevant to all teams, whether at the senior management or middle management echelon or at the worker-maintenance areas in an organization; or in formalized permanent teams within an organization's structure or temporary project teams or task forces. A particular challenge to teams is to maintain flexibility in situations where membership configurations change on a frequent basis, with new members joining and others leaving, as in temporary task forces or project committees.

The key intervention on the face-to-face team level consists in formally building up and maintaining team skills. Team building is the title given to a wide range of activities which are aimed at improving a work team's effectiveness. Team skills comprise four activities in order of importance (Beckhard, 1972; Nadler et al., 1998):

a   Setting goals and priorities
b   Analyzing and allocating work
c   Examining the team's process, and
d   Developing the interpersonal relationships among team members

Team building is the key intervention because it deals with members' participation, with the team's goals and work allocation and how the team can be productive. Other interventions focus on less comprehensive issues and provide team process skills in communication, problem-solving, decision-making, member roles and functions, cultural rules of interaction, norm evaluation, conflict management, leadership style and the exercise of influence, and initiating and managing change (Schein, 1999). Team development provides a framework for understanding the growth stages of the collective personality that is the team (Wheelan, 2015) and through cultural analysis uncovering the hidden assumptions that constitute its relationship to its external and internal environment (Schein, 2009).

A working party established by a bishop to create a pastoral plan for the diocese invited an OD consultant to work with its members because the group was experiencing interpersonal difficulties. Meetings were proving to be stressful; members frequently felt hurt by others' comments and several were reported to be on the verge of resigning. After being briefed by a delegation of the working party, the OD consultant designed a process for a two-day review meeting. At the outset he invited each member to write down what he or she perceived the working party's mission and purpose to be. He did this to ground any later exploration of interpersonal relations in the working party's mandate, the way it structured its tasks, and the way the process worked. When members shared their perceptions of the working party's mission and purpose, both the consultant and the group noticed that there were practically as many versions of the mission as there were members, and that many of the perceptions were incompatible. It emerged that the purpose of the working party had changed since it was originally established, and that some members were working from a new definition, some from the original one and others from a variation on both. The two-day meeting was then devoted to clarifying and articulating a common purpose for the working party and its work. Very little time was subsequently devoted to the subject of interpersonal relations. The consultant, presenting the team-building framework outlined above, pointed out that if the goals and mission of the group had remained unclear, then any work on interpersonal relationships within the group would at best be temporary and the problems would resurface. Subsequent reports indicated that interpersonal relations did improve as the working party launched into its work with a clearer and agreed statement of purpose.

The four tasks of setting goals and priorities, analysing and allocating work, examining the team's process, and developing the interpersonal relationships among team members can be viewed from the perspective of the manager, the team member, the OD consultant and outcomes (Table 3.6).

Level III – Interdepartmental group

From the team's point of view, to be effective and enter the organization's life is to work within a larger system. This third level is made up of any number of face-to-face working teams which must function together to accomplish a divisional purpose, such as manufacturing, sales, or marketing, or it is a collection of individual work teams that provide a strategic business unit function for an organization. The interdepartmental group level needs to:

1. have the ability to sense critical information not directly experienced
2. pass beyond the barriers of individual teams in order to implement programmes through coordination
3. project at a range beyond their direct contact, that is deal with people not in their immediate group team or functional department, and
4. manage work, information and resource flows

In large organizations where size and distance dissolve immediate personal relationships, it is imperative that this level function well. From management's view, the team's task within the group is to perform as a team, while having a sense of belonging to the interdepartmental group from which it receives the scarce resources enabling it to function. When this third level is working effectively, the interdepartmental group or division is capable of obtaining information and converting it into decision processes, enabling the implementation of complex programmes or operations. The task of this level is to map the flow of information and partially completed work from one unit to another. Management requires that these units form a coordinated aggregate. The process of performing a complex function and making an appropriate distribution of scarce resources, such as personnel and money, is the key venture of the group level. It is a highly political situation in which the in-built structural conflicts of multiple interest parties need to be resolved. As an interdepartmental group, this diversified mass of differing functions and interests must negotiate an outcome that adequately reflects the balance of power among competing coalitions and a just distribution of resources. An essential element in Level III dynamics centres on issues of power and how power is exercised in the allocation of resources and the accessibility of information.

From management's view, the technical issues at this level require an ability to locate dysfunctions. Dysfunctions occur in the flow of transferring information and partially completed work or services from one team to another. The entire function must be viewed, understood and successfully handled in order to produce the product or service. Because of a huge number of individuals engaged in particular functions in a large organization, this process is often very difficult to see. The interdepartmental group's process then must focus on becoming a functioning work unit to build on successes and learn from mistakes. Difficulties also arise at this level from the lack of reflective and corrective skills. Discovery of negative information is difficult because it is often hidden in the interfaces that exist between one team and another. The organizational rewards system often does not reflect the actual needs of particular functioning units within the larger group.

Severe dysfunctions on an interdepartmental group level are most often solved through the use of an OD consultant who can help the group configure its information and its materials handling processes, and restructure itself, if necessary, to a new configuration. Knowledge of content is essential. For example, a consultant must be conversant with the content of the technology in an information flow or decision-making process. Level III interdepartmental group dysfunction does not, of necessity, take place only within the work flow process, but often can take place within the resource flow.

A common expression of failures at Level III is the perennial issue of information technology enabled change. Research and experiences over decades have shown that a) most investments in information technology fail to deliver on time and within budget and b) that this failure is due to the lack of integration between the technology and the human and organizational dimensions of organizations. A primary dynamic of this failure is the existence of sub-cultures within organizations, especially executive and technical occupational communities, each of which has its own assumptions, language and perspective on information technology (Schein, 1996). The inherent difficulties of enabling these occupational communities to communicate with one another on information technology have proved to be complex and enduring. The framework of organizational levels enables the dynamics of information technology in organizations to be identified in how IT affects the work of individuals, teams, the access and sharing of information across the interdepartmental group and contributing to organizational effectiveness and competitiveness (Coghlan, 1998).

The key intervention on this interdepartmental group level consists of internal mapping. This framework focuses a process whereby individual heads of work units or team leaders are asked to plot the work flow through their section, and to do this in such a way that from the beginning of a work process to its finish, all the intermediate links between different functioning teams are plotted, and all the members of the group then have a chance to jointly own the dysfunctional areas and work in small task forces to address the dysfunctions. This process requires each manager to put down each input and output from their own area on a large sheet of newsprint. These sheets are connected together in an interdepartmental group meeting and the quality and effectiveness of each point of connection between teams are evaluated. The correction process of dysfunction is to set up a marker or flag at each point of dysfunction and put together a task force of affected individuals to correct the dysfunction. Most often the dysfunction is *between* working teams and not in them.

A construction company which manufactured modular factory/warehouse units and competed with companies which manufactured stand-alone units uniquely suited to each operation provides an example of this intervention. The problem posed was that through the process of manufacturing the modules and making adaptations to fit customers' requirements faster than competitors, deliveries were not being made as expeditiously as industry rivals. Accordingly, a consultant gathered the heads of each major departmental area and facilitated a detailed mapping of each step in the process from input to output. Time delays and the reasons for them were identified. The inadequacies of meeting others' needs as well as the points of differences and conflict between the department areas were carefully worked out. After some thoughtful reflection it became apparent that while there were unique requirements for each customer, there were some common elements among customers. If Sales sat down with Engineering to address customers' needs, oftentimes, pre-designed engineering solutions were available and could fit the customer's wishes without requiring extremely time-consuming engineering projects. Because of this mapping process intervention the time it took to build modified units dropped significantly.

Another important intervention at this level is the use of large group processes (Bunker and Alban, 1997; Holman and Devane, 2007), such as 'search/future search conferences', 'whole scale change', 'open space' where organizational members from all functional and geographical areas come together for a number of days and:

- review the past
- explore the present
- create an ideal future scenario
- identify common ground and
- make action plans

The significance of these approaches is that they enable the whole system to engage in strategic thinking and planning in an integrated manner in a defined period of time in a manner that is dialogical, participative, draws on metaphoric approaches as well as rational ones and builds ownership of strategy and change agendas.

The tasks at the interdepartmental group level can be viewed from the four perspectives (Table 3.7).

TABLE 3.7 Perspectives at interdepartmental group level

Perspective	
Leader	How do I lead effective coordination across the organization and minimize any inter-functional conflict and political turf-protection that jeopardizes the enterprise? What technologies do we invest in to achieve effective coordination?
Member	How do I work across functions? What technologies do I have to coordinate information across functions?
OD consultant	What coordinating technologies are in place? Are they effective? How well do functional areas understand other areas? How do the occupational communities engage in working together? Would a large group intervention be appropriate?
Outcome	Coordination across functions, technologies, operations, business units, geographical units, sub-cultures, occupational communities…

Senior management group

There is a certain amount of discussion as to whether senior management teams are actually teams or not. Hambrick (1994) suggests that the constellation of executives at the top of an organization may not constitute a team, but rather a group. In the same vein, Katzenbach (1998) outlines a number of myths pertaining to senior management groups which negate the notion that these groups are teams. While staying with the term 'executive team', Nadler, Spencer and Associates (1998) highlight synthetic and cosmetic teamwork, under-designed teams, consensus management, good plough–wrong field, inertia and succession overhang as the main problems with senior management groups. In the light of these issues it is more useful to think of the senior management group as a collection of individuals, each representing a constituency and with his/her own goals and preferences – the leader with the board (Hambrick et al., 1998) and the senior managers with their departments.

Finglestein and Hambrick (1996) identified three critical issues with respect to an understanding of senior management groups. First, the composition of the senior management group needs to be clear – who is a member and why. Second, the power dynamics among a group of executives at the top of an organization are central. Third, the nature of the interaction within the senior management group is key.

Composition: While it is clear that this group is at the strategic apex of the organization, its membership may vary according to the nature of the strategic decisions under consideration. In relation to particular areas of decision, different individuals may be included or excluded according to their area of expertise and hierarchical position within the organization. The selection of members, the boundaries of who is included and/or excluded, and indeed the formation of group norms tends to be set by the chief executive.

Power Dynamics: The distribution of power among the members of the senior management group is not equal. The play of power among a CEO, line managers, staff analysts, support staff and others is acted out, not only through an active voice in decision-making, but also through advice-giving, sponsorship and alliances in the internal coalition which forms the structure of an organization. When strategic decisions are unstructured and ambiguous, the role that power plays is greater. There is greater potential for competition for scarce resources, self-interest and institutional enhancement. Accordingly, conflict can not only be about substantive issues relating the content and process of the policy, but also be emotive. Amason (1996) concludes that quality of decision in the senior management group depends on the encouragement of substantive conflict with a restraining of emotive conflict.

There is a complex relationship between the CEO and the members of the senior management group. CEOs are the leaders of the groups. They design the composition, structure and process of the group. When the group meets, they chair and shape the dynamics. As a senior management group typically does not spend much time together and its members work apart from each other most of the time, CEOs also shape the dynamics when the group is not in meeting. At the same time, the group members are dependent on their CEOs, whose decisions are final. Their tenure is uncertain and their continued membership of the senior management group depends on their CEOs. Senior managers have limited exit options; they can only move down or out so they need to build a good working relationship with their CEOs.

Interaction: When executives interact in a senior management team or group on unstructured tasks such as policy formation, implementation and review, the dynamics are complex. There are social complexities whereby with a high ego involvement there is as high potential for disagreement and a need for individuals to be able to stand back from their own perspectives and biases. There are political complexities as a great deal may rest on the individuals in terms of their careers.

In our view, Level II is defined by the common task and interaction in a small group or team, whether formal or informal, permanent or temporary. When the senior management group engages in the process of strategy formation, implementation and review it can be understood in terms of a Level III membership attempting Level II process working on Level III and IV content. That is to say, the issues of strategic and policy analysis and decision, organization and coordination of resources and action are discussed and acted upon by a working group which forms a political coalition from the functional areas of members which they represent as it engages in strategic conversation. Therefore, group and team process issues of how goals are set, how the group process works, how information is communicated, decisions are made and so on are pertinent and critical to how the content issues of strategic analysis, decision, implementation and review are considered and put into practice.

Level IV – Organization

The fourth level is the organizational goals, policy or strategy level. It is the final fusion of the three previous levels together to form a working, cohesive organization which functions as a complex adaptive system in a discontinuous world. Organizations operate at the edge of chaos and must exhibit a capacity for self-organization in the face of multiple complexities. In their view equilibrium means death and therefore the creation of variety is paramount for organizations to learn and adapt to the many unexpected changes.

The organization's task is to:

1. be cohesive;
2. live in a competitive environment;
3. exchange a product or service to obtain scarce resources;
4. reflect on its own strengths and weaknesses; and
5. engage in a proactive relationship to determine the opportunities and threats from the external environment.

Strengths and opportunities are matched in a selection process which determines programmes, services, products aimed at accomplishing the goals of the organization and servicing the external environment with its products and services. An awareness of the cultural assumptions which underlie an organization's policies, strategies, structures and behaviours contributes to the successful completion of the tasks at this level (Schein, 2009).

TABLE 3.8 Perspectives at organization level

Perspective	
Leader	Where are we going?
	What does the horizon look like?
	What's over the horizon?
	What advantages do we have over the competition?
	Do we understand whom we serve?
	Do we have the capabilities to achieve our goals?
Member	How do I contribute?
	Do the plans include me?
OD consultant	Do they know the competition?
	Do they understand the customer?
	Is there good strategic thinking?
	Is there good involvement of all?
Outcome	Does the organization learn and adapt in a changing environment?

The key intervention is open systems planning, performed in terms of the organization's core mission, with its internal and external constituencies making demands on the organization. Open systems planning comprises elements of identifying key environmental stakeholders and analysing the demands they are currently making on the organization, the projected demands they will make, the current responses to those demands, creation of a desired future and action planning (Beckhard and Harris, 1987; Nadler, 1998). In Part III we develop the open systems perspectives in terms of five strategic foci – framing the corporate picture, naming corporate words, determining corporate alternatives by analysing, choosing and implementing corporate actions, and evaluating corporate outcomes. The central theme of the book is to link these processes to the process of change, whereby the strategic foci are the means by which managers and the consultants enact change in their organizations.

A pharmaceutical company started out as a single product company, manufacturing a calcium supplement. As the product was successful and the operation grew, a conscious programme of acquisitions was begun by the founding entrepreneur. A company that manufactured a chairlift for stairs and one that manufactured eyeglasses were purchased. These organizational components would generally be classified as being in the medical or health field although they were not in pharmaceuticals. After the initial period of significant growth, there was a period of flat sales at the company because the resulting wide range of activities was difficult to manage. A new president was brought in, who in turn hired professional managers with whom he was familiar. The new president brought his senior management group into his office to discern the company's core mission. They decided to be an ethical pharmaceutical company and began a systematic placement of themselves in that business. The first approach was the development of new ethical prescriptions from R&D. The period from the initiation of the basic research to the production of a marketable product lasted fourteen years. A second approach evolved to fill the gaps by acquiring from abroad other products that could be manufactured and sold in the US under license. This process could produce a marketable product in three years, which indeed happened. This strategy combination of R&D and product licensing was used systematically to shape the organization from within and simultaneously develop its competitive advantage. The organization placed itself in a particularly competitive marketplace while developing a strong market position with strong new products.

In developing the core mission, the company found out it could not sustain being a broad-based medical company. First, a comprehensive medical company was too broad with too many different product lines, supply chains, distribution channels, and marketplaces on which to focus as a single organization. Second, it realized that the product the company was selling was sold over-the-counter through pharmacies and that this, in turn, was a very different market from the ethical drugs prescribed by physicians and sold in pharmacies under prescription. Both these insights contributed to the refinement of the company's core mission. The company decided that the most lucrative market was the specialized ethical drugs sold through pharmacies under physicians' prescriptions. The result of this decision was to sell off businesses producing products which were no longer consistent with the company's mission, and use the funds from the sales to obtain products which would be within the pharmaceutical specialty. The long phase of research and testing in order to obtain certification that a drug was safe for use was such that it was not possible to make up ground quickly on competitors. The several years of basic research followed by several years of testing meant that most new products would only come to market more than ten years after inception. Careful discussion and thought-provoking focus enabled the company to decide to purchase the rights to drugs already in the testing process in foreign countries, therefore reducing the 'catch-up' time substantially.

The strategy of using foreign drugs is a precise example of setting an interim state between the present and future states. In this situation the ability to start from scratch and develop new ethical drugs was still a distant dream so the staged approach was necessary for the company to cohesively adapt to a changing competitive environment. An intermediate point, which represented movement in the desired direction, was to acquire drugs already in existence with some original testing finished, and bring them into the marketplace on a quicker basis by doing only the additional testing required by the United States FDA, a process which shortened the wait period and gave the pharmaceutical company an intermediate lifeline.

Inter-organizational networks

A dynamic within the organization level is the increasing development of participation in inter-organizational networks, such as strategic alliances in inter-organizational collaboration supply chain management through the extended manufacturing enterprise (EME). The extended enterprise is a business value network where multiple collaborating companies, such as manufacturers, which own and manage parts of the enterprise, bring value to the marketplace (Coughlan and Coghlan, 2011). The purpose and motive for a *strategic network* (such as supply chains, EMEs, joint ventures, strategic alliances) are economic with a primary focus on reducing transaction costs and on increasing competitiveness. At the same time they have the potential to transition from strategic to becoming a learning and transformational network (Coughlan and Coghlan, 2011)

The 'key' individual, team, group/division and organization

We have made the critical distinction between organizational levels and echelons and pointed out that they are not the same. There is a strong connection. Positioning on an organization's hierarchy has an impact on functioning or dysfunctioning. When an individual has a problem the higher he/she is on the echelon the greater the impact is on the organization. The charismatic founder/entrepreneur is legendary in having an impact on an organization's life, style and functioning. The higher one is on the echelon or the more power a team has the greater the influence is to bring about change. The problem of an interdepartmental group or divisional leader is more than a Level II issue for his or her team. The representatives of an organization in building and sustaining inter-organizational networking are central to the creation and maintenance of trust and good inter-organizational relations.

To develop that idea further we refer to the notion of the 'key' individual (individuals who by virtue of power, position, charisma or expertise can influence more than other individuals). The notion of the key individual allows for how leadership is spread around an organization and how it is embedded in teams and groups, rather than in the heroic individual (Raelin, 2003).

Similarly within an organization, there is the notion of the 'key' team and the 'key' group. In engineering organizations, the lead engineering group may be the key group. In manufacturing organizations, over different stages of the life-cycle the key group may shift from design engineering to production to sales. In universities there is typically competition between academics, administration and finance as to which is the key group. In competitive markets where organizations compete for clients and customers, there are 'key' organizations (i.e. those organizations which are pre-eminent, the market leader from which other organizations tend to position themselves). In organization development, process interventions must be owned in the organization from the top. If an intervention is to be successful the issues around key individuals must be understood and dealt with first.

Conclusions

In this chapter we have discussed organizational membership through the notion of the four levels of behaviour and distinguished it from echelon. We have also outlined the organizational processes which take place at each level. We have characterized these processes in terms of a key word to define the essence of each level: Level I *matching needs*, Level II *functioning team*, Level III *coordination*, and Level IV *adaptation* (Table 3.4). Finally we have noted that within the issues of each level there is a twin focus: actions which enable completion of the relevant tasks at each level and actions which facilitate the significant inter-relationships between each level.

This construct of four organizational levels is essential for understanding the dynamic inter-relationship between individuals, teams, aggregations of teams and an organization's strategic endeavours in a complex world of discontinuous change. It integrates the disciplines of individual and group psychology with those of strategic management, technology and industrial relations. In our view, it is located at the cutting edge of organization development and the management of learning and changing.

Reflexive engagement activity 3.1

In the mode of the clinical approach, what insights do you have about how the tasks at each level are met in your organization? Can you verify the insights that you have about this?

1. Do you know what matching means in different hierarchical positions or functional locations in the organization?
2. Do you know what the team challenges are for teams in your organization? Do they differ across different teams? How do you know?
3. Do you know what the interdepartmental coordination challenges are across your organization? Are there particular teams that don't coordinate effectively with other teams?
4. How is the organization positioned strategically to meet present and future market challenges?

Case: Omega Foundation

In an OD intervention in the Omega Foundation, a European healthcare organization which provides residential care for people with physical and sensory disabilities, organizational levels were a central consideration.

In 1997 Omega was going through a period of intense change. Internally, this resulted in changes in governance structure, in policies and procedures, in employment practices, and in methods for funding operations. A major internal force for change was identified in customers' (the service users) changing needs and expectations regarding the service provided by Omega. In response to these forces for change, an organization development project was initiated, with an agreed-upon objective of creating a shared learning experience for participants, which would be grounded in Omega values and mission, and enable it to develop capabilities and processes for continued organizational learning and change.

The aim of the project was to: a) create conditions in which the stakeholders could engage in dialogue and listen to each other's perceptions of major organizational mission and vision components, i.e. on what was important in Omega's work; and b) how it could create actions from the conversations in order to move purposefully into the future.

Each individual, whether resident, staff member, trustee, volunteer, member of a management committee, had a relationship with the organization. This relationship was experienced very differently by members of the different groups and varied from individual to individual. Some individuals related to others as part of staff teams. Others related to the organization as individuals with responsibility, while many others were recipients of the care services provided. The project aimed at strengthening the relationships among these different stakeholders in ways that were appropriate to each of the different constituencies by creating an open space in which conversation and listening could take place. The project also aimed at addressing the functional and residential groups and teams in which individuals worked and lived. Therefore, there was attention to the strategic and operational issues of how each centre functioned, how committees worked and how professionals worked together to deliver the service to the residents. It also examined how the different groups coordinated their efforts, whether it be the resident, staff and management committee within a centre or the many centres within the national organization, or between the head office and the local centres. Finally, the ultimate aim of the project was to help the strategic and operational adaptation of the whole organization in a changing world. The OD project attempted to create an open space for conversation across and between all levels. The project created a structure to facilitate conversation about the present and desired future states of the organization, to enable stakeholders to take ownership of the change issues and to begin empowerment to map courses of action.

Questions for reflection and discussion

1. Map what you think are the different expressions of the individual and team levels in Omega.
2. What insights do you have into the complexities of Level III in Omega? How can you verify these insights?
3. What insights do you have into how Level IV in Omega comprises the effective workings of Levels I, II and III? Where's your evidence?
4. How would you structure working with each level in an OD project as outlined above?

References

Amason, A.A. (1996) Distinguishing the effects of functional and dysfunctional conflict on strategic decision making: Resolving a paradox for senior management teams. *Academy of Management Journal*, 39(1), 123–148.

Argyris, C. (2010) *Organizational Traps*. New York: Oxford University Press.

Beckhard, R. (1972) Optimizing team building efforts. *Journal of Contemporary Business*, 1(3), 23–32.

Beckhard, R. and Harris, R. (1987) *Organizational Transitions*, 2nd edn. Reading, MA: Addison-Wesley.

Bolman, D. and Deal, T. (2013) *Reframing Organizations*. San Francisco, CA: Jossey-Bass.

Bunker, B.B. and Alban, B. (1997) *Large Group Interventions*. San Francisco, CA: Jossey-Bass.

Coghlan, D. (1998) The interlevel dynamics of information technology. *Journal of Information Technology*, 13, 139–149.

Coughlan, P. and Coghlan, D. (2011) *Collaborative Strategic Improvement through Network Action Learning*. Cheltenham: Edward Elgar.

Finglestein, S. and Hambrick, D.C. (1996) *Strategic Leadership: Top Executives and their Effects on Organizations*. St Paul, MN: West.

Hambrick, D.C. (1994) Top management group: A conceptual integration and reconsideration of the 'team' label. In L.L. Cummings and B.M. Staw (eds), *Research in Organizational Behavior*, Vol. 16. Greenwich, CT: JAI Press, pp. 171–213.

Hambrick, D., Nadler, D.A. and Tushman, M.L. (1998) *Navigating Change*. Boston, MA: Harvard Business School Press.

Holman, P. and Devane, T. (2007) *The Change Handbook: The Definitive Resource to Today's Best Methods for Engaging Whole Systems*. 2nd edn. San Francisco, CA: Jossey-Bass.

Katzenbach, J.R. (1998) *Teams at the Top*. Boston, MA: Harvard Business School Press.

McGregor, D. (1960) *The Human Side of Enterprise*. New York: McGraw-Hill.

Miller, J.G. (1978) *Living Systems*. New York: McGraw-Hill.

Nadler, D.A. (1998) *Champion of Change*. San Francisco, CA: Jossey-Bass.

Nadler, D.A., Spencer, J. and Associates (1998) *Executive Teams*. San Francisco, CA: Jossey-Bass.

Raelin, J.A. (2003) *Creating Leaderful Organizations*. San Francisco, CA: Berrett-Kochler.

Rousseau, D.M. (1985) Issues in organizational research: Multi-level and cross-level perspectives. In L.L. Cummings and B.M. Staw (eds), *Research in Organizational Behavior*, Vol. 7. Greenwich, CT: JAI Press, pp. 1–37.

Schein, E.H. (1978) *Career Dynamics: Matching Individual and Organizational Needs*. Reading, MA: Addison-Wesley.

Schein, E.H. (1995) *Career Survival: Strategic job and role planning*, San Francisco, CA: Pfeiffer.

Schein, E.H. (1996) The three cultures of management: The key to organizational learning. *Sloan Management Review*, 37(1), 9–20.

Schein, E.H. (1999) *Process Consultation Revisited: Building the Helping Relationship*. Reading, MA: Addison-Wesley.

Schein, E.H. (2009) *The Corporate Culture Survival Guide*. 2nd edn. San Francisco, CA: Jossey-Bass.

Schein, E.H. and Van Maanen, J. (2013) *Career Anchors: The Changing Nature of Careers*. New York: Wiley.

Stapley, L. (2006) *Individuals, Groups and Organizations Beneath the Surface*. London: Karnac.

Wheelan, S.A. (2015) *Creating Effective Teams: A Guide for Members and Leaders*. Thousand Oaks, CA: Sage.

Zand, D.E. (1997) *The Leadership Triad: Knowledge, Trust and Power*. New York: Oxford University Press.

4

INTERLEVEL DYNAMICS

The notion of organizational levels is common in organization development and change texts. Many of these texts have their chapters constructed around interventions at the different levels, for example, individual interventions, group interventions, inter-group interventions and total system interventions (Anderson, 2015). It appears that this approach uses organizational levels as a set of convenient headings under which various OD activities can be categorized. Organizational levels in this context become a rather static notion. In the latter part of the last century, the focus was on individual, team and organization but not on the systemic interconnectedness and inter-relationship between them. By contrast, we are endeavouring to describe the dynamic nature of the four organizational levels as central to the process of organizing. A significant element in this dynamic nature is the relationship between levels. Therefore, when we talk about any particular level, we are simultaneously dealing with an interlevel reality.

The conceptual basis for the interconnectedness of organizational levels is found in systems dynamics (Senge, 1990; McCaughan and Palmer, 1994; Williams and Hummelbrunner, 2013). As system practitioners point out, the key insight in a systems approach is to see inter-relationships occurring in feedback loops rather than seeing linear cause-and-effect chains. For instance, an individual's relationships within a team are both affected and caused by the team's relationships with individual members. Within organizational systems, the interconnectedness of departments, functions, positions on the echelon, demonstrate the centrality of complex feedback loops, each having an effect on the other. In the framework of the four organizational levels, each level is related to the other three. The individual is affected by his/her relationship to the team, by how the team works in the interdepartmental group and by how the organization functions in its external environment. The face-to-face team is affected by how the individual functions in his/her relationship to the organization and vice versa, how the interdepartmental group functions, and how the organization succeeds in its mission. The interdepartmental group is affected by how the organization relates to its environment, how its constituent teams function, and how the individuals and the organization match their respective needs. In our view these dynamic relationships are constitutive of the organization as a living system.

Interlevel dynamics, or levels of aggregation as they are sometimes called, enrich the perspective of organizations as living systems, as they focus on patterns of interaction among people, and so are open to the complexity and unpredictability that all human relationships potentially have. We cannot be mechanical about relationships: we can only adopt an organic approach which tries to work collaboratively with people rather than to control them. The patterns of participation in organizations, namely the individual with the organization and vice versa, the individual with fellow team members and vice versa, teams with other teams within the interdepartmental group, and the organization with its external environment and vice versa, are determined by the system itself. They can work together in the interest of the whole or work against one another and fragment the whole. They have their own internal cognitional activity which shapes what we call culture and they select what they consider to be important, sometimes to the frustration of senior management. Above all, they are capable of learning and changing. How they do so is the subject of this book. A premise underpinning the integration of interlevel dynamics and action research in this book is that interlevel dynamics are integral to creating 'communities of practice' and 'communities of inquiry'.

The interconnectedness between positions on the echelon and levels of complexity exists in the role of the key individual. The key individual is a general term to connote those whose role involves crossing boundaries from one subsystem to another and linking one subsystem to another, as instanced by Likert's (1961) famous linking pin framework. The team leader, supervisor, manager, administrator crosses the boundary from his/her area of responsibility to those of other functions or higher management. That is a crossing of boundaries on the hierarchical echelon. At the same time, these individuals are interacting in interlevel dynamics. They bring individual issues to a team, and team issues to the interdepartmental group. When an individual represents his/her own team to a broader function, he/she crosses from a team to an interdepartmental group level, and the dynamics of that interaction may lead to a reassessment of the individual level. Examples of such interlevel interaction are described by Lewin (1948) as the 'gatekeeping' role, by Allen (1977) as the 'technological gatekeeper', and by Ancona and Caldwell (1988) as external functions such as 'sentry', 'scout' and 'ambassador', whereby information is brought into the team from the external environment. New information, especially disconfirming information, may cause the individual to be rejected by the team, thereby producing conflict in the team. We will return to the notion of the key individual in Chapter 7 when we examine how the process of changing moves across the four levels.

Level I effects – functional and dysfunctional – on other levels

The matching needs task at Level I implies an interconnectedness between the individual and the organization. The individual brings his/her life tasks to the organization and enters into a psychological contract with the organization. The feedback loop from the organization's management communicates that the person is of value and is worthy of compensation. Thereby the formal contract of employment is set up and enacted through conditions of employment, socialization, training and development, career planning, promotion opportunities and other human resource management processes.

Dysfunctions at Level I can come from either side of the relationship. Issues particular to an individual can come from a person's maladaptive coping with the dynamics of the life-, work-, and family-cycles of adult development (Schein, 1978). From management's side, managerial assumptions about human motivation, actual management behaviour, and the conditions of employment and compensation create the conditions for, or inhibit, an effective Level I (McGregor, 1960).

Level I can affect any of the other three levels. Depending on the individual's place in the organization's echelon this effect can be more or less significant. If a dysfunction on the individual level concerns the chief executive, then the Level II senior management group, the coordination of the entire organization at Level III and the organization's competitive performance at Level IV are affected. When an individual level dysfunction occurs at the operational level, the effects may be more localized. Figure 4.1 depicts Level I dysfunction influences on other levels.

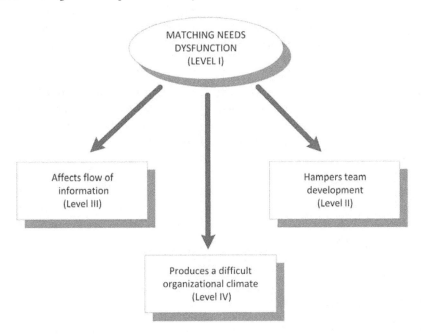

FIGURE 4.1 Level I dysfunctions affecting other levels

How Level I affects Level II

As the individual enters into a face-to-face working team (Level II), issues of team membership predominate for the individual. The individual struggles to satisfy particular emotional needs – identity, power, control and influence, individual needs vs. team goals, and acceptance–intimacy (Wheelan, 2015). How these issues are resolved on a continuing basis sets the psychological contract between the team and the individual member. From management's view, the task is to be effective in achieving the team's tasks, and the focus is more on uniting around common goals and effective process. When individuals do not integrate into a team the outcome can be team dysfunctioning (Level II) or dysfunctioning in the matching needs relationship at Level I among the team members. Yet if a dysfunction persists for a long period of time or does not yield to team process interventions, then most often Level I dysfunction is operative.

How Level I affects Level III

As individuals interact with a wider and more complex system, depending on their position in the organization, there is a growing sense of alienation and of non-belonging. The average individual's identification with his/her own team, section or function typically means that the individual's interaction with the interdepartmental group primarily operates through the membership of a team. As already mentioned, this scenario is different for key individuals, such as supervisors and middle and higher level management. In this context, Level III dynamics centre around issues of information availability, resource allocation and inter-team power alignment as management attempts to orchestrate the aggregation of multiple teams at Level III.

In a university the president functioned in an authoritarian top-down detailed analysis mode of operating. He worked that way himself and throughout his ten-year tenure that philosophy spread through the university. His successor worked from a participative model, whereby problem-solving and decision-making through consensus were implemented. He had an uphill battle in transforming the norm from the individual controlling his/her own area in isolation to one where interdependence required interactive information-sharing and decision-making by consensus. This was apparent throughout all levels of the university as well as up and down through the hierarchy. The ten years' practice of guarding one's turf and working in isolation was extremely difficult to overcome.

How Level I affects Level IV

The chief executive of an organization plays a key role in forming the organization's strategic position in its external environment.

Howard Head was an engineer and also an inventor and entrepreneur who developed a new material for producing skis at a time when all skis were made of wood. In establishing the Head Ski company in 1950 in Baltimore, he exerted strong influence on the company and how it was perceived. As an example, he originally had wanted his skis to be black so that colour would not detract from the design and marketing would be centred on the engineering and the performance of the skis. In Howard Head's mind the success of the company was directly proportional to the success of professional skiers using Head skis – if he had had his way the only customers would be professional skiers. This insight into Head, the engineer, is essential to understanding the Head Ski Company.

Level II effects – functional and dysfunctional – on other levels

Team dynamics occur throughout the organization. They are found in the workings of the senior management group, teams within each department, the organization of the cleaning shifts, formal and informal committees, task forces and so on. The face-to-face team level is connected to the individual, interdepartmental group and organizational levels. Figure 4.2 depicts Level II dysfunction influences on other levels.

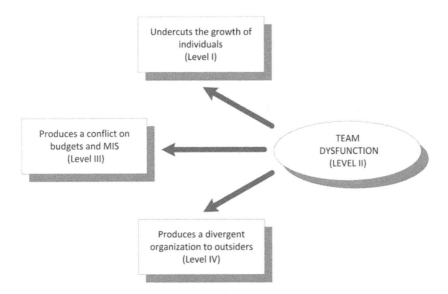

FIGURE 4.2 Level II dysfunctions affecting other levels

How Level II affects Level I

A team's norms may result in behaviour that discriminates against particular individuals and create a dysfunction from the team back to the individual. The famous Asch experiments have shown how a group can enforce conformity on individuals even to the point of the individuals doubting sensory evidence. Such pressure from the group can enforce conformity on individuals to participate in the group's defensive routines by colluding with a sense of success (groupthink) by not surfacing questions of concern or by not raising issues which are considered to be undiscussable (Argyris, 2010).

A sales installation team of a large telephone company included one woman in an otherwise all-male team. The men were avid sports enthusiasts and constantly made use of sporting analogies and imagery. In fact, the sports chat was the price of admission to the team's conversations. The female colleague who had no interest in sports and was barraged by sporting models felt that she was intentionally being made to feel excluded. The lack of sensitivity on the part of the males led to the withdrawal of the woman from active participation in the team. From her perspective she explained her difficulties to her MBA organizational behaviour professor, who suggested that she confront the men's conduct in front of the team and talk out the issues involved. The ability to raise and articulate the issues enabled the woman to return to her team, confront the men with their behaviour in a gentle way, and show how it produced a feeling of exclusion in her. While this confrontation resulted in some sensitivity and opened the door for a greater participation in the team on the woman's part, it did not eclipse all the prejudice and behavioural practices which had been built up in an all-male organization over a long period of time. The exclusionary climate had grown over many years as the role of operators had been limited to women and the role of installers had been limited to men.

How Level II affects Level III

In a large organization, the interdepartmental group's effectiveness depends on the quality and timeliness of information and resources from the teams which make up the interdepartmental group, so that any interdepartmental group level dysfunctioning may be due to a particular team's dysfunctioning in achieving its own tasks. For instance, when a finance department delays purchase or payment for purchases, new purchases are not received on time for particular projects. A finance team's context is always at the interdepartmental group and organizational levels: receiving information; providing it for other parts of the organization; making judgements regarding financial criteria for the operation (Level III) and relating it to external auditors, the board of management, and the leader (Level IV).

How Level II affects Level IV

The interlevel interaction between the team and organizational levels can be found in those teams whose role is to work on policy and strategy, e.g. senior management groups, sales teams, and other boundary functional teams.

A construction company, in its building division, was going through a difficult period. Competition was focused on custom building whereas the company manufactured modular buildings so a meeting with the sales and engineering departments was called. In a separate management training session, which coincidentally included the same members, Rashford acted as facilitator. The first session comprised an exercise of tinker toys to encourage the development of team skills and the senior management group at first elected to stay together as a group. As the exercise proceeded the company's president got up, left the group and began to pace the room on his own. He then returned to the group with a view on what the group should use the toys to build and how it could sell the idea (the task of the exercise). The group complied. In the review and discussion that followed, participants reflected that the president's behaviour exhibited in the exercise was his common way of behaving and that the company's senior management group operated in this manner also. In fact, the real issue in the company's inability to thrive in custom building was that the divisions represented by senior management wanted to do their work as individuals and did not have the skills to work together. Working together was essential in order to produce custom building for the customer. Armed with this insight the senior management group began a concerted effort to work closely together, resulting in significantly improving decision-making and positively affecting the whole organization through better strategic choices. Success ensued.

Level III effects – functional and dysfunctional – on other levels

The interdepartmental group level is the most political of levels and is where interlevel interaction is most critical. Interdepartmental group level dynamics are commonly enacted in team level settings where representatives of different functions or departments meet to coordinate and review plans and activities. Success at this level requires political manoeuvring and bargaining in order to achieve an adequate political balance between information availability, resource allocation, and the maintenance of power and influence of particular interests. An instance of the interdepartmental group level interacting with the individual level occurs whenever department heads experience their suggestions and proposals blocked, and their frustration with the inability to get ideas through leads them to withdraw from the arena and perhaps leave the organization. Figure 4.3 depicts Level III dysfunction influences on other levels.

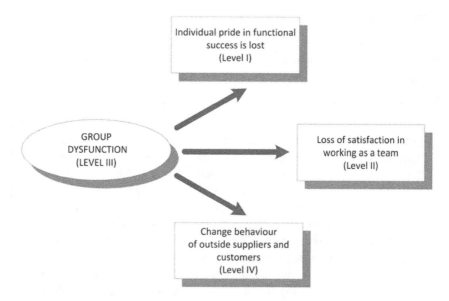

FIGURE 4.3 Level III dysfunctions affecting other levels

How Level III affects Level I

The effect of Level III on Level I is most often seen in the budgeting process or the management of information. The organization that finds resources scarce and begins to change the allocation process will soon affect one team more than another. Individuals begin to worry about their relationship with the organization. The ability of the organization to be a place of personal growth appears to diminish.

How Level III affects Level II

The working of the interdepartmental group can affect the working of a team. Obvious examples like late or incomplete information at the interdepartmental group can impede the effective task completion by a team which is dependent on the reception of that information accurately and on time.

An organization's senior management group set up a team to design and coordinate a company-wide training programme on environmental awareness. After six months' work the team invited Coghlan to do some team-building work because morale was low: one member had resigned and others were near the point of following her. The consultant met the team and inquired into the team's process – its goals, its way of working, and so on. What became very apparent to the consultant was that this team had been very active and had fulfilled its mandate effectively. At the same time its work did not appear to be having an impact on the organization. Few members were taking up the opportunity for the training that the team was organizing. What emerged was that although the senior management group had given the team its mandate and told it how important its role was, this had not been communicated to the rest of the organization. Consequently the training programme was perceived across the organization as outside the mainstream priorities of the organization and therefore something that one could take or leave as one chose. Subsequently, the team met the senior management group and discussed this lack of clarity. This situation illustrates how the team's problems lay not in the Level II processes within the team but rather in the interface with the senior management group, whose own behaviour in not communicating the importance of the training to the organization as a whole had led to a crisis within the team.

How Level III affects Level IV

Interdepartmental rivalry or conflict can sabotage an organization's ability to compete in its external market. An industrial dispute can cripple an organization when it loses its share of the market during the closure or its good name for reliability suffers so that when the dispute is ended it finds it difficult to recover its former position. The terms of settlement may put severe strain on the organization's resources.

The effect of Level III on other levels can be significant.

A greeting card manufacturing company using large quantities of paper purchased on rolls measured in tons set up an interdepartmental group management information system to detect paper losses in production. Each roll was purchased within parameters of length and thickness while conforming to weight specifications. The company wanted to increase its production by controlling and reducing the amount of waste. As paper moved along the production process, whenever presses were out of register or there were other failures, the length of the amount of paper that had to be scrapped was measured and detailed against the weight of the original roll, which led to a reduction in waste. The printing foremen and their teams were put under pressure to not produce waste (Level III affecting Level II). At the same time, there was considerable tension between the production and card design functions as production blamed card design for repeatedly developing difficult-to-register designs due to the added precision necessary for accurate colour interfacing (Level III affecting Level II in another function).

The control of scrap and the measurement of the length of paper to provide a better manufacturing control mechanism turned out to have the desired effect, but not in the way it was expected. The paper manufacturer, through its sales people who worked in the card company heard that now the length of each roll was measured in order to ascertain the magnitude of loss. Fearful of losing the greeting card company's business, the paper manufacturer evaluated its own processes and found it had allowed thicker paper than desirable: despite being within specifications, paper rolls had been shorter, resulting in fewer cards produced by the card company for the same weight whereas the card company wanted length for more cards. The paper company changed its manufacturing process in order to produce a thinner paper with the same strength but with a longer roll length. As a consequence, the card company dramatically improved its productivity producing more cards. This example of the card company's Level III affecting Level IV resulted in an improved strategic position relative to its competitors. In this case, the competitive position of the paper manufacturing company also improved.

Level IV effects – functional and dysfunctional – on other levels

The organizational level depends on the individual, team and interdepartmental group levels working adequately. The organization's attempt to exist, to survive and to fulfil its mission in a competitive environment requires a strategic balance between the subsystems within it. It is contingent on coordination at the inter-departmental group level (Level III), so that the many departments, functions and interest groups maintain a working relationship which contributes to the organization's ability to fulfil its mission (Level IV). Such coordination depends on each team being effective in its own area of responsibility (Level II), which, in turn, depends on an adequate formal and psychological contract between the individual and the organization (Level I).

Often, Level IV dysfunction emanates from the competitive environment and then affects the other levels. When a radical shift in the market necessitates a change in the material being used, engineering and manufacturing functions are drastically affected. Figure 4.4 depicts Level IV dysfunction influences on other levels.

How Level IV affects Level I

A special relationship exists between the organizational policy level and the individual level. The individual's identification with the organization's mission and culture is dependent upon how the organization functions in its external environment and how that then gets transferred back through the three levels. The ability to function at Level IV requires a sense of mission, stability and viability. When this is threatened, individuals review their most basic commitment to the organization. The relationship between these two levels is typically referred to as 'organizational climate'.

In a national health service, when funds from the exchequer were reduced in an effort to control public spending, there was less money to go around the different

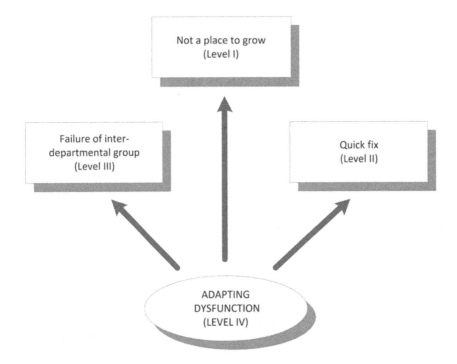

FIGURE 4.4 Level IV dysfunctions affecting other levels

sectors of the health service (Level III). This resulted in particular units receiving less money and having to work on reduced resources, both financial and personnel related (Level II). Consequently, many units were placed under a great deal of strain. This in turn resulted in a growing anger and alienation among nursing staff, a decrease in the matching needs relationship and many seeking to leave the system and work elsewhere (Level I).

How Level IV affects Level II

Environmental forces can play a significant part in the functioning of a senior management group and is often mediated through the interdepartmental group. A discussion on how the changing environment is affecting the organization can evoke protective action in the senior management group's behaviour as each function represented tries to protect its own group from forthcoming changes.

How Level IV affects Level III

Mergers and acquisitions provide particular challenges between levels IV and III (Dauber, 2012; Marks and Mirvis, 2010). What was hitherto a Level IV organization becomes a Level III unit within the merged or acquired organization. The challenges arise from disparate groups being thrust together, the forced merging of cultures and traditions and the change demands made on what is considered to be the minor partner.

Conclusions

In this chapter we have shown how the four organizational levels are implicitly interconnected. Each level is linked to each of the others (Figure 4.5). An understanding of how the loops feed back from one level to another is essential for the manager or consultant in assessing the workings of each level and in preparing and implementing interventions.

Reflexive engagement activity 4.1

Take an issue in your organization with which you are familiar:

1. Name the issue from the perspective of the organization for its performance and success.
2. Now work diagonally along the shaded boxes. What demands does it make on interdepartmental group coordination? How does it impact on the work of teams? What are the consequences for individuals?
3. In the mode of the clinical approach, where would you put your energies to address the issue and heal any dysfunctions?
4. Develop strategies to address the issue at each level.

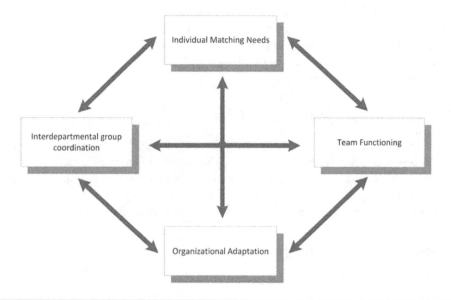

FIGURE 4.5 Interlevel dynamics

	Individual	*Team*	*Interdepartmental Group*	*Organization*
Individual				
Team				
Inter-departmental Group				
Organization				

TABLE 4.1 Reflexive engagement activity 4.1

Case: The IT investment (Adapted from Coghlan, 2000)

An IT consultant was invited to an organization to advise its senior management on the selection of an updated IT system. He initially met the managing director, and then in turn interviewed the managers of the manufacturing, marketing and finance functions respectively, each of whom were members of the senior management group. He also met the IT director, who was not a member of the senior management group.

From these interviews he formed the following picture. The senior management group was intensely political as some members disliked other members and did not readily share information with one another. Furthermore, they were unanimous in their distrust of the managing director. In fact the individual managers had little sense of what was going on in functional areas other than their own; none of them had much idea of what they required of a new IT system. Each commented that they left IT matters to the IT director. On the other hand, the IT director felt very frustrated. He experienced that while IT issues were being left to him, he could not get enough information or policy direction from the senior managers on which to make recommendations. It subsequently emerged that the capability of the current IT system, which was now to be replaced, was largely under-utilized. The IT director's expectation was that this would happen again with the new system and a significant capital investment would not reap its potential benefits.

In this situation it was clear that the organization's IT agenda was secondary to other organizational issues. In other words, any efforts to resolve the technological issues of choosing a new IT system might well be doomed to failure unless some key organizational issues were resolved first.

Questions for reflection and discussion

1. What are the Level I, Level II, Level III and Level IV issues in this organization?
2. What insights do you have into how they affect the issues of IT investment?
3. What insights do you have into how the level issues identified in Q. 1 affect one another? Where's your evidence?
4. At what level do you think the IT consultant might intervene to address the issues?

Case: Network Action Learning Improvement Initiative (Adapted from Coghlan and Coughlan, 2015)

A company in the transportation industry needed to develop a network of suppliers and outsourcing of component parts. This growth in outsourcing underscored the significance of supplier relationships and managing the supply base had to become an even more critical task. To compete, new competencies and relationships had to be developed and, so, the company began a two-year collaborative improvement initiative during which it engaged interactively with key suppliers. The initiative involved interactions at a number of levels: between the company and the group of suppliers as an EME; and between it and individual suppliers as a set of dyads.

The system integrator (SI) invited the suppliers to a workshop where the underlying objective was to help the suppliers to feel that they were not alone in facing issues such as mutual understanding, goal sharing, order management, quality management, cost reduction and change order management. The invitation was to become part of a much larger effort, in which they believed and were taking part. Supplier companies' concerns were of a different kind however. They were interested in knowing the difficulties that the other companies saw in engaging in collaborative improvements. They spoke about the different relationships that suppliers had with the SI and of how they were fearful of change. The network held monthly workshops, preceded and followed by interim dyad-level and internal firm-level meetings. The participants in the monthly workshops at network level included both the system integrator and supplier staff, all of whom were in a position to influence the activities.

The focus of these face-to-face meetings and conference calls was to provide updates on improvement initiatives at dyad and firm levels, to question and to reflect on the progress, and to work out a project plan. The internal, firm-level, meetings evolved around these improvement projects. The participating staff questioned progress, planned the next steps and, as necessary, engaged in training. Together, these three levels of interaction fed from and into each other iteratively.

The SI and supplier engaged in a first initiative that was designed both to enable the firms to improve their collaboration and also to develop a shared understanding of collaborative processes based on their direct experience. They undertook to improve lead-times for equipment and for parts deliveries. This initiative ran for two years and involved facilitated monthly meetings of managers from both firms. These meetings were complemented by regular meetings at network level where the appropriateness of the monthly workshop was confirmed as both useful and essential.

The shared objective of the second initiative was to reduce lead-time for the delivery of equipment parts by six months. They also targeted document sharing, aiming to be more transparent and traceable. As the teams agreed to adopt the overall approach used in the first initiative they made swift progress in planning the corrective action. During this stage, SI identified changes in its working relationship with the supplier as the supplier became more proactive, and was making things happen rather than waiting for direction. The SI listened to the supplier's views and ideas, and both reached agreement on subsequent activities and responsibilities. It realized that reciprocal benefits of sharing activities with the supplier could help to achieve initiative goals and also to create a platform for further improvements.

Questions for reflection and discussion

1. What are the levels present in the EME action learning group?
2. Place yourself in the role of one of the SI's purchasing managers. What interlevel issues do you face in this action learning process?
3. How are interlevel dynamics useful in understanding and managing EME processes?

References

Allen, T. (1977) *Managing the Flow of Technology*. Cambridge, MA: MIT Press.
Ancona, D. and Caldwell, D. (1988) Beyond task and maintenance: Defining external functions in groups. *Group and Organization Studies*, 13(4), 468–494.
Anderson, D.L. (2015) *Organization Development: The Process of Leading Organizational Change*. 3rd edn. Thousand Oaks, CA: Sage.
Argyris, C. (2010) *Organizational Traps*. New York: Oxford University Press.

Coghlan, D. (2000) Interlevel dynamics in clinical inquiry. *Journal of Organizational Change Management*, 13(2), 190–200.

Coghlan, D. and Coughlan, P. (2015) Effecting change and learning in networks through network action learning. *Journal of Applied Behavioral Science*, 51(3), 375–400.

Dauber, D. (2012) Opposing positions in M&A research. *Cross Cultural Management*, 19(3), 375–398.

Lewin, K. (1948) Group decision and social change. Reprinted in M. Gold (ed.) (1999), *The Complete Social Scientist: A Kurt Lewin Reader*. Washington, DC: American Psychological Association, pp. 265–284.

Likert, R. (1961) *New Patterns of Management*. New York: McGraw-Hill.

Marks, M.L., and Mirvis, P.H. (2010) *Joining Forces: Making One Plus One Equal Three in Mergers, Acquisitions, and Alliances*. New York: John Wiley & Sons.

McCaughan, N. and Palmer, B. (1994) *Systems Thinking for Harassed Managers*. London: Karnac.

McGregor, D. (1960) *The Human Side of Enterprise*. New York: McGraw-Hill.

Schein, E.H. (1978) *Career Dynamics: Matching Individual and Organizational Needs*. Reading, MA: Addison-Wesley.

Senge, P. (1990) *The Fifth Discipline*. New York: Doubleday.

Wheelan, S.A. (2015) *Creating Effective Teams: A Guide for Members and Leaders*. Thousand Oaks, CA: Sage.

Williams, B. and Hummelbrunner, R. (2013) *Systems Concepts in Action*. Stanford, CA: Stanford University Press.

PART II

Interlevel learning and changing

In Part II we introduce the subject of organizational learning and changing and invite you to a reflexive engagement in terms of $L=P+Q$ by adopting a clinical perspective to processes of learning and changing. We are using the term 'changing' as a gerund rather than 'change' as a noun so as to be focused on the ongoing engagement of individuals, teams, the interdepartmental group and the organization in changing and learning. In the three chapters in this section we explore the interlevel dynamics of organizational learning and changing. In Chapter 5 we introduce some fundamental notions that help us to understand what learning and changing in organizations mean. We ground these in a notion of systemic health and in the process of learning and changing as cycles of continuous coping and adaptation as information is received into an organization, processed and transformed into outputs. In Chapter 6 we explore processes of large systems changing as interlevel dynamics. In Chapter 7 we map how changing begins, enters and moves through an organization in and across the four organization levels.

5

THE PROCESS OF LEARNING AND CHANGING

In Chapter 2 we grounded our understanding of organizations in the process of organizing and explained how this is a richer perspective to take than the more static notion of organization. Within the same perspective we now approach the process of learning and changing. We invite you to a reflexive engagement in terms of $L=P+Q$ by adopting a clinical perspective to systemic learning and changing.

Underpinning all processes of learning and changing are activities of taking in information, processing it, making decisions and taking action. How any system, whether you as an individual or the organization in which you work, does this characterizes its health. Developed from constructs in the field of mental health, the four elements of a healthy system are: a sense of identity and purpose, the capacity to adapt to changing external and internal circumstances, the capacity to perceive and test reality, and the internal integration of subsystems (Bennis, 1962; Schein, 1980, 2013). Consequently, we can frame systemic organizational health as a cycle of continuous coping and adapting as information is received into an organization, processed and transformed into outputs (Schein, 1980, 2013). We will develop this notion in the following chapter.

Learning

It is useful to distinguish between different types of learning. One is where we learn to solve a problem by finding a solution that works within a given frame of reference. Argyris and Schon (1996) call this type of learning *single loop* learning, which is the form of learning by which we solve routine problems and make improvements to our organizations. It is based on the principle of linear causality, if A then B. This form of learning is essential for the continuous improvement of production and service delivery and the more effective functioning of organizations. There are times, however, when the steps we take to solve a problem or improve a service do not achieve that end; indeed it may make the problem worse. In these situations we are challenged to question the questions we are currently asking and to reframe the way we formulate the questions or define the situation. Argyris and Schon call this form of learning *double loop* learning, and define it as the process of learning how to learn. In their view double loop learning is central to organizational learning and is critical to uncovering organizational dysfunctions. Argyris and Schon also discuss *deutero*-learning, which is, in effect, about developing the practice and skills of double loop learning. Double loop learning can be a once-off event and can inhibit future learning. Accordingly, learning from previous contexts of learning or failures to learn so that new strategies for learning can be created are characteristics of *deutero*-learning.

Organizational learning

Organizational learning refers to what and how the total organization (not merely what individuals or groups within the organization) can do to increase or maintain the capacity to act in the face of changing internal and external circumstances. There are two basic challenges in learning: exploring new possibilities and exploiting what we have learned (March, 1991). *Exploration* refers to the exploration of new possibilities and includes things captured by terms such as: search, variation, risk taking, experimentation, play, flexibility, discovery and innovation. *Exploitation* refers to the exploitation of old certainties and includes such things as: refinement, choice, production, efficiency, selection, implementation and execution.

For double loop learning to take place in organizations managers need to learn to question their theories-in-use and basic assumptions (Argyris and Schon, 1996). While organizations have formal goals and strategies that they espouse govern their behaviour, they typically have covert assumptions that actually are at least as significant in driving behaviour. These assumptions find expression in the routines of the organizing. Some of these routines may actually inhibit double loop learning. Argyris (2010) refers to these as 'defensive routines'. These routines are actions that aim to prevent people from experiencing embarrassment and are self-reinforcing and self-proliferating systems of self-protection. They are skilfully implemented and lead to organizational defensive routines which protect them and keep them from being discussed.

Learning mechanisms

Contemporary organizational learning literature is focusing on how organizations develop organizational learning mechanisms (Lipshitz et al., 2007). These mechanisms typically refer to planned organizational structures and processes that encourage dynamic learning, particularly to enhance organizational capabilities. The mechanisms can apply at individual, group, organizational or inter-organizational levels and can aim to initiate, facilitate, monitor and reward learning. Organizational learning mechanisms can be designed and managed in various ways

(Fredberg et al., 2011). These various ways have been described as a set of learning design dimensions, each of which fulfils a necessary learning requirement for achieving learning and performance. As such, the learning design dimensions are a basic set of alternative solutions from which managers can choose in order to meet the learning design requirements.

Utilizing a design thinking perspective triggers the creation of learning mechanisms – composed of structures and processes – as an integral part of a changing initiative. Contemporary literature on learning is focusing on ways of organizing with a long-term perspective in mind (Lawler and Worley, 2012; Mohrman and Shani, 2011). Such development is embedded in the creation of organizational agility via a tapestry of learning mechanisms (Shani and Docherty, 2008; Mohrman and Shani, 2011). These mechanisms typically refer to planned organizational structures and processes that encourage dynamic learning, particularly to enhance organizational capabilities (Oliver, 2009). The mechanisms can apply at individual, group, organizational or inter-organizational levels and can aim to initiate, facilitate, monitor and reward learning (Schechter, 2008).

Shani and Docherty (2003, 2008) present three types of learning mechanisms: cognitive, structural and procedural:

- *Cognitive learning mechanisms* provide language, symbols, theories, values and concepts for thinking about and understanding learning issues. For example, single and double loop learning concepts can help to identify a starting point and to evaluate a change of state resulting from an action (Argyris and Schon, 1996). Critical to attending to learning is to grasp the general empirical method of how the mind works in questioning experience, processing and weighing data and forming judgements (Coghlan, 2012). The conscious application of the learning perspective represents a language and concepts with which to frame, to think about and to reflect on an ambition, and which require relationships and procedural steps to realize (the focus of the following mechanisms).
- *Structural mechanisms* comprise organizational, physical and technical infrastructures, such as action learning sets (Pedler, 2008), parallel learning structures (Bushe and Shani, 1991), quality teams, continuous project groups (Enberg et al., 2006), inter-organizational supply chain groups (Coughlan and Coghlan, 2011), feedback channels, databases, intranets, document sharing systems and the physical layout of the work space.
- *Procedural mechanisms* are the institutionalized procedures that promote and support learning, such as learning meetings and action learning programmes (Marquardt, 2011). Recognition and recording of interactions among key functionaries facilitate this capturing and application of the learning achieved.

Roth, Shani and Leary (2007) describe how, in a biopharma company, they set up learning mechanisms in order to build learning capabilities. The cognitive mechanism involved the company understanding that there was knowledge more than knowledge about medical science, i.e. it is also about leadership. The structural mechanisms that were established and formalized were a knowledge facilitation method for learning across groups and functions and knowledge facilitators were trained with formal accreditation. Methods for cross-team learning were set up and followed through as procedural mechanisms with interviews, interventions, evaluation and reporting.

Organizations have choices as they determine the direction, scope and structure of learning mechanisms, and the notion of sustainable development suggests that organizations need to be open to alternative mechanisms. They may draw on existing capabilities and build their own learning mechanisms, or build a new mechanism that seems to have worked elsewhere, or choose any combination of the above. As such, a unique tapestry of learning mechanisms is likely to evolve in changing. The critical issue is not so much which choices are made, or what specific tapestry of learning mechanisms get designed as the learning process followed in making choices.

Organizational changing

As we introduced above, we are grounding the processes of changing as activities of taking in information, processing it, making decisions and taking action. As Schein (1980) demonstrates, the information that is being sensed and taken in may be disconfirming and be a demanding challenge to the status quo. Accordingly, there may be a hesitancy or resistance to the disconfirmation, a fear or anxiety to embark on the necessary or desired changing, and structural and procedural barriers to embedding the outcomes of changing. In the remainder of this chapter and the following two chapters we focus on these issues.

Orders of changing

We may distinguish different orders of changing. Changing that improves existing operations, such as continuous improvement is often referred to as first-order, adaptive or continuous changing. Equivalently, changing that involves redefining the organization and its business may be termed second-order, generative, transformational or discontinuous changing. Here we use first-, second- and third-order changing as our terms.

First-order changing occurs when a specific change is identified and implemented within an existing way of thinking. For example, Bartunek, Crosta, Dame and LeLacheur (2000) describe management-led action research in a bank on a problem of communication problems with clients. Throughout the processes of participative data gathering, data analysis, feedback and action planning, intervention and evaluation, the named problem was addressed and improvements made.

It is realized that sometimes, concrete problems are symptoms of complex attitudinal and cultural problems that must be addressed and that problem resolution involves organizational transformation. *Second-order* changing occurs when first-order changing is inadequate and that changing requires lateral thinking and questioning and altering the core assumptions that underlie the situation. In another example, Bartunek, Crosta, Dame and LeLacheur describe a manager-led change project which initially aimed at addressing improving a manufacturing system by increasing volume while maintaining flexibility as well as enabling automated material control and improved planning. As the data was being analysed, it became evident that these changes would involve creating a radically new way for the company to do business. Accordingly through the changing process, materials personnel, assemblers, testers and supervisors/managers participated in analysis and feedback resulting in the implementation of a new integrated manufacturing system. Due to the success of this project, a similar methodology was applied to other changing projects in the company. Second-order changing is equivalent to changing the culture (Schein, 2009). Second-order changing can be implemented as a once-off event becoming normative and embedded in the system as unchangeable. The creative leap or lateral thinking gets embedded in operational practice and takes on a first-order character. Hence there is a need for organizations to develop the ability to renew themselves continually.

Third-order changing occurs when the members of an organization learn the habit of questioning their own assumptions and points of view, and developing and implementing new ones as complex adaptive systems (Burnes, 2004; Miller and Page, 2007). Third-order change goes beyond willingness to question our existing way of thinking in that it entails a continuous openness to information gathered from the environment and from within the organization that leads to accepting that reframing the very mission and vision are possibilities. Third-order changing occurs when complex adaptive systems alter their essence in pursuit of survival.

Programmes of changing

Mitki, Shani and Stjernberg (2000) cluster change programmes as limited, focused and holistic:

- *Limited change programmes* are aimed at addressing a specific problem, such as team building, communication improvement, management development, operational improvement and so on.
- *Focused change programmes* are ones that identify a few key aspects, such as time, quality, customer value, and then use these, by design, as levers for changing the organization system-wide.
- *Holistic change programmes* are aimed by design to simultaneously address all (or most) aspects of the organization.

Buono and Kerber (2008) make a useful distinction between three approaches to changing: directed change, planned change and guided changing:

- *Directed change* is where there are tightly defined goals and leadership directs and commands.
- *Planned change* is where there is a clear goal and vision of the future and leadership devises a roadmap to reach it and influences how it is reached.
- *Guided changing* is where the direction is loosely defined and leadership points the way and keeps watch over the process.

Table 5.1 demonstrates how Mitki, Shani and Stjernberg's and Buono and Kerber's frameworks provide a way of framing how some changing projects have and continue to have limited and focused programmes and may address first-order challenges. Holistic and guided changing are more likely to be needed for second-order challenges.

Engaging with change

Traditional change theory has been built around Lewin's (1948) model that the change process has three stages or sets of issues: being motivated to change, changing, and making the change survive and work. Any change process can be conceptualized as comprising three stages, – i) a stage of seeing the need for change and assenting to its relevance (what Lewin called 'unfreezing') and Schein (1980) 'disconfirmation', ii) a stage of changing from the present state to a changed state (what Lewin called 'moving'), and iii) a stage of making the change survive and work (what Lewin called 'refreezing'). In Lewin's view attention to all three stages are essential. Lewin's theory is frequently considered to be out of date because a) it appears to assume a more stable world where planned change occurs periodically and linearly rather than discontinuously as in today's world (Burnes, 2004) and b) in many situations we are forced to change first and think about it afterwards, so moving may precede unfreezing. Accordingly we present four psychological stages of change – denying, dodging, doing and sustaining – which in our experience accommodates both scenarios.

TABLE 5.1 Orders of limited, focused and guided changing

Change Programmes	Change Approaches	Orders of Changing
Limited	• Directed approach • Planned approach	Focus is likely to be first order.
Focused	• Directed approach • Planned approach	Focus is likely to be first order.
Holistic	• Guided changing	Focus is likely to be second order with emphasis on conversation about change and changing.

Four psychological reactions to changing

We present four psychological stages of changing – denying, dodging, doing and sustaining – which in our experience accommodates both scenarios. In Chapter 7 we show how these stages are enacted in the implementation of changing.

First stage: denying

The *denial* stage begins when the data supporting changing are first brought into the organization, i.e. when disconfirmation first starts. It can be a denial of the need for changing in the face of others' assertion of the need to change or a need for changing caused by environmental forces. This stage centres round processing information, disputing its value, relevance or timeliness. The change agent may be anywhere in the organization and will meet with denial from above and below. The more unexpected the disconfirming information is, the more likely it is to be denied. The need for changing is disputed as denial involves the rejection of the change information as not being relevant or pertinent. If change is being mandated without explanation or because there is no time, then organizational members may comply with the change directive while at the same time denying its relevance.

Resistance to changing comprises cognitive and emotional elements that arise from the context of the change or the individual's inability to deal with changing. The starting place for dealing with resistance is to consider it as a healthy, self-regulating manifestation which must be respected and taken seriously by managers and consultants. Denial must be treated in this manner. On the cognitive dimension, the substantive issues of why changing is needed, the degree of choice which exists about whether to change or not, the nature and strength of the forces driving changing, the effect of changing on individuals and teams must be presented in such a manner that the individual can assess the perceived impact of changing in the light of as full information about the change as is possible. On the emotional dimension, listening to fears, empathically understanding different perspectives on changing and creating the facilitative climate whereby individuals can be enabled to acknowledge and come to terms with personal emotional forces inhibiting participation in changing is a necessary process for managers and consultants. In short, for movement to occur there has to be sufficient psychological safety whereby the change data can be accepted as valid, relevant and pertinent. In other words, some unfreezing has begun to take place.

At the same time, the acknowledgement of the need for changing is somewhat generic. The acknowledgement that changing is required is not necessarily internalized immediately. A reluctant acknowledgement shifts the impetus for changing to other parts of the system. When this happens changing has shifted to a dodging stage. It must be acknowledged that some may remain in the denial mode and continue to persist in denying that changing is needed. For such members the changing process may move on without them, and at a later stage they have to reassess their position. We refer to these people as 'outliers' and discuss their involvement in the changing process in Chapter 7.

Second stage: dodging

The *dodging* stage begins when the accumulated evidence shows that changing is likely to take place. It is acknowledged reluctantly that some changing is needed, but that changing is required in other parts of the system, – 'Others have to change'. There can be a searching for countervailing data, which allow the individual or team to avoid or postpone having to change. Individuals and teams can seek ways to avoid or postpone changing or remain peripheral to it.

It is at the *dodging* stage when passive-aggressive behaviour is more typical (McIlduff and Coghlan, 2000). Anger is directed at change agents – 'those who are making me change'. If an individual experiences the culture of the organization as not supporting direct expression of anger and opposition, then passive-aggressive behaviours may follow during which time individuals will not participate actively in change programmes. They may physically attend meetings and training events but do not participate, and in their passivity communicate unexpressed hostility and opposition. At the same time they vent their opposition and lack of support to peers and friends outside of formal organizational situations. Coghlan and Rashford (1990) pointed to ways in which alienated members engage in distorted and faulty thinking about managerial behaviour. This means that individuals and teams, when they feel under threat, tend to over-generalize, deny the positive, be selective in what they perceive, jump to conclusions and act on the basis of emotional reasoning.

On the cognitive dimension, an individual or team can confuse the issue by presenting the weakness of the approach to the changing. There may be a more serious issue that needs to be dealt with first. This attempts to shift the action to a different focus. Another method to subvert is to change the form. If the discussion is on work flow change, change it to personnel. If it is on human resources, change it to bulk capital budget funding or to the expense budget.

The generic approaches to dealing with resistance outlined in the denying section above are also applicable to the *dodging* stage. The issues on the cognitive and emotional dimensions must be dealt with through a process of consultation, listening and serious consideration of the concerns expressed. Movement out of the *dodging* stage comes either when, out of the consultation process, ownership of the need for changing is accepted and the changing process can begin, or after some time has elapsed, when other have been implementing the change and the implications and effects of the change are perceived differently and perhaps appreciated or at least perceived less negatively.

Third stage: doing

The *doing* stage is where the need for changing has been acknowledged and owned to the degree that explorations of what changes are required, how, where, at what cost and at what cost to whom are undertaken. The *doing* stage is not comprised of any one action; it is a whole series of actions – assessing the forces driving and restraining changing, interpreting data, articulating a desired future, having intermediate stages, creating and following a change plan, generating commitment, managing the transition, negotiating and bargaining, implementing, reviewing, and so on (Beckhard and Harris, 1987; Nadler, 1998). It may be spread over a considerable time. As the changing process unfolds issues of where changing must occur in the present system, how that changing should be made, and what cost must be diagnosed, decided upon and implemented. The changing process tests the readiness and capability of the system to change.

Within a complex system, the changing process necessitates dealing with controversy and disagreement regarding different assessments, negotiation and bargaining within the system and dealing with the conflict that inevitably arises in such a context. Conflict at the doing stage is more focused than at the denial and dodging stages as it occurs within the context of a change plan and in this regard is different from conflict at the dodging stage. The issue is not whether changing is required, but what changing is required in what parts of the system and affecting what subsystems. Indeed, on particular issues regarding possible solutions to a change problem, there may be a reversal to denial and dodging. Each proposal may initiate its own change stages, so that within the broader changing process, a particular proposal may generate denial and dodging and require to be dealt with in those terms.

There are three directions the *doing* stage can take. One is something of an optimistic view, whereby the changing process takes off and it is a matter of jumping on the wagon. A precaution needs to be observed not to change anything that is not germane to the need for changing. It is not uncommon to think that because changing is taking place, any change can be made. The second direction is a more common one, whereby doing involves negotiation as to what changing take place, how and at what cost. The third direction leads to a sense of futility that while there is a lot of activity, it does not address the real issues. At the moment where action should give a sense of satisfaction, there is an undercurrent that the organization has no identity or is losing its identity or value. It is at this point, that the changing issue may alter to encompass a more fundamental transformation of the organization. We will take up this point in the following chapter.

Fourth stage: sustaining

As normative behaviour is difficult to change, some reinforcement of changed habits is necessary to ensure changing survives and the new state is sustained. The successful completion of this stage is the integration of the change into the habitual patterns of psychology, behaviour and operations, and to exploit it. In organizational terms, this stage is best defined as the implementation of operating procedures and is a key stage of any changing process. It is the focusing of energy to follow through on programmes and projects. Sometimes new manners of proceeding, new information systems or even new endeavours mark this stage. At this point the organization needs to be attuned to the fact that changing is part of life. The organization will have in place the ability to sense changes in the environment and to adapt quickly to them. In this respect, sustaining or refreezing does not attempt to create a new stability or close down future changing, but maintain an openness to continuous forces for changing.

Modern organizations in environments subject to constant change, such as industries with rapid technological development expected by consumers or industries dependent on volatile customer tastes such as fashion, actually may not even experience this stage because the pace of change is so high (Christensen, 1997, 2003). As complex adaptive systems surviving in fast-changing environments, these organizations need to be in constant higher-order changing mode and never fall into 'refreeze' mode. Instead of going to a sustaining phase, these organizations remain in a constant reformulated doing stage.

Conclusions

In keeping with understanding organizing as a social construction, new understandings about the process of organizational learning and changing and new forms of organization development (OD) emerged in the late twentieth century, influenced by the new sciences and postmodern thought and constructivist philosophy and views of organizations as meaning-making systems (Burnes and Cooke, 2012). Accordingly, contemporary OD views reality as socially constructed with multiple realities that are socially negotiated rather than a single objective reality that may be diagnosed. Data collection is less about applying objective problem-solving methods and more about raising collective awareness and generating new possibilities which lead to changing. Contemporary OD emphasizes changing the conversation in organizations by surfacing, legitimating and learning from multiple perspectives and generating new images and narratives on which people can act.

Gervase Bushe and Robert Marshak (2009, 2015) explore the emergence of new forms of OD in the postmodern world and frame classical OD as 'diagnostic OD' where reality is an objective fact and diagnosis infers collecting and applying data by using objective problem-solving methods to achieve changing to an articulated desired future. As an alternative, they propose what they called 'dialogic OD', where organizations are viewed as meaning-making systems, containing multiple realities, which are socially constructed. Accordingly, the understanding of OD is that it is an approach that creates the space for changing the conversation in organizations.

Senior managers, organizational members and OD consultants need to have some understanding of learning and changing in order to work them effectively. In this chapter we have outlined what we consider to be essential core constructs of learning and changing. We noted how there are different orders of learning and changing for any system, whether individual, team or organizational. We emphasized the role of design by establishing learning mechanisms that consolidate and sustain learning and changing. Finally, we introduced our own research on the psychological reactions to changing. In Chapters 6 and 7 we will show how these changing frameworks work in how changing is introduced into and moves through a complex system.

Reflexive engagement activity 5.1

In the mode of the clinical approach:

1. Can you identify something that your organization has learned?
2. How do you know it has learned?
3. Do members of the organization know that and what they have learned? What's your evidence for this learning? What order of learning was it?
4. Are there learning mechanisms in place to ensure the learning survives and can be exploited?
5. What enablers and inhibitors of learning have you identified? How do you know?

Reflexive engagement activity 5.2

In the mode of the clinical approach, with respect to a changing project in an organization with which you are familiar, whether in the past or currently ongoing:

1. Was/is the programme limited, focused or holistic? What insights do you have into whether the designation (whether implicit or explicit) was/is appropriate as a response to the challenge that was/is driving the need for change?
2. What approach was/is being taken – directed, planned or guided changing? Was/ is that an appropriate approach given the challenge and the designation? What's your evidence for this understanding?
3. If this was in the past what learning was captured? What order of learning was this? If this is in the present and is currently in progress, what insights are you having about it? How do you know? Is there a need or opportunity to reframe the focus or approach? How might you do this?

Case: The new university president's effort to institute participative decision-making

An incoming president of a major university faced several challenges as he attempted to alter the system of top-down individual decision-making espoused by the previous incumbent. Coming from a different environment, and knowing that he would need strong bottom-up support to institute the broad changes he envisioned, the new president was determined to encourage a culture of greater faculty participation. He hoped there would be support for the novel vision he had for the university but at the same time realized that the existence of dissenting voices and opinions was inevitable. As part of the process he held a four-day off-site retreat for key members of the administration and faculty with the presence of an OD consultant to facilitate a common understanding of goals. The retreat had several objectives. One important objective was to learn more about the previous situation. A second objective was to engage in dialogue to communicate his vision and test its acceptance and feasibility. A third was to begin to change the culture to encourage dialogue and exchange of ideas thereby erasing the perception that faculty opinions were not taken into consideration. Reactions of different individuals present at the four-day retreat provide an apt illustration of the four psychological reactions to changing as pattern changes that usually occur over an extended period of time were compressed due to the circumstances.

The setting of the retreat favoured honest exchange of points of view, and differences of opinion were stated with surprising openness. It became apparent in the first hours that very few of the participants had already bought into the new vision, i.e. very few were in the 'doing' stage. Most were either in the 'denying' stage or in the 'dodging' stage. Those denying were wedded to the previous set of institutional objectives, with some eloquently articulating its advantages even in a changing environment. Those dodging seemed to be aware of the drawbacks of continuing with the previous model but seemed also unsure of the benefits of a new set of objectives. The discussion that ensued was very important not only in that it offered the opportunity for those already in the 'doing' stage to clarify questions articulated by those who were denying and dodging, but also in that it allowed the new president to discern valuable insights regarding interpersonal and interdepartmental issues affecting individual points of view.

Several times during the discussions in the first couple of days, the tension between some members of the senior management group spilled out and caused concern in the larger group. These tensions provided a block to engagement and an impediment to deeper exploration of possibilities for two sets of reasons. The first were interpersonal disagreements which were overcome eventually through concerted open-mindedness and intense communication. The second reasons were fundamental differences in view of process as selected members of the senior management group believed strongly in the top-down command-and-control process that the new president, most of the leadership group, and the broader constituency wanted to make more participative. The few participants defending this view, including one senior academic officer, maintained a denial stance. Conversely, the president noticed a gradual movement from denying to dodging from some participants, and from dodging to doing by others as buy-in seemed to be steadily occurring.

While the energies of both the senior management group and the faculty-administration group were occasionally being directed towards personal conflicts rather than to their visions for the future, it was clear to the president that progress was being made. Each time such interpersonal conflicts were resolved the discussions resumed with more participants reaching the 'doing' stage. At one point, the OD consultant alerted the president that a senior member of the cabinet seemed to be absent from the process. When confronted, this senior cabinet member reacted aggressively and an argument ensued in everyone's presence. The OD consultant pointed out that likely denying would persist and alternative remedies might be advisable. Realizing that key individuals were still denying the desirability of a more participative process to reach change, the president took action by personally discrediting those members of the senior management group who still were wedded to the previous style. This led to an increase in the new president's credibility with the broader group as those who favoured a more democratic bottom-up approach felt empowered and energized. By the end of the retreat the majority had moved into a 'doing' stage and it became clear to the president that the few remaining dissenters would not be an active part of the change going forward as they had not left the 'denying' stage. The broad communication and open discussion had the added benefit of solidifying the conviction of those who had walked into the retreat already in the 'doing' stage so by the end of the four days their demeanour was consistent with 'sustaining'.

Questions for reflection and discussion

1. Can you discern from the case any elements that may have helped the new president discern individuals following respectively denying, dodging and doing patterns during the retreat?
2. How did the incoming president deal with outliers, especially those who remained with a toxic denying demeanour?
3. Of actions taken by the new president, which do you think were most effective in getting the remaining attendees to move from denying and dodging to doing? Which were less effective?
4. How do levels interact with one another in this case?
5. Please assume for the moment that this situation were not an academic, but rather a corporate institution, i.e. another type of organization, e.g. a high-tech organization. Would anything in the situation or the president's actions be different? If so, what?

References

Argyris, C. (2010) *Organizational Traps*. New York: Oxford University Press.
Argyris, C. and Schon, D. (1996) *Organizational Learning II*. Reading, MA: Addison-Wesley.
Bartunek, J.M., Crosta, T.E., Dame, R.F. and LeLacheur, D.F. (2000) Managers and project leaders conducting their own action research interventions. In R.T. Golembiewski (ed.), *Handbook of Organizational Consultation*, 2nd edn. New York: Marcel Dekker, pp. 59–70.

Beckhard, R. and Harris, R. (1987) *Organizational Transitions*. 2nd edn. Reading, MA: Addison-Wesley.

Bennis, W. (1962) Toward a truly scientific management: The concept of organizational health. *General Systems Yearbook*, 7, 269–282.

Buono, A. and Kerber, K. (2008) The challenge of organizational change: Enhancing organizational change capacity. *Revue Science de Gestion*, 65, 99–118.

Burnes, B. (2004) Kurt Lewin and complexity theories: Back to the future. *Journal of Change Management*, 4(4), 309–325.

Burnes, B. and Cooke, B. (2012) The past, present and future of organization development: Taking the long view. *Human Relations*, 65(11), 1395–1429.

Bushe, G.R. and Marshak, R. (2009) Revisioning organization development: Diagnostic and dialogic premises and patterns of practice. *Journal of Applied Behavioral Science*, 45(3), 248–268.

Bushe, G.R. and Marshak, R.J. (2015) *Dialogic Organization Development: The Theory and Practice of Transformational Change*. San Francisco, CA: Berrett-Koehler.

Bushe, G. and Shani, A.B. (Rami) (1991) *Parallel Learning Structures*. Reading, MA: Addison-Wesley.

Christensen, C. (1997) *The Innovator's Dilemma: When New Technologies Cause Great Firms to Fail*. Boston, MA: Harvard Business School Press.

Christensen, C. (2003) *The Innovator's Solution: Creating and Sustaining Successful Growth*. Boston, MA: Harvard Business School Press.

Coghlan, D. (2012) Understanding insight in the context of Q. *Action Learning: Research and Practice*, 9(3), 247–258.

Coghlan, D. and Rashford, N.S. (1990) Uncovering and dealing with organizational distortions. *Journal of Managerial Psychology*, 5(3), 17–21.

Coughlan, P. and Coghlan, D. (2011) *Collaborative Strategic Improvement through Network Action Learning*. Cheltenham: Edward Elgar.

Enberg, C., Lindkvist, L. and Tell, F. (2006) Exploring the dynamics of knowledge integration: Acting and interacting in project teams. *Management Learning*, 37(2), 143–165.

Fredberg, T., Norrgren, F. and Shani, A.B. (Rami) (2011) Developing and sustaining change capability via learning mechanisms: A longitudinal perspective on transformation. In R. Woodman, W. Pasmore, A.B. Shani (Rami) (eds), *Research in Organizational Change and Development*, Vol. 19. Bingley: Emerald, pp. 117–161.

Lawler, E.E. and Worley, C.G. (2012) Designing organizations for sustainable effectiveness. *Organizational Dynamics*, 41, 265–270.

Lewin, K. (1948) Group decision and social change. Reprinted in M. Gold (ed.) (1999), *The Complete Social Scientist. A Kurt Lewin Reader*. Washington, DC: American Psychological Association, pp. 265–284.

Lipshitz, R., Friedman, V.J. and Popper, M. (2007) *Demystifying Organizational Learning*. Thousand Oaks, CA: Sage.

March, J.G. (1991) Exploration and exploitation of organizational learning. *Organization Science*, 2(1), 71–87.

Marquardt, M. (2011) *Optimizing the Power of Action Learning*. 2nd edn. Palo Alto: Davies-Black.

McIlduff, E. and Coghlan, D. (2000) Understanding and dealing with passive-aggressive behaviour in teams and organizations. *Journal of Managerial Psychology*, 15(7), 716–736.

Miller, J.H. and Page, S.E. (2007) *Complex Adaptive Systems: An Introduction to Computational Models of Social Life*. Princeton, NJ: Princeton University Press.

Mitki, Y., Shani, A.B. (Rami) and Stjernberg, T. (2000) A typology of change programs and their differences from a solid perspective. In R.T. Golembiewski (ed.), *Handbook of Organizational Consultation*, 2nd edn. New York: Marcel Dekker Inc., pp. 777–785.

Mohrman, S.A. and Shani, A.B. (Rami) (eds) (2011) *Organizing for Sustainable Effectiveness*. Bingley: Emerald.

Nadler, D.A. (1998) *Champion of Change*. San Francisco, CA: Jossey-Bass.

Oliver, J. (2009) Continuous improvement: Role of organizational learning mechanisms. *International Journal of Quality and Reliability Management*, 26(6), 546–563.

Pedler, M. (2008) *Action Learning for Managers*. Surrey: Gower Publishing.

Roth, J., Shani, A.B. (Rami) and Leary, M. (2007) Insider action research: Facing the challenge of new capability development. *Action Research*, 5(1), 41–60.

Schechter, C. (2008) Organizational learning mechanisms: The meaning, measure, and implications for school improvement. *Educational Administration Quarterly*, 44(2), 155–186.

Schein, E.H. (1980) *Organizational Psychology*. 3rd edn. Englewood Cliffs, NJ: Prentice-Hall.

Schein, E.H. (2009) *The Corporate Culture Survival Guide*, 2nd edn, San Francisco, CT: Jossey-Bass.

Schein, E.H. (2013) Notes toward a model of organizational therapy. In. L. Vansina (ed.), *Humanness in Organizations*. London: Karnac, pp. 91–100.

Shani, A.B. (Rami) and Docherty, P. (2003) *Learning by Design*. Oxford: Blackwell.

Shani, A.B. (Rami) and Docherty, P. (2008) Learning by design: Key mechanisms in organization development. In T. Cummings (ed.), *Handbook of Organization Development*. Thousand Oaks, CA: Sage, pp. 499–518.

6

THE INTERLEVEL DYNAMICS OF ORGANIZATIONAL CHANGING

In Chapter 5 we introduced the subject of learning and changing. Now we turn to the subject of organizational changing. For us, the process of organizational changing is characterized by the engagement and integration of change in individuals, teams, the interdepartmental group and organizational behaviour and performance, whether that changing be first, second, or third order. The process involves an evolution in understanding the organization's meaning, in its way of reading reality, and in making, implementing and evaluating choices. We will focus on these latter activities in Part III.

In the previous chapter we introduced the notion of systemic health in terms of four elements: a sense of identity and purpose, the capacity to adapt to changing external and internal circumstances, the capacity to perceive and test reality, and the internal integration of subsystems. We also framed systemic organizational health as a cycle of continuous coping and adaptation as information is received into an organization, processed and transformed into outputs (Bennis, 1962; Schein, 1980, 2013). We now develop this cycle as a framework for organizational changing and learning.

The adaptive coping cycle of organizations

The adaptive coping cycle has six steps beginning with a change in some aspects of the organization's external or internal environment and ending with a more adaptive, renewed organization (Figure 6.1). While these steps are separated conceptually, in practice they overlap and occur concurrently as an organization is in constant interaction with its environment:

1.   Sensing a change in the internal or external environment.
2.   Getting the information to the right place where it can be processed and acted upon.

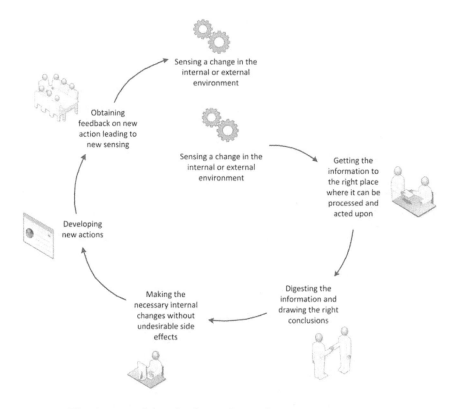

FIGURE 6.1 The six steps of the adaptive coping cycle

3. Digesting the information and drawing the right conclusions.
4. Making the necessary internal changes without undesirable side effects.
5. Developing new actions.
6. Obtaining feedback on the new action leading to new sensing.

These six steps lay the foundations of considering organizational changing and learning. The movement through the six steps involves sensitivity to process – how information is taken in, shared and heard, how decisions are made, how vision is articulated, how commitment is built, where interventions are judged to be necessary or desired and so on so that the changing is made effectively. It also involves interlevel dynamics as information is gathered and processed, decisions are made, their consequences are followed through by a complex interaction of individuals, individuals in teams and working groups, and between teams.

Sensing a change in the internal or external environment

The first step of the adaptive coping cycle occurs when disconfirming information is identified and changing is put on the agenda. The identification of the forces driving change is critical as, in the long run, whatever changes are made must provide an adequate response to these forces. The forces for changing may be coming from the external environment, such as globalization, competitor strategy or changing customer needs. The forces for changing may also come from within the organization, such as the need for restructuring, the need to divest unprofitable lines, to adapt the balance of product portfolios, or to develop new management skills, to take a few examples.

The process of taking in disconfirming information, assessing it and acting on it constitutes the evocation of the question 'why change?' As Schein argues in an HBR interview (Contu, 2002), any disconfirmation must be accompanied by 'survival anxiety' and a sense of psychological safety in order for changing to get going. As this first step of the adaptive coping cycle involves iterations of individuals and teams as the changing issue enters the organization and gets a hold, individuals and teams may have to deal with issues of denial and dodging as the members of the system who are exposed to the changing issues in its initial stages respond to the data.

This first step of the adaptive coping cycle may fail because of the absence of sensing structures, an overemphasis on either internal data only or external data only, perceptual defences which distort data and differing sensing structures where subsystems see and think different things. Critical interventions could focus on building formal sensing structures, exposing senior managers to the experiences and perceptions of organizational sub-cultures, and uncovering defensive routines and distortions. In terms of interlevel dynamics, a manager or an OD consultant could work with how individuals and teams perceive and respond to the change agenda and how perceptions and responses move from individuals to teams and across teams to the wider system.

Getting the information to the right place where it can be processed and acted upon

The second step of the adaptive coping cycle is that of taking the disconfirming information into the teams of the organization where it can be processed. The critical question is, of course, where is the 'right' place? What parts of the organization need the information and can make sense of it?

This step may fail because relevant information remains in a particular subsystem and is not shared, because there is lack of communication between those who sense the change and those who make decisions, or because information is distorted or because information is used as a power tool rather than a problem-solving tool. Organizational defensive routines that seek to maintain face-saving or embarrassment-avoiding strategies may inhibit the exploration of the information as valid and generate denying and dodging (Argyris, 1985). Interventions could focus on the interdepartmental group, whereby creation of networks and information channels, creating reward systems for information sharing and punishments systems for withholding, exaggerating or distorting information and dialogue meetings are developed so information gatherers and decision-makers could develop mutual understanding.

Digesting the information and drawing the right conclusions

The ability of working groups and teams to make sense of the information is obviously critical. Dysfunctions on this step can be short-term linear thinking rather than systems thinking, and may be characterized by denial and other defensive routines, inter-functional conflict and cognitive biases and distortions. Managers and OD consultants could work with members of the working groups in developing systems thinking, uncovering distortions and defensive routines and helping develop dialogue skills. These activities are critical interlevel processes as individuals and teams work through the implications of the changing information.

Making the necessary internal changes without undesirable side effects

This step is what is generally perceived as being the actual changing process, though as we have seen, the previous steps are equally essential to the process. The critical tasks are to articulate a desired future, move from the present to the future and manage the intervening period of transition.

The key critical aspect of this stage of the adaptive coping cycle is the management of changing within the organization and the effective use of OD approaches to lead and enable the members of the organization to internalize the changing process and make it work. Accordingly, attention to behavioural dynamics within and between individuals, teams, and the interdepartmental group as the changing agenda is presented and responded to across the system is critical to the success of the changing venture. This involves designing learning mechanisms in order that changing and learning may be sustained.

Developing new actions

The changing process must impact the actual production or service activities of the organization. The outcome of the changing process may be new products, or management exercised in a new or different way, and so on. The changing efforts must be directly related to (a) the actual mission of the organization, and (b) the forces pushing for changing. So new or different processes which emerge from the changing process must relate to what the original disconfirmation of experience pointed to and be congruent with the mission of the organization. New information systems may need to be implemented as a consequence of renewed relationships with suppliers and customers.

Such new action may make demands on individuals in what they do and how they do it, on teams in what they do and how they do it, and on the balance of power, influence and resource allocation across the interdepartmental group. The new situation needs to be consolidated in both the formal and informal organizations.

Obtaining feedback on the new actions leading to a new sensing cycle

In the external forum, the market provides feedback on the success or failure of the new actions. Customers respond positively to the new or improved product or service. Sales increase; costs decrease. In the internal forum, once the change is in place it must be stabilized and maintained. There is an awkward balance or tension in institutionalizing changing while maintaining openness to further changing. This step constitutes the sustaining stage, both systemic (as the changed state becomes normative within the organization) and relational (as the change is reinforced by key stakeholders).

The focus of review is learning from experience. Darling and Parry (2000) illustrate in their application of 'after action review' (AAR) to the US American military how post-mortems can move from being a review of the past to a living practice that anticipates issues and generates emergent learning *in* action. This learning involves both content and process learning. What has the organization as a collective system learned from the experience of the changing process? What learning mechanisms have been installed and how are they working? Individuals may be learning, but that is not a guarantee that the system learns. Any organization may go through many adaptive coping cycles and repeat its dysfunctions. Subsystems may go through the cycle without the system learning. For the managers and OD practitioners, the process of organizational learning involves reviewing the steps of the adaptive coping cycle and the movement of the changing agenda through individuals, teams and between teams.

Any organization can have dysfunctions on any of these six steps. It can fail to sense changes in the environment or it can misinterpret them. It can fail to transmit the relevant information to those parts of the system which can act upon it. The information may fail to have the impact of creating change. A change may not result in a renewed output or there may be inadequate feedback of the effect of the changed service on the customer or client, which enables the organization to reassess its strategic role and function. It may do some of the steps well. Each step in the adaptive coping cycle contains the potential for pitfalls and problems. While the maintenance of continuous coping and adaptation needs to be built at all four levels, as we discussed in Chapter 2, the cutting edge of the successful enactment of the adaptive coping cycle is at the interdepartmental group level. Without interdepartmental coordination mechanisms, information may remain locked in one department, either for political reasons or because the information is framed in technical terms that others cannot understand. For the system to remain healthy and to cope and adapt productively with the demands of the discontinuous global economy, each step requires specific attention.

The process of large system changing

While the adaptive coping cycle outlines how an organization engages in continuous coping and adaptation the process of deliberately developing new actions,
whether limited, focused or holistic, or directed, planned or guided changing
requires specific focus.

Mohrman et al. (1989) define large-scale change as 'lasting change in the character of an organization that significantly alters its performance' (p. 2). Large-scale
change has three dimensions:

- Deep changes which entail shifts in members' basic beliefs and values in the
  way the organization is understood.
- Pervasive changes which involve a major proportion of an organization's
  structures and processes, both formal and informal.
- Complex change refers to the size of the system changed and the size of the
  change effort necessary to alter the performance of the organization.

So when large-scale change is applied to large systems then the size of the
organization, and the depth and pervasiveness of the change come into play. For
us, depth and pervasiveness of change in a large system is defined by the integration
of change in individual, team, interdepartmental group and organizational behaviour
and performance, especially if that change is holistic and higher order and involves
a realignment of identity and strategic action (which we discuss in Part III).

How do large systems engage in changing? There is a growing consensus born
out of a great deal of research and action as to what leaders need to do. This
consensus names a number of key activities that form a generic model of system
change (Beckhard and Harris, 1987; Kotter, 1996; Nadler et al., 1998; Pasmore,
2011) (Figure 6.2). These activities typically comprise: i) determining the need for
changing, ii) designing the vision of the desired future state(s) beyond the
change, iii) assessing the present in terms of the future to determine the work
to be done, iv) managing the transition state through the implementation stage and
v) reinforcing and sustaining the changing. These activities act as a framework for
examining factors that threaten intervention success and which may generate
reflection on creating more positive outcomes from changing endeavours (Pasmore,
2011).

Determining the need for change

From the sensing, importing and digesting activities of the adaptive coping cycle,
the key step is to inquire into the context for changing, what Nadler et al. (1998)
calls 'recognizing the change imperative'. It may seem obvious that naming the
need for changing and its causes is essential. The forces for changing may be
coming from the external environment, such as major shifts in capital markets,
global market patterns, new competitors who have a new basis for competition,

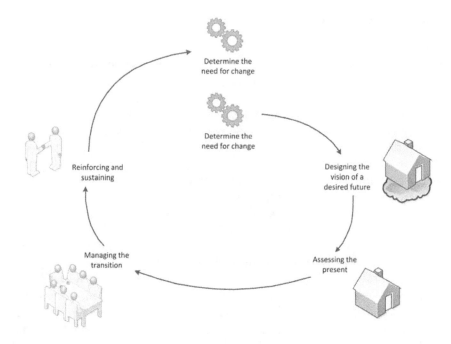

FIGURE 6.2 The process of large system change

innovations in products and processes, external developments which change the rules of the game, and changes in customer characteristics and demands. They may be coming from the internal environment, such as budget overruns, low morale among staff, excessive dysfunctional political inter-group rivalry and so on. The digesting of the meaning of these forces identifies their source, their potency and the nature of the demands they are making on the system. These forces for changing have to be assessed so that major change forces are distinguished from the minor ones. Organizational leaders should not be waiting for such forces to become apparent; they need to be actively 'looking beyond the horizon' (Hesselbein et al., 1995).

A second key element is the pressure of time and making the change in a particular window of opportunity. These pressures evolve from the sequencing of events, cycles of events or order of appearance in a market place. Being first makes a lasting impression. In this context the pressure of timing is everything.

A third key element in evaluating the need for change is the degree of choice about whether to change or not. Choices are not absolute. While there may be no control over the external forces demanding change, there is likely to be a great deal of control over how to respond to those forces. In that case there is likely to be a good deal of scope as to what changes, how, and in what time-scale the change can take place. The degree of choice may be mitigated by how quickly competitors respond to driving forces. There needs to be shared diagnosis into how these forces for change are having an impact and what choices exist to confront them.

There are critical interlevel dynamics in the activities of assessing the need for change (Figure 6.3). The change process has to begin somewhere. Who first senses that change is required may be anyone in the organization. As we will discuss in more detail in the following chapter, the gatekeeper, whether someone in direct dealing with customers or a high level executive engaging in economic forecasting, who first perceives that need for change must have the confidence to import the information and take it to those in executive positions and persuade them to adopt his/her insight. If those in the executive positions deny or dodge the relevance of that insight, then the individual may give up or else reconsider how to present the case for change more forcibly. When the senior management group adopts the need for change and begins to act, it has then to win over other teams in the system. Each of these movements – from individual to team to interdepartmental group – is an iterative process. In other words, when the team adopts an individual's position, that adoption reinforces the individual. When other teams adopt a particular team's position, that reinforces that team, and, of course, when customers adopt a new product, that reinforces the organization. Pasmore (2011) identifies one of the reasons change efforts fail is that there may be a 'drift through discourse' or an ambivalence arising from evolving discourse. Accordingly, senior managers need to ensure that the conversations across levels are not meaningless or convey an assumption of being pointless or therapeutic.

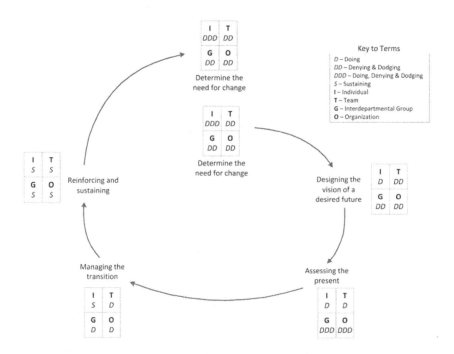

FIGURE 6.3 Interlevel dynamics of large system change

Founded in 1851 in Philadelphia, Saint Joseph's University is a comprehensive university with approximately 7500 students. Located in the competitive northeastern US it is one of many private universities competing for the same students. The mission of Saint Joseph's University traces its origins through the 450-year tradition of Jesuit education as well as over 160 years as a Jesuit college in the Philadelphia PA area. Traditionally Saint Joseph's had been centred on undergraduate education as the university prided itself in small class sizes and a high student–professor interaction. The commitment to graduate and lifelong learning programmes throughout most of its history occurred through a part-time evening division. This, in effect, generated two Saint Joseph's Universities coexisting side by side, a situation which had persisted from the turn of the century until about 1986, when a new president came to the university with a desire to overcome issues of stagnant growth and poor economic performance. Furthermore, although its reputation was strong as the only Jesuit University in the Philadelphia area, there were significant competitive threats as there were nearly six dozen other higher learning institutions in the immediately adjacent region, ten of which were Catholic. From the experience of successful graduate programmes in a prior institution, the president opened the discussion for change.

An OD consultant may be brought in at the point where questions are being asked about how to extend the need-for-change question through the organization. Interventions may attend to how individuals and teams perceive the need for change and what their sources of resistance are. Such interventions may uncover the absence of structures for sensing changes in the environment, a focus on internal or external data only, and perceptual defences whereby data is distorted, and where different subsystems attend to different data. Critical interventions would focus on building formal sensing structures – planning groups, data-gathering groups, etc. and inter-functional dialogue where assumptions and perceptions of data are shared and heard.

At Saint Joseph's University the senior management group's initial reactions to the president's change initiative were mixed. New facilities would be required for adult learners. New faculty would be costly. Structural changes would be necessary as university departments heretofore had not had responsibility for graduate programmes. Slowly the senior management group came to embrace the need for change and began the process of internal communication and gradual implementation. It in turn then met strong resistance in their respective academic departments. Gradually the change was accepted by most of the organization.

Designing the vision of the desired future

Once a sense of the need for changing has been digested and established, the most useful focus for attention is to design a desired future state or states. This is like an architect who shows the future picture with vision but leaves room for new ideas or for others' contributions. This process is essentially that of articulating what the organization, unit or subunit would look like after change has taken place. This process is critical as it helps provide focus and energy because it describes the desires for the future in a positive light. It is also positive as it leaves room for additional input. On the other hand, an initial focus on the problematic or imperfect present may overemphasize negative experiences and generate pessimism. In addition, plans that are too grandiose or seen to be out of range can also generate pessimism or apathy. Working at building consensus on a desired future is an important way of harnessing the political elements of the system.

When organizations embark on second-order changing they do so in the expectation that there will be a steady state in the new order. This steady state or states may be envisaged in terms of a higher-order operating level (however that may be defined), and can be maintained through iterative corrections. Third-order changing emerges when an organization arrives at the new state and is confronted by continuing changing. For the most part third-order change does not emerge until second-order changing has been embarked upon and cannot be planned for from a first-order platform.

Clearly, the process of defining the future involves interlevel dynamics. If the vision comes from the chief executive, then there are interlevel dynamics from that individual to the senior management group and then to the interdepartmental group and on to the organization. As the leader takes his/her vision to the senior management group and works at persuading its members to adopt it, the movement is from the individual to the team. If the vision is created by the senior management group, then the process begins with the team and moves to individuals within that team, is reinforced in the group and then goes to the interdepartmental group and on to the organization. So the iteration of issue presentation, perception, assessment of impact and response ebbs and flows from individual to individual, team to team and so on.

Interventions would focus on what the most appropriate way to articulate and communicate vision might be, particularly within the senior management team and between the senior management team and the other teams of the organization.

Returning to the Saint Joseph University case: after several years, faculty groups and some administrative groups in the university felt the changes had been imposed in a top-down fashion and therefore were not representative of the wants and desires of a broader constituency. In an attempt to identify a new vision that could gain the support of multiple stakeholders, external OD consultants were hired to assist. When the group went off campus to begin the process, the toxic interlevel dynamics brought the process to a standstill. Conflicts among the senior management group members as well as some conflict between the senior management group members and the consultants almost destroyed the process. These conflicts focused on whether or not the process could achieve the desired end. Significant progress was made by confronting issues between the individuals, and by deliberately reducing faculty's fear they would not be heard. Additionally, the president learned which actions of his were contributing to the conflict. As a result, he modified his behaviour, and the senior management group and faculty were able to engage in the process with a new level of openness. As a result, a new collective vision of the university's future that could be embraced by the group emerged.

Assessing the present in terms of the future to determine the work to be done

When the desired future state or states are articulated, the focus is placed on the present reality and questions like 'what is it in the present which is redundant for or a threat to the desired future state that needs changing and what is to be carried forward?' are asked. Because the present is being assessed in the light of the desired future, it is assessing what needs changing and what does not. It may judge that, for the change to effectively take place, a change in current structures, attitudes, roles, policies or activities may be needed. As any change problem is a cluster of possible changes, it may need to group particular problems under common headings, i.e. HRM policies and practices, service delivery, information management, reward systems, organizational structure and design and so on. Then it describes the problem more specifically, and asks, 'Which of these requires priority attention? If A is changed, will a solution to B fall easily into place? What needs to be done first?' This step is about taking a clear comprehensive accurate view of the current state of the organization, involving an organizational diagnosis which names:

- the priorities within the constellation of change problems
- the relevant subsystems where change is required

Another element in describing the present is to describe the relevant parts of the organization that will be involved in the changing. This description points to the critical people needed for the change to take place. Examples of who needs to be involved might include specific managers, informal leaders, IT specialists and so on. Their readiness and capability for change must be assessed. *Readiness* points to the motivation and willingness to change, while *capability* refers to whether they are able, psychologically, technically and otherwise, to change.

At this stage it may be clear whether first- or second-order changing is required. Changing begins with a limited or focused agenda and opens up into a holistic one. As we described in Chapter 5, by first-order changing is meant an improvement in what the organization currently does or how it does it. By second-order changing is meant a system-wide change in the nature of the core assumptions and ways of thinking and acting. The choice of whether to follow a first- or second-order changing process may be as much determined by organizational politics or organizational capability as by the issues under consideration. How the key organizational actors interpret the forces for change and how they form their subsequent judgement as to what choices they have are important political dynamics.

Interlevel processes are critical to this step. Assessment of the present may create defensiveness in individuals, teams and between teams. There may be tendencies to attempt to shift blame for change problems from one team onto another. In assessing readiness and capability, a critical aspect may be how teams are capable or ready or how much capability and readiness there is between teams. This may refer to political dynamics between teams or to issues around such topics as information management or IT compatibility. Relevant subsystems refer to individuals, teams and to the interdepartmental group. In second-order changing the assessment of the present inquires into whether the organization has the capability and readiness to make the quantum leap to the unforeseen future.

Interventions need to focus on conversations within teams and between teams to agree on criteria for evaluation of the present strengths and weaknesses, with the accompanying focus on reducing the influence of interdepartmental politics, defensive routines and conflict. A particular focus for such intervention might be dialogue between the business functional areas and the IT specialists as to the current and potential role of IT.

To continue with the Saint Joseph's University case: When the small group that had been away for four days returned to campus the desire was to repeat the process with larger groups of these constituencies. Shared vision exercises carried out in the small group were now repeated with a large group of stakeholders from both within and outside the university. These groups included more faculty, more administrators, students, parents, donors, alumni and support staff. The outcome of the process with the larger groups was very similar to the small group experience. The process itself generated excitement about a possible new future. As people became excited about the possibilities, fear of letting go of the past slowly declined. In fact some of the excitement came from regaining some aspects of the distant past that had been perceived as lost. Concerns expressed centred on finding resources to accomplish the new goals. The president had his eyes opened. He was not afraid of the future but was afraid that people would not embrace a graduate programme as a component of the university's future. He came to see that people were not only ready to embrace the new order, but had better ideas than he did on how to structure graduate programmes within the current university structure, thus helping to ensure their success. This intervention changed the president's thinking and how he acted when working with faculty and administrative teams.

Managing the transition

The transition period is both a period of time and a state of affairs. The critical task is to move from the present to the future and manage the intervening period of transition. This transition state between the present and the future is typically a difficult time because the past is found to be defective and no longer tenable and the new state has not yet come into being. So, in essence, the transition state is somewhat particular, as the old has gone and the new has not yet been realized, and so needs to be seen and managed as such. It is a messy time and state of affairs, where unanticipated events interrupt the formalized plan or its schedule.

As Beckhard and Harris (1987) argue, there are two aspects to managing this transition state. One is having a strategic and operational plan which simply defines the goals, intermediate stages, activities, structures, projects, resources and experiments that will help achieve the desired state(s). As no amount of changing can take place without commitment, the second aspect is a commitment plan. The commitment plan focuses on who in the organization must be committed to the change if it is to take place. There may be particular individuals whose support is a prerequisite for the change and a critical mass whose commitment is necessary to provide the energy and support for the change to occur, particularly in second-order changing. There are those who contribute new ideas and enhance innovation. The political dynamics of building commitment involves finding areas of agreement and compromise among conflicting views and negotiating cooperation.

Interlevel dynamics are pivotal to the processes of the transition state as individuals and teams address the implications and implementation of the change agenda. As the change agenda affects the work of individuals in what they do and how they do it, individual commitment is essential. Nadler et al. (1998), in their description of the characteristics of how organizations respond to incremental and discontinuous change, notes that in redirecting and overhauling approaches senior managers are typically replaced, not because of failure to perform but because they don't fit the new situation. Those managers who are flexible to new roles and approaches tend to survive. As the change agenda affects the work of the permanent teams and typically requires the creation of new teams, introducing new members and work in temporary committees or project groups, team commitment is critical to the changing process.

In particular, temporary task groups which are formed to guide the changing process through activities such as steering the process, listening to opinions around the organization, planning and facilitating dialogue meetings and so on are critical. These task forces or project committees need to function well as Level II units and be able to engage in Level III interactions as they work across the different functional and cultural areas of the organization.

In a similar vein, the changing agenda involves the interface of multiple teams with respect to information sharing, problem identification and resolution, resource allocation, and collective bargaining. Inter-team dynamics can enable or hinder the successful management of the change process.

Building commitment is essentially an interlevel process. Individuals identify with their teams, profession or occupational community or trade union, so efforts to build commitment involve interventions with teams and across teams, particularly if inter-team relations are likely to have a negative impact on the progress of the change. Strategies to manage resistance and build the commitment of middle managers are particularly important.

Pasmore (2011) identifies persistent problems that occur in undertaking change. He refers to emergent issues and unanticipated side effects and to 'irrational, emotional and political' responses and resistance to changing. He also points to lack of leadership and inadequate experience in those leading the changing.

To continue with the Saint Joseph's University case: as implementation of the new goals began, groups and individuals within the university were required to change. It became clear that to sustain and reinforce these changes two things needed to happen. First, the changes that were occurring needed to relate directly to what had been the outcome of the group process. Second, the resources available were used to help the university make progress towards goals desired by the group.

Three times over the next year, group sessions were held that were called 'walk-throughs'. The sessions laid out explicitly what had been set as goals, what had been accomplished, and what yet remained to be done. Input from the group was solicited through questions as well as written evaluations. These experiences proved to be very important for the constituent groups to feel connected to the change process and to remain involved. It gave members an opportunity to see how bigger issues could and would affect them. In fact, the feedback led some things to change before any formal change initiative was even begun. The 'walk-throughs' included a wide base of the university's workforce who saw what was coming and began to implement change even before they were officially told to do so.

Reinforcing and sustaining

Because change generates so much energy and emotion there is a danger that both managers and organizational members will relax if the tension of change appears to be over. The personal energy and hard work of senior management in particular tends to go into the earlier stages of getting change in and moving. But there is need to focus on making the change stick, making it work and survive. It is important that senior managers make reinforcing and sustaining part of their personal agendas. Hence the importance of building learning mechanisms into the design and implementation of the whole changing project.

Reinforcement involves consolidation, which Nadler (1998) see as critical in the period immediately after implementation when the changes have not yet been locked into operational practice. He advises that the focus be placed on middle managers so that they take responsibility for measuring the success of the change, refining it and consolidating it through communication, staffing and HR policies. Measuring the success of the change involves formal evaluation processes. When senior management initiates an evaluation process it needs to be clear what the evaluation is for, what the targets of evaluation are and how the evaluation is to be conducted. In addition, senior managers need to show interest and involvement in the work of middle managers.

Sustaining is a longer-term focus than reinforcement or consolidation as it attends to keeping the momentum going. Processes such as team review meetings, interdepartmental group meetings, review conferences, and return visits by external consultants support formal sustaining structures which ground the change such as restructuring, job and role redesign, performance reviews and reward systems.

As we outlined in the previous chapter, organizations which are in third-order changing never go to a sustaining phase but remain in a constant reformulated doing stage.

Review and learning

Review and learning permeate all five activities, i) determining the need for change, ii) designing the vision of the desired future state(s), iii) assessing the present in terms of the future to determine the work to be done, and iv) managing the transition state through the implementation stage and v) reinforcing and sustaining the change. While reinforcing and sustaining refer to consolidating the changing, review and learning refer to the outcome of reflection on the experience of engaging in each of the activities and of the process as a whole. The critical dimension to change is how review is undertaken and managed. Review is essentially reflection on experience and in any such reflection the critical questions are asked, not to evoke guilt or blame, but to generate learning as to what is taking place and what needs to be adjusted. If review is undertaken in this spirit then the likelihood of individual or team defensiveness can be lessened and learning can take place.

Sustaining

Sustaining change is based on how learning mechanisms were designed into the changing process at the outset. Cognitive structural and procedural mechanisms hold the outcomes of the learning and changing in place. Docherty, Kira and Shani (2009) describe a phased model of developing social sustainability: becoming aware and receiving insights, mobilizing resources, building commitment and setting direction, designing, experimenting and implementing changing, and finally establishing a state of sustainability. Social sustainability is understood to mean that human, social, economic and ecological resources are balanced and integrated in the long term and that the changed work system is sustainable (Mohrman and Shani, 2011). Many of these concerns point to a common problem in sustaining changing, which is the financial sustainability or as Pasmore refers to it 'resource starvation' (2011: 261). Pasmore cautions against 'losing focus' and the dangers of shifting priorities and turnover of the key changing champions.

As we have detailed already, there are three types of inquiry in review (Fisher et al., 2000) (Figure 6.4). The first inquiry loop focuses on behaviour and actions. How skilful was the organization in each of the five activities and in the overall process of change? Can the critical events be identified? What was learned for future changing processes? The second inquiry loop focuses on the strategies underpinning the behaviour and actions. In hindsight do the strategies and plans make sense? From where do they emerge? If skilfully implemented would they stand a chance of being successful? Would the strategies need to be changed to achieve a better outcome? The third inquiry loop focuses on the intentions which the strategies and actions aimed to fulfil. Who are we? Is it what we wanted to be? Given the outcome how do the original intentions now look? Were they realistic and achievable? Do these intentions need to be adapted, changed or continued?

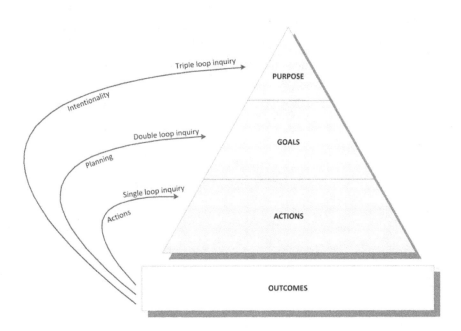

FIGURE 6.4 Single, double, and triple loop inquiry

Perspectives on large system changing

The perspectives of leader, member, OD consultant and outcome may be applied to the five activities of large system changing.

Leader

For leaders the change imperative for first-order changing comes primarily from the non-attainment of targets and market changes (Table 6.1). They set out where they want the organization to be, what needs to change, develop and lead a change plan, build commitment, manage the transition and reinforce and sustain momentum. In situations of discontinuous change they intuitively sense a new world coming over the horizon and start designing change towards a future which is difficult to envisage and which may never settle into a steady state.

TABLE 6.1 Change from leader's perspective

Leader's perspective	First-order/incremental change	Second–third-order/discontinuous change
Determining the need for change	Not meeting goals Market changes	Intuitive sense of a new world Structure of changing market
Designing vision of desired future(s)	New state of operational effectiveness	Vision of new world
Assessing the present in terms of future	What needs to be developed What needs to be cut out What needs to change	What needs to be developed What needs to be cut out What needs to change
Managing the transition state	Implementing a change plan Management structures Building commitment	*Second order* Implementing change plan with no landing point Flexible management structures Building commitment *Third order* Implementing change plan with no landing point Flexible management structures Building commitment to continuous change
Reinforcing and sustaining	How not to slip back How to sustain momentum	*Second order* How not to slip back How to sustain momentum *Third order* How to sustain momentum for continuing change

Members

For members the change imperative questions open up questions of awareness of the strategic issues of the organization (Table 6.2). If they have no such knowledge then they question the underlying assumptions of the changing, tend to seek people or functions to blame. They typically have no comprehension of the rationale for discontinuous change. Through the change process they participate in the activities of the change process – assessment, problem-solving, negotiating, adapting roles and behaviour, and coping with the uncertainty. They are reinforced in presenting new ideas.

OD consultants

OD consultants work with the senior management and members of the organization facilitating each of the five activities (Table 6.3). They are concerned with

TABLE 6.2 Change from member's perspective

Member's perspective	First-order/incremental change	Second–third-order/discontinuous change
Determining the need for change	Awareness of strategic and operational issues	Lack of comprehension
Designing vision of desired future(s)	Future place and role in the organization	Lack of comprehension
Assessing the present in terms of future	Providing feedback Participating in assessment	Comprehending the rationale for radical change
Managing the transition state	Participating in change process Adapting to changing organization Coping with uncertainty and stress	*Second order* Participating in change process Adapting to changing organization Coping with uncertainty and stress *Third order* Participating in change process Adapting to changing organization Coping with uncertainty and stress
Reinforcing and sustaining	Providing feedback on perceived success of change from operational viewpoint	*Second order* Finding a place and role in changed organization *Third order* Finding a place and role in continuously changing organization

TABLE 6.3 Change from OD consultant's perspective

OD consultant's perspective	First-order/incremental change	Second–third-order/discontinuous change
Determining the need for change	Accurate diagnosis Widespread acceptance of need for change	Accurate sensing
Designing vision of desired future(s)	Level of involvement in creating desired future(s)	Buy-in to vision of new world
Assessing the present in terms of future	Assessment of what needs to change Political dynamics of assessment	Assessment of what needs to change
Managing the transition state	Progress of change process Commitment building Problem resolution	*Second order* Progress of change process Commitment building Problem resolution *Third order* Progress of change process Commitment building Problem resolution Coping with uncertainty and stress
Reinforcing and sustaining	Reinforcement and sustaining mechanisms in place Continuation after end of consultant contract	*Second order* Consolidating changed state *Third order* Remaining flexible for continually changing

content and process issues. Their content concern focuses on the accuracy of the diagnosis and sensing of the need for change, the content of the desired future(s) and of the change plan. Their process concern attends to the involvement of the members of the organization, the progress of the change plan, how commitment is built up and how learning takes place.

Outcomes

The outcomes are that each activity is successful in moving the organization through its change process (Table 6.4).

Conclusions

The adaptive coping cycle marks the process by which all systems learn and change. The ability to sense disconfirming information, to import it and digest its

TABLE 6.4 Change from outcome perspective

Outcomes	First-order/incremental change	Second–third-order/discontinuous change
Determining the need for change	Accurate diagnosis Widespread acceptance of need for change	Accurate sensing
Designing vision of desired future(s)	Level of involvement in creating desired future(s)	Buy-in to vision of new world
Assessing the present in terms of future	Assessment of what needs to change Political dynamics of assessment	Assessment of what needs to change
Managing the transition state	Successful management of transition Commitment to change Renewed organization	*Second order* Successful management of transition Commitment to change Renewed organization *Third order* Successful management of transition Commitment to change Renewed organization
Reinforcing and sustaining	Change goals achieved Shared learning from experience	*Second order* Change goals achieved Shared learning from experience *Third order* Change goals achieved Shared learning from experience Skills at continual change

implications, to make necessary changes while reducing or managing side effects and exporting new products or services that are in keeping with the original perceived change and obtaining feedback on the success of the changes through further sensing are core skills. Once managers have embarked on a change they address the five activities of changing: determining the need for changing, designing the vision of the desired future state, assessing the present in terms of the future to determine the work to be done, managing the transition state through the implementation stage, and reinforcing and sustaining the changing. Both the adaptive coping cycle and the five activities of changing involve the management of interlevel dynamics.

Reflexive engagement exercise 6.1

Capturing the adaptive coping cycle

Adopting the clinical approach, track a changing project through the adaptive coping cycle and name the ways in which engagement in the steps of the cycle worked well or didn't:

1. From where in the organization was a change in the internal or external environment sensed?
2. Was the information brought to the right place where it was processed and acted upon? How do you know what the right place needed to be? What interlevel processes were engaged? How? To what effect?
3. Who digested the information and drew what conclusions? Did the information succeed or fail to have the impact of creating change? What interlevel processes were engaged? How? To what effect? How do you know?
4. What changes were made? Were they an adequate response to the original forces for change? What interlevel processes were engaged? How? To what effect? How do you know?
5. What new actions were developed? What interlevel processes were engaged? How? To what effect?
6. How did the organization obtain feedback on the new action? What interlevel processes were engaged? How? To what effect? How is it attuned to further sensing? How do you know?
7. Applying $L=P+Q$ to this changing, what are you learning about organizational changing as you subject changing theory to your questioning experience? What's the evidence for your understanding?

Reflexive engagement exercise 6.2

Review exercise for implementing large system change

Reflecting on a change process in an organization with which you are familiar, answer the following questions:

Step 1

Determining the need for change.

- What are the external forces driving change?
- What are the internal forces driving change?
- How powerful are these forces?
- What choices do we have?

Step 2

If things keep going the way they are without significant intervention

- What will be the predicted outcome?
- What is our alternative desired outcome?

Step 3

- What is it in the present that we need to change in order to get to our future – what is done, how work is done, structures, attitudes, culture...?

Step 4

- What are the main avenues which will get us from here to there?
- What are the particular projects within those avenues? Long, medium, term...
- How do we involve the organization in this project?
- Where do we begin?
- What actions do we take to effect maximum effect? Medium effect? Minimum effect?
- How will we manage the transition?
- How do we build commitment? Who is/is not ready/capable for change? How will we manage resistance?
- Who will let it happen, help it happen, make it happen?
- Do we need additional help – consultants, facilitators...?

Step 5

- What review procedures do we need to establish?
- How do we articulate and share what we are learning?

Applying $L=P+Q$ to this changing, what are you learning about organizational changing as you subject changing theory to your questioning experience?

Case: The growing HVAC engineering and contracting firm

Consider the case of a fast-growing Heating, Ventilation, and Air Conditioning (HVAC) firm in a major metropolitan area in the United States to illustrate the adaptive coping cycle of organizations within the context of interlevel dynamics of organizational changing. The firm helps construction managers deliver HVAC systems within specifications of indoor thermal comfort and air quality, and specializes in designing, building, retrofitting and maintaining energy-efficient heating and cooling systems for all types of buildings. Projects are highly technical endeavours at the interface between architectural engineering (construction) and mechanical engineering (thermodynamics and heat transfer) so technological expertise and sound project management are necessary to ensure high quality delivery on time and within budget. In its early years the firm went through a period of explosive growth earning several awards for excellence, expanding its capabilities from engineering design to a full menu of product offerings through acquisitions and alliances, and securing several significant public and private contracts. This fast growth required repeated adaptation to evolving external demands and development of internal capabilities, providing a series of examples of the organization's adaptive coping cycle, of which we examine one below:

1. *Sensing a change in the internal or external environment.* Originally an engineering design company representing manufacturers, the two founding mechanical engineers, one with an MBA and another with an entrepreneurial background, perceived an opportunity for growth through vertical integration. Backward integrating to manufacture components of the systems they designed would allow the company to benefit from synergies in design and manufacturing, therefore differentiating itself from other design firms. Forward integrating to become providers of construction services (being subcontracted by builders to deliver and install heating and ventilation systems) would permit the company to benefit from certain changes in public policy that favoured minority-owned businesses. As a result the leaders not only actively sought opportunities for partnership but also were receptive to new ideas that came their way. We focus on one such case.

2. *Getting the information to the right place to be processed and acted upon.* Both forward and backward integrating required significant expansion in the scope of the company and, consequently, in the activities and responsibilities of the two founders. Here we consider backward integrating into manufacturing as an opportunity to merge with a struggling large-scale sheet metal manufacturing operation presented itself. This information needed to be processed not only by the leaders, but also by the departments with most interaction as such a merger would provide several strategic advantages to the fledgling design company. First, by manufacturing their own sheet metal products for air distribution, the company guaranteed supply and the internal company structure was re-examined. Second, product quality was ensured. Lastly, the company was able to better insulate from price variability. The 'right place' to process the information on backward integrating was the top management team consisting of the two founders and the senior management team of each of the areas which interfaced with the sheet metal plant.

    Systems thinking was a necessity as the scope of the company expanded and there were several points to consider including such external issues as the possible negative reactions of other suppliers and the uncertain reaction of clients (which could be positive or negative). Internally, it was necessary to be able to manage a manufacturing operation and and improve internal systems and structures to allow for continued growth. Additionally a significant challenge would be to integrate two completely different cultures as the manufacturer was over one hundred years old and did not have a fast-growth entrepreneurial spirit.

3. *Digesting the information and drawing the right conclusions.* After careful consideration the two co-founders felt that despite the expected difficulties, this was a unique opportunity and that the company should indeed go ahead and merge with the sheet-metal fabrication operation, which was substantially larger than their own organization. They felt confident that they could reach an agreement which would be financially acceptable to both organizations' stakeholders while still maintaining the company's minority-controlled characteristic, which was very helpful in obtaining government contracts. They then proceeded to examine how to integrate the two companies.

4. *Making the necessary internal changes without undesirable side effects.* In order for the acquired company to be successfully integrated and to overcome expected difficulties, several changes were necessary. First, because the size of the company grew by a factor of five, accounting and personnel systems needed to be completely reprogrammed. Second, the manufacturing processes required automation in order to face the evolving competition. Both of these changes required significant investment but the main difficulty was integrating the cultures. The classic tension between manufacturing's desire to have predictable low-cost runs colliding with the design and engineering penchant for developing unique solutions for several clients was only one of the unforeseen consequences of the change. Others related to the geographic distances involved as communication suffered and to ownership of problems as there was some degree of finger-pointing.

    A programme to integrate personnel from the two companies and foster a common culture was instituted. This included a company-wide retreat for all employees. The effects were transformational for two weeks, but then the entire company reverted back to original behaviours, a discouraging result. Another initiative was one-on-one interventions with each employee and the formation of committees for increased collaboration between departments. Unfortunately employees would coalesce during meetings but later fall again into isolation. In short, despite all the care and planning some negative side effects from the acquisition seemed at first unavoidable, leading the founders to try alternative paths.

5. *Developing new actions.* New actions followed the recognition that some unexpected consequences needed to be corrected. Explicit top-down intentionality in off-site events and one-on-one interventions failed to provide lasting cultural change through increased cross-departmental cooperation because many of the employees tended to revert back to previous behavioural patterns when under pressure. On the other hand raising the stakes by targeting large projects and daunting tasks that forced individuals and departments to collaborate or fail, such as securing a high-rise project that tested the limits of the firm, led to increased cohesiveness. Individuals and departments banded and

worked together as they understood that success would help everyone but could only be achieved through cooperation. Advancing new technologies that required extensive training and interaction among employees also helped.

Additionally, the successful acquisition of the sheet metal operation depended on robust information systems to permit cross-referencing among the various different functions of both organizations: a necessary condition for the two organizations to become one was the integration of the systems. Automation of processes through high-end accounting, estimating, filing and project management software helped as the six-month period of installation, training and absorption gave employees a sense of ownership and resulted in strong buy-in. Most employees felt a sense of ownership and responsibility for the creation of a new reality and the few that rejected the process eventually left or were removed.

Surprisingly the founders realized that in several cases key employees at middle-level positions or lower were more easily converted than some top-level managers. For example, the sheet metal plant manager was a very experienced and competent professional who needed to adapt to a more nimble and less predictable routine and did so with difficulty. With each successful project undertaken buy-in grew.

6. *Obtaining feedback on the new actions to a new sensing cycle.* With many moving parts, the execution was not flawless during the transition period. The relationship between personnel in the acquired operation and the existing staff slowly improved as each party learned more about the other's needs to deliver successful outcomes. Even without structured systems in place to adjudicate disputes, internal feedback was positive as an emphasis on a common goal was increasingly crystallized. The immense expense of getting both organizations to function profitably drained company resources, but synergies from blending the old traditional methods of the acquired manufacturing company with the innovative methodologies of the acquiring engineering firm yielded a high-margin differentiated technology which yielded high returns. The marketplace accepted the technology offerings and company stakeholders rallied around the resulting transformational accomplishments. Furthermore, by being battle-tested in cultural immersion, the firm created a unique competence in interacting with larger firms through nimble and effective strategic partnerships. The beginnings of a new cycle became evident when the next opportunity for company expansion presented itself.

Questions for reflection and discussion

1. Many internal and external forces were affecting the growing HVAC engineering company and the case focuses on one major change. From the text, how many other change forces and factors can you identify?
2. Which of these would warrant intentional change on the part of the company? On what do you base this understanding?

3. As you consider the reflexive engagement process, consider the importance of Q in this case. What evidence from the case do you have that the founders asked themselves the right questions before taking action? What questions do you think they missed?
4. How would you go about effecting lasting change if you were leading the company? Show evidence of your choice.

References

Argyris, C. (1985) *Strategy, Change and Defensive Routines*. Marshfield, MA: Pitman.

Beckhard, R. and Harris, R. (1987) *Organizational Transitions*, 2nd edn. Reading, MA: Addison-Wesley.

Bennis, W.G. (1962) Toward a truly scientific management: The concert of organizational health. *General Systems Yearbook*, 7, 269–282.

Contu, D.L (2002) Interview with Edgar Schein – The anxiety of learning. *Harvard Business Review*, 80(3), 100–106.

Darling, M. and Parry, C. (2000) *From Post-mortem to Living Practice: An In-depth Study of the Evolution of the After Action Review*. Boston, MA: Signet.

Docherty, P., Kira, M. and Shani, A.B. (Rami) (2009) Organizational development for social sustainability in work systems. In R. Woodman, W. Pasmore, and A.B. Shani (Rami) (eds), *Research in Organizational Change and Development, Vol. 17*. Bingley: Emerald, pp. 77–144.

Fisher, D., Rooke, D. and Torbert, W. R. (2000) *Personal and Organizational Transformations Through Action Inquiry*. Boston, MA: Edge/Work Press.

Hesselbein, F., Beckhard, R. and Goldsmith, M. (1995) *The Leader of the Future*. San Francisco, CA: Jossey-Bass.

Kotter, J.L. (1996) *Leading Change*. Boston, MA: Harvard Business School Press.

Mohrman, A., Mohrman, S., Ledford, G., Cummings, T., Lawler, E.E. and Associates (1989) *Large Scale Organizational Change*. San Francisco, CA: Jossey-Bass.

Mohrman, S.A. and Shani, A.B. (Rami) (eds) (2011) *Organizing for Sustainable Effectiveness*. Bingley: Emerald.

Nadler, D.A. (1998) *Champion of Change*, San Francisco, CA: Jossey-Bass.

Nadler, D.A., Spencer, J. and Associates (1998) *Executive Teams*. San Francisco, CA: Jossey-Bass.

Pasmore, W.A. (2011) Tipping the balance: Overcoming persistent problems in organizational change. In A.B. Shani (Rami), R.W. Woodman and W.A. Pasmore (eds), *Research in Organizational Change and Development, Vol. 19*. Bingley: Emerald, pp. 259–292.

Schein, E.H. (1980) *Organizational Psychology*. 3rd edn. Englewood Cliffs, NJ: Prentice-Hall.

Schein, E.H. (2013) Notes toward a model of organizational therapy. In L. Vansina (ed.), *Humanness in Organizations*. London: Karnac, pp. 91–100.

7

PHASES AND LEVELS OF ORGANIZATIONAL LEARNING AND CHANGING

In Chapter 5, we described individual learning and changing in organizations and introduced four psychological reactions. Then in Chapter 6 we explored the interlevel processes in large system changing. In putting these two themes together in this chapter we see how the psychological reactions occur as the learning and changing processes are initiated and as they develop within an organization. As changing moves through an organization, there is a domino effect as the key individual takes the change issue to a team, and the team takes it to the inter-departmental group and so on until the changing affects the entire organization, both internally and externally. The changing process in a complex system involves individuals and teams, hearing the news of the proposed change, perceiving it, assessing its impact and deciding how to respond. The support of a critical mass is needed for movement to occur and changing to take place. This support is built over time and so there is need to understand how changing moves through the organization over a time period.

Interlevel dynamics of organizational learning

As organizations are dynamic interlevels systems, organizational learning involves complex iterations of learning across and between the four levels. The challenge is that people in organizations act collectively, but they learn individually. This creates a tension, if not a frustration, for organizational learning. Organizations learn through individuals who learn; individual learning does not guarantee organizational learning. But without it no organizational learning takes place

How then can we understand how organizational learning relates to individual learning and vice versa? Crossan, Lane and White (1999) provide a useful frame-work. They present organizational learning as a dynamic iterative process between the individual, the group and the organizational levels. They integrate three elements in their framework in terms of 4 Is (intuiting, interpreting, integrating and institutionalizing) as iterative learning across three levels. *Intuiting* occurs at the individual level and refers to the grasping of patterns, possibilities, similarities and differences and in the work of the experienced professional becomes tacit knowledge. *Interpreting* also occurs at the individual level and refers to more conscious elements of developing cognitive maps within specific domains or environments. *Integrating* occurs at the group level where shared understanding is worked at through conversation among group members in order to attain coherence. *Institutionalizing* is the process whereby the organization consolidates the learning.

The 4 Is hold the tension between exploration and exploitation. The tension between exploration and exploitation is viewed as feed-forward and feedback mechanisms. Feed-forward (exploration) is characterized by interpreting-integrating and requires a shift from individual learning to team/group learning. Feedback by institutionalizing-intuiting works from the organizational to the individual level and may be problematic as institutionalization may inhibit or drive out intuition.

These processes do not necessarily move smoothly from one level to another. They are highly political (Lawrence et al., 2005). We do not automatically accept others' views without examining them first. Even more so, groups or teams do not accept the stated learning of other teams without subjecting them to critical assessment. Accordingly, the framework that takes account of different reactions and responses to learning and change that we presented in the previous chapter is useful. The clinical perspective involves being attentive to movement across the 4 Is and questioning how the feed-forward or backward is working or not and what is enabling or inhibiting exploration and exploitation.

We will now detail how the reactions to changing interact with the four levels. Since there are countless activities and interactions in a large system's changing process, we have grouped them together to form a seven-phase sequence in order to bring structure to this process (Table 7.1). This approach maps how the changing moves through an organization – across the four levels – taking account of how individuals, teams, the interdepartmental group and the organization deny and dodge before doing. While it appears that these phases are linear, they are not. They move iteratively, back and forth in circular loops as the conversations on the changing agenda unfold throughout the organization.

It may also appear that these phases form the structure for a social engineering approach through cascading whereby senior management's dictates for change are pushed downwards for compliance through the organization. (They indeed may be used in this manner, as we will see in the A&P case in Chapter 15.) We, however, see these phases as a structure for understanding the conversations and interactions necessary for participation in and internalization of change. The quality of the conversation required is such that individuals, teams and the interdepartmental group engage in exploring and listening to one another and mutually influencing each other. So individuals and teams are open to influence from one another as the changing agenda moves in spiral loops through an organization.

TABLE 7.1 Players in organizational change and the phases of large system change

Phase	Change gatekeeper	Key individual	Team members	Team outliers	Group members	Group outliers	Organization	Organizational outliers
Ground zero	Denying Dodging							
Change awareness	Doing	Denying Dodging						
Initiation	Doing	Doing	Denying Dodging					
Manoeuvring	Sustaining	Doing	Doing	Denying Dodging Persistence	Denying Dodging			
Integration	Sustaining	Doing	Doing	Doing Compliance	Doing	Denying Dodging Persistence	Denying Dodging	
Achievement	Sustaining	Sustaining	Doing	Doing	Doing	Doing Compliance	Doing	Denying Dodging
Follow-through	New denying	Sustaining	Sustaining	Sustaining	Sustaining	Sustaining	Sustaining	Doing Compliance
Sustaining	New dodging	New denying	Sustaining	Sustaining	Sustaining	Sustaining	Sustaining	Sustaining

Phase 0 – Ground zero: the need for change enters the organization

Change enters the organization through an individual. In *intuiting* the individual goes through his or her own reaction to the need for changing by initially denying the validity, relevance and pertinence of the data calling for change. Once it is recognized that the changing will occur, the issue of acting on the insight can be dodged and left to others. For changing to progress this has to give way to a realization that the information is real and threatening, i.e. the organization may be in peril or lose some opportunity if something is not done. The individual, in this instance, can be anywhere in the organization and is, in effect, performing the 'gatekeeping' role or acting as 'scout' by bringing to the team the special information from the environment it needs to perform its task.

The individual who first senses the need for change may or may not be a key individual in the organization's hierarchy. He or she may be at the strategic level where the analysis of market trends leads him or her to question how the organization is currently functioning. Or it may be that an individual may be in direct contact with customers or clients and brings feedback to the organization on the organization's product or service as experienced by customers or clients. If that individual is not a key individual then a key individual (manager, team leader) must be approached and persuaded to take on the change issue. In terms of the adaptive coping cycle the individual is importing the sensed information to where it can be acted upon. In Crossan's terms, it is *interpreting* what had been *intuited*. The gatekeeper by this point has worked through the denying and dodging phases and is now in the doing phase, while people within the organization to whom the information is being brought are still in the denying phase.

Phase 1 – Change awareness: the key individual denying and dodging

The process from gatekeeper to key individual may have to work through several layers of the organization's hierarchy until it reaches a key individual powerful enough to act on it. At each juncture, the individual presented with the change issue goes through the initial reactions of denying and dodging before reaching the stage of doing and acting on the information. If the key individual is threatened by the change issue or by the gatekeeper's approach, the change process may be blocked and proceed no further. Ownership by the key individual concludes this phase, that is, when the key individual decides to act upon the issue.

It is not unusual for change to enter an organization through the key individual. This may occur through meetings with other leaders, such as with other CEOs or presidents, where information is exchanged and a realization of the need for change arises. Sometimes the key individual may be meeting with superiors at corporate or a higher level.

Phase 2 – Initiation: the key individual doing and the team denying and dodging

When the key individual has worked through the psychological reactions of denying and dodging regarding the change issue, he or she moves to the doing stage and presents the changing data to the appropriate team for consideration and action, emphasizing the necessity for changing and beginning to define the dimensions of changing. This is the beginning of Crossan's integrating stage. He or she places an emphasis on the degree of choice and the ultimate control over the change, and why changing is necessary at this time. In second-order change the emphasis is on selling a vision of a new order.

The process of denying and dodging is repeated in the team as the individual members deny (believe change is not required) and dodge (believe they do not have to do it now), before entering into the period of doing. The tendency 'to shoot the messenger' who has brought the bad news must be recognized. This phase is concluded when the team, as a team, recognizes the issue as critical and acknowledges the need to do something. Ownership of an articulated issue ends this phase, not just as defined by an individual, but as articulated by the team through consensus. There will be individuals who do not support the changing but are not powerful enough to block or stop it.

Phase 3 – Manoeuvring: the key individual and team doing and the interdepartmental group denying and dodging

This phase involves bringing multiple teams together at the interdepartmental group level to confront the issue of changing. Not only does this refer to interactions between the senior management group and other functional teams but also between the temporary task forces and committees set up to guide the changing process and functional teams. The process of first denying and then dodging is repeated within the individual teams that make up the interdepartmental group. Each team tends to view the change issue from its own viewpoint and may deny the validity, relevance and pertinence of the change. It will be evident in the organization that at Level III some functions will have to diminish and some will have to grow, e.g. some teams are more critical than others, some activities will be let go and others developed, etc.

The rationale behind the denying may focus on the information system, i.e. that the present form of data gathering is not providing the information that is needed to lead to the change. Denying at the interdepartmental group level typically means the emergence of differing and conflicting interpretations of the data supporting the change. It is argued that the information driving the change is not accurate or reliable and is found to be open to differing interpretations. The political interrelationship between teams may be a factor in denying, as for instance, when one team denies the need for change because the change is being promoted by a rival team.

When the decision support system is questioned the dodging is taking place, as when the coordination of the interdepartmental group is not effective and teams are blaming other teams for inefficiencies. This is when dodging needs to be addressed by internal mapping processes. The interfacing of teams – workflows, information processing – are the most relevant ones for identifying areas of trouble. The critical aspect of evaluating the need for change and getting ownership is to see the problem in a new way. Workflow mapping is a means of extending the boundary of the group's search for information to solve the problem. Each functioning team must become conscious of what other teams do and how what they do interacts with what others do. The dodging stage at this level confronts the assumption that if everyone else did their work, their team would have no problems. This phase ends with agreement on the articulation of the problem and the process steps needed to introduce change. Typically this involves correct identification of the critical people needed to make the change and description of what the new steady state might look like. In second-order change some key people may not yet be part of the organization, so initial consideration of the introduction and integration of new people who have not been part of the process begins.

A significant element of this third phase is the articulation of bargaining outcomes as a prelude to negotiation. In unionized settings when the collective bargaining process between management and unions is undertaken, it can be said that the interdepartmental group is at the doing stage. Collective bargaining negotiates what changes will take place, how, at what cost and to whose benefit. This phase concludes with ownership and with what effect the change will have on the organization's stakeholders, both internal and external.

In our experience there is a danger of regression, particularly at Phases 2 and 3. As the key individual experiences the team's denying and as the team experiences the interdepartmental group's denying, it is often noticed that the individual or the team can lose confidence and slip back into a dodging mode. Not everyone buys into the change agenda. Some choose to remain peripheral to it. It is in this regard that we are introducing the notion of 'outliers'.

Outliers are those individuals who do not buy into changing in the first round. If the team that is instituting the changing is a senior team, some outliers can be managers from areas or departmental groups that have the most to lose from changing. It is essential to double back and bring these outliers from denying and dodging into the doing phase. One technique that can be helpful with these outliers is to do a 'walk-through'. This exercise takes all members of the team and presents the findings of the first change with which the interdepartmental group has just dealt. Then the senior management group provides an evaluation of why the steps were chosen and what happened when the change was presented to the interdepartmental group. This is followed by an evaluation of the forces resisting change and the forces supporting change. This dialogue can at times unfreeze members who are outliers or it may uncover a perspective that requires management to step back and rethink its position. In this instance, management may revert to denying and dodging.

The changing process is always more difficult in a senior management group. The group member simultaneously reflects his or her own views while being a representative of an interdepartmental group. The presence of an OD consultant can be significant in addressing outliers and helping the manager and the team process what is going, while reinforcing for the senior manager the need for change and the need to remain firm in his or her convictions for changing. The purpose of the conversations at this phase is to engage the interdepartmental group in changing. Through conversation new ideas may emerge and the changing agenda may be enlarged and amended to include emerging perspectives and points of view.

Phase 4 – Integration: the key individual, team and interdepartmental group doing, the organization denying and dodging

The organization's adaptive behaviour commences at this point as the organizational change forces its impact on the organization's external functioning and relations. Initially, in this phase, the question is how other organizations and stakeholders will perceive them and the organization, if changing occurs. At this point, assumptions about the inter-relatedness of competitive organizations are questioned. At first, such an inter-relatedness can be denied and when the denying is accepted, the question of what the least amount of change is acceptable is asked. Accurate competitive analysis leads to ownership of the interlinking of organizations in competitive markets. The open systems planning approach maps the impact of the changed and changing organization on its customers or clients, competitors and the market in general. The organization will be involved in extensive marketing activities in order that the changed organization's products or services will meet customer or clients' needs. Successful change requires an understanding of stakeholder demands and behaviour as well as a proactive stance in their regard.

The senior management group working over time with all of the changes may have overlooked the interdepartmental group outliers. They are the members of the interdepartmental group who are still dubious about changing. They are not supporting the process, but are mostly very quiet about their disagreement. This is an important check at this point in the process. The solution can be to run a 'walk-through' in which the total interdepartmental group is brought together, placed at working tables, presented with the previous change process and given a chance to evaluate it in small group discussions. When the discussions are finished, input is collected by paper or voice. This can help collect the outliers into the support group of doers or hear their corrective input.

Phase 5 – Achievement: the key individual sustaining, the team, interdepartmental group and organization doing

The key individual goes into a sustaining stage when his/her energy shifts from initiating the change effort to keeping the organization focused on changing. The energy of the key individual is now refocused to look for ways of sustaining change. This may involve working with the consultant as to what structures and reward systems may be required to keep the change in place and seeing how other organizations have done it. The focus at this point is on the process of restructuring new functions, setting new norms and making the changed state normative, rather than a focus on the content of the change. These new elements are the part of changing that must be sustained. Here it is important to determine if any of these critical aspects are not being sustained and, if so, what means are at hand to sustain them. This phase is concluded when the key individual, satisfied that all that can be done has been accomplished, enables the team to own the sustaining issues so he or she can look at new data and sense other emergent issues.

Phase 5 deals with the organizational level and the people affected by the change from outside the organization who are now, willingly or not, affected by the change outcome. These people can be suppliers, brokers, customers, the labour market, neighbours or community officials, capital markets and brokers, and any other individual or groups of individuals who relate to and interact with the changed organization.

In Phase 5, we now have, at the organization level, outliers who are a group of people at the edge of the change process still having doubts. It is often helpful to have a follow-up 'walk-through'. The follow-up 'walk-through' enables the outliers to listen to what was intended, what has been accomplished, and to look at ways to further enhance the outcome. For some of these, such as customers, the 'walk-through' can be accomplished only through advertising and other forms of communications. Most often, the outliers will consist of people who have the most to lose from changing. When they see the reality of change, their fears will sometimes be reduced or they will be lost to the changed organization.

If the key individual is a creative person and, as such, recognized the need for change in the earlier stages and helped the organization adapt, that same creativity at this point may cause the individual to lose interest in the sustaining process. While progressing to the stage where he or she can see the end point, he or she can lose interest and become bored with getting the organization to sustain the change. Yet, this is a time to show concern and to continue to enable the change process.

Phase 5 is the critical phase in which questions surface of whether or not first- or second-order change is required. The adequacy or inadequacy of the change as perceived and implemented is reviewed in the context of its effects on the long-term perspective of the organization and its ability to engage in continuous change.

Phase 6 – Follow-through: the key individual and team sustaining, the interdepartmental group and organization doing

The team goes into the sustaining stage when the process regarding the terminal point of change is defined. The key team defines the end, the phases, and the time deadlines, i.e. the who, the what, the when, and the how the change can be sustained. Then it is freed to play an enabling role as the momentum is under way and there is continuity in the entire organization. In high-tech organizations in a web-based world, there may not be time for this phase and there may not be a 'normal' time or period of equilibrium. In many cases the next changing initiative has already begun.

If the changing fits the needs of adaptive coping, the organization is free to leave the change mode and move into a more normal state since the momentum is under way and there is continuity in the entire organization. If the changing is not sufficient to meet the change needs, e.g. if there is a lack of satisfaction within the organization or a lack of ownership of the change process, the question of whether a second-order change is required must be asked. It is not uncommon, at this point, for an organization facing second-order change to revert to Phase 2 in which the key individual has to convince the team of the necessity of second-order change and deal with its members' denying and dodging. In second-order change, things are not neat and well defined. Yet the change is played out in a cycle of similar phases: recognition of the imperative for changing (dodging), developing a shared direction, implementing changing (doing), and sustaining (sustaining).

Phase 7 – Sustaining: the key individual, team, interdepartmental group and organization sustaining

The *sustaining* stage has occurred when there is a new relationship between the organization and peer organizations, when stakeholders come to accept the new relationship and interact with the organization in the new way, and when the structures, reward systems and review processes are in place. This is the institutionalizing stage in Crossman's terms. In the initial stages of sustaining, a good deal of energy must be devoted to ensuring changing has worked by monitoring feedback, both from within and outside the organization. Feedback is available through attention to each of the four levels. At this point the learning organization makes use of the organization's openness to learning as the ability to change is a confirmation of organizational learning.

After some time, when it is felt that the change is in place and has worked, there is a drop in energy. The organization is moving and it has its own impetus. The organization is fat and happy. Through its normative behaviour it reinforces its culture and thereby sets up the mode for future denying.

The Saint Joseph's University case presented in Chapter 6 also illustrates the phases and levels of large system change in operation. The new president, entering at ground zero, became aware of the need for change and initiated the process. He first brought the issues to his senior management groups where he received a mixed reaction (Initiation Phase). Some denied the need for change; others dodged by presenting difficulties as described in the case at the end of Chapter 5 – indeed, the four-day retreat described in that case was a watershed event early in the new president's tenure. New facilities would be required for adult learners. New faculty would require more resources and structural change as the departments of the university did not have responsibility for graduate programmes. Slowly the senior management group came to embrace the need for change and began implementation (Manoeuvring). They in turn then met resistance in their departments. This resistance was not immediate, but evolved over a period of time. As resentment set in the faculty-administrative retreat described at the end of Chapter 5 was planned.

This initial four-day retreat meeting established a forum and process whereby a core group of the university moved into a doing stage and began a university-wide process of vision generation, which drew in outliers and over several years facilitated buy-in to change and to a new mission and identity by the whole university community. The process itself generated excitement about a possible new future. As people became excited about the future the fear of letting go of the past decreased. In fact some of the excitement came from regaining some aspects of the past that had been lost. As implementation of the new goals began, groups and individuals within the university were required to change. It became clear that to sustain and reinforce these changes two things needed to occur. First, that the changes that were occurring relate directly to what had been the outcome of the group process. Second, that the resources used were helping the university make progress towards goals desired by the group. Three times over the next year group sessions called 'walk-throughs' were held. The sessions laid out explicitly what had been set as goals, what had been accomplished, and what yet remained to be done. Input from the group was solicited through questions as well as written evaluation pages on the tables. These experiences were very important for the constituent groups to feel connected to the change process and to remain involved. Thus Integration was achieved.

Several years passed as Saint Joseph's achieved its goals and surpassed them. Outlying groups of faculty were treated to walk-through experiences to show the attainment of the stated goals. The realization of a new 'Saint Joseph's University' was taking place. Enrolment was up; student qualifications were up and graduate studies became a part of each department. The Sustaining phase had been reached.

As outlined previously some organizations do not move to sustaining but remain in continuous doing. As we discussed earlier, this may be due to perpetual discontinuous change in the environment where sustaining is a precursor to death because conditions are continually evolving. Examples of industries and sectors in which this is the case are those with very rapid technological innovations which are disruptive to incumbents (Christensen, 1997, 2003) and those which depend on somewhat volatile consumer tastes such as motion picture and gaming entertainment, and fashion. Participants in industries in which either supply or demand conditions are volatile and subject to unexpected sudden change need to be willing and able to expeditiously engage in systemic change.

Conclusions

Large systems do not learn and change instantly. Changing has to begin some-where. The seven phases of changing provide a framework for one clear fact of experience which is rarely considered in the change literature, namely, in organi-zational changing, people change at different paces. This is partly as a result of access to information, i.e. the leader is likely to have a sense of the need for change before others further down the echelon because he or she has access to the infor-mation. A sales team may be convinced of the need for change from interaction with customers and then have to persuade the senior management team to take on the issue. The seven phases framework is built on the sequence that when one party is aware of the need for change and begins initiating change, another party may be caught unaware and typically responds by denying and dodging.

In our consulting and teaching experience we have found that, while the seven phases may look linear, they are not. Each phase may comprise multiple loops as interventions are made to build commitment and action and help those who are dubious of the change (whom we have called 'outliers') to move from denying and dodging to doing. That there are individuals and teams in the outlier role provides valuable feedback on the organization's capacity, readiness and willingness to change. The multiple activity loops within each phase depend on management's ability to create minimal survival anxiety and maximum psychological safety. Knowing in advance that denying and dodging are likely to occur provides change leadership with its own psychological safety. These behaviours are common experiences in a change process. Knowing that they are coming is one form of preparation.

While the seven phases may provide a framework for senior management to cascade a change agenda downward through the organization, we caution against this approach. Rather we argue that the seven phases provide a framework for understanding the perspectives and reactions of organizational members (whether as individuals or as teams) as they engage in conversation about what, why and how the organization changes. Each conversation allows for new ideas and new perspectives to emerge. So rather than the seven phases being the vehicle for understanding the process of compliance, they are the vehicle for appreciating the processes of conversation.

Through the seven phases members of organizations can easily recognize what phase their organization is currently in and identify with the descriptions and issues of each phase. In large organizations, sustaining the change process over a period of time across the four levels requires management and knowledge of the terrain. The seven phases give structure to this process.

Changing involves a letting go of familiar and accepted ways of seeing and doing things. It can take a lot for us to acknowledge that change is needed. We will even deny the need for changing. Then we dodge it and leave it to others. When that position cannot be sustained, we begin to see what is required, what needs chan-ging, how, when, at what cost, etc. As relevant changes are made, they need to be sustained so that change survives. These seven phases show how members of an organization can be at denying and dodging stages of the change process because they have access to information that others do not have. The phases also describe how in an organization change moves through the key individual, teams and the interdepartmental group towards the entire organization.

An OD consultant can facilitate the individual manager, the team, the group and the organization to attend to the processes within the change effort and identify and work through the stages and phases of the change. A process consultation approach allows the members of the organization to understand what is going on and to develop the key diagnostic and problem-solving skills to manage change themselves. The OD consultant collaborates with the members of the organization in designing the particular activities that help deal with the issues of each stage that move the individual, the team, the group and the organization through the change phases.

Reflexive engagement activity 7.1

Reflecting on a change in progress in an organization with which you are familiar, revisit Reflexive engagement exercise 6.1:

- Review how the change entered the system, with whom…
- Track how the change moved from that individual to the wider system.
- Note how individuals/teams and groups received and responded initially to the changing agenda.
- Note how responses changed/did not change over time.
- Where is the progress of changing now?
- What now needs to be done?
- Applying $L=P+Q$, what are your insights into the pattern of the progress of this change from changing theory?

Case: AT&T Long Lines Division after the break-up

Large-scale system change is by definition complex, involving changes in processes and support systems which depend on human acceptance, adaptation and eventual adoption. While Table 7.1 depicts the actions of all players (and consequently all levels) in every phase of large-scale system change, most situations will involve a subset of the players included in that table. We believe good illustrations of the flow of player actions across all phases in large system change include as many steps and stages as possible. As a result we invite you to consider the case below, which occurred decades ago, but which in our mind provides a powerful illustration of all the phases described in Part II.

This case is about the Long Lines Division of the AT&T Company shortly after the court-mandated Bell system break-up which became effective in January 1984. The case is complex because it involves large projects conducted by AT&T in the period in which the organization was required to adapt to momentous externally induced change. In short, telephone services in the United States had previously been provided by a monopoly, AT&T, which was also vertically integrated backward in that it had a subsidiary producing telephonic equipment. After the court order, the company was split into independent Regional Bell Operating Companies (the RBOCs) which would be responsible for local telephone services and owned the direct hardwire access to individual consumers, and a new company, still called AT&T, which would retain control of the manufacturing subsidiary (Western Electric), the research arm (Bell Labs), and would be responsible for long distance land-line telephone communications. As a result of the break-up, AT&T effectively lost what were captive buyers of equipment and systems and now needed to interface with separate regional land-line telephone companies in a competitive marketplace to provide the physical infrastructure for successful communications services. The case examines the transition phase that AT&T went through as it adapted to market relationships with the RBOCs. It describes the various phases of change as the company adapted to the new competitive environment and managed long-term large-scale communications installation projects which extended over long distances and lasted five or more years. Because adapting to the new reality was so difficult the case aptly illustrates the phases of change throughout the four levels with the intervention of a consultant (adapted from Rashford and Coghlan, 1994).

Phase 0 Ground zero: the problem surfaces

During an executive MBA class on the subject of organizational levels, the topic of discussion was complex change processes in large organizations. One of the students was the vice-president for Engineering of a regional division of AT&T, then responsible for long-distance communication circuits used by regional telephone-operating companies throughout the US. The class discussion centred on large systems change and the difficulties in detecting errors and correcting them in a timely manner in complex long-duration projects. The V-P observed that cost overruns in construction projects had been a source of difficulties for the company. Projects would begin with allocated funds which at later stages would often turn out to be insufficient to complete a particular project, thereby, impeding delivery of a functioning set of long-distance communications circuits to the operating companies. It was at this stage that the V-P fully recognized that there was a problem. Interestingly, part of the freedom to admit that a problem existed came from the implicit realization that a solution to the problem was possible. The vice-president, as the key individual, moved from denying to dodging at this point.

Phase 1 Change awareness

Further discussion led the V-P and Rashford, the professor, to set up a consultation project for a two-year period to study the project management process. The contract was for a process consultation to facilitate the analysis of the problem by the company's staff and to work with the management team to design a process to solve it.

Phase 2 Initiation: meeting the team and setting the parameters

This phase involved the interdepartmental group leaders admitting in their face-to-face working team that problems existed. The interdepartmental group leaders represented every function of engineering, from current design to installation engineering. The first meeting of the team was the most traumatic. The initial reaction was intense denial that there was a problem, together with a belief that if there were one, it could be solved without a consultant. The consultant was perceived as extra baggage and tolerated as the V-P's professor. Therefore, he should be endured but largely ignored. The notion that an outsider be brought into the company was a sign of failure in and of itself, and therefore not acceptable.

Working through denial

The discussion of the 'problem' soon became technical and the use of jargon and special engineering language proliferated. The consultant who was to participate as a process observer incidentally had a background in military electronics and began participating in the technical discussion. This caught the team by surprise and some of the defences came down. The team slowly accepted that the consultant might indeed understand the issues involved, admitted that there was a problem, and began the process of setting out a course of action in which the consultant could play a part. One individual went as far as to suggest that if the consultant had not embarked on a teaching career he might well be working for the company and the rest concurred. The consultant was, at this point, admitted as a fellow technician and not as a process consultant, which in this particular group seemed to be a pre-requisite for acceptance.

The need for focus soon became apparent. The consultant inquired about the most recently completed project and sought to find out what could be learned from that project. The discussion centred on the fact that the project had since been turned over to a group of operators who were to run the equipment (which was providing the communications circuits from point A to point B), and that the people trying to operate it did not have appropriate testing equipment. The testing equipment was necessary for the operations group to be effective and therefore was an integral part of the project. The funds originally allocated for the testing equipment had been spent in cost overruns in the early phases of building linkages between point A and point B. In the past all financing had been internal, instead of through market transactions between different companies, so these end-of-project cost overruns had always been absorbed with little or no drama.

Working through dodging

The discussion grew heated at this point and it seemed as though participants were trying to find somewhere to put the blame. Each area was interrogated to see who was at fault. This went on for some time and the consultant intervened. He set up a make-believe process in which a culprit was chosen to take the blame. The person was asked to get down on his knees and say 'I am sorry'. The consultant led the way and showed how to adopt the contrite position as it was named. The group was silent and then began to laugh. Soon the pointlessness of blaming became apparent. If one found the culprits and they were punished or shunned, this would not solve the problem or change the situation. The interdepartmental group leadership team, in this way, came to process the situation and started to plan for the change process.

Phase 3 Manoeuvring: getting the interdepartmental group leaders to see the issues and dealing with outliers

This phase began with the definition of the basic problem and an outline of the issue. Systematic analysis had yet to begin. It is the nature of complex processes that no one individual can see the full consequences of their actions, yet each individual can see where they stand to lose as a result of the process and defence mechanisms arise quickly.

The second meeting was set up as an all-day meeting. Each person was to bring a large chart with all the inputs to and outputs from their functional area. Traffic analysis would show their hand-offs or outputs to the design engineering group. They, in turn, would show their hand-offs or outputs to the equipment manufacturers who were not part of the company. The design group would also do the hand-off to the Federal Relations group for obtaining FCC permission and frequency allocations. This process of detailing the full project took up the entire morning. The team went to lunch and had a drink to celebrate the morning's success. One member decided to continue the celebration in lieu of lunch.

The outlier phenomena: a personal issue sets the interdepartmental group leaders back

After the lunch break the individual who had been celebrating had his area come up for presentation and review. His chart had been rolled up during the morning session and was now revealed to be blank. The individual in a slurred speech told the team angrily that the process was useless, that he did not agree with it, never had and that he was the most senior and should know what was best. He stormed out of the room. After the initial awkward silence the remaining team members discussed what was happening. He was a valuable individual but over the past year had brought much destruction to the team through an abuse of alcohol. His spouse had recently died of cancer and he had begun to drink heavily and to miss work.

It soon became apparent that what the team thought was a team management issue was indeed a personal issue. A meeting was held in which the V-P and some other team members who had the required data confronted the individual and enabled him to seek company-assisted help. The project was put on hold. Distinguishing a Level I issue from a Level II or III issue is difficult at best.

Phase 4 Integration: getting the interdepartmental group leaders involved in the change

The next meeting of the interdepartmental group leadership team took place a month later. The leaders of the teams began to put the internal maps together again. In the process of putting the internal maps on paper and talking about the relationships between different functional areas, some new information emerged. Some of the hand-off processes, reports that were filed and moved to the next group, were done for functions which no longer existed and therefore were not needed. The team receiving the report would file it and do nothing with it even though the team members generating it had spent significant time and resources preparing it. At this very preliminary stage of internal mapping, problem areas were soon identified as areas which existed between different sub-functions and the hand-offs between those sub-functions. One group's output became another group's input and the mismatch between those outputs and inputs turned out to be very large indeed. The group leadership, reflecting on the internal mapping process, realized the significance of the problem and the extent to which change was required. This analysis only involved the interdepartmental group leaders of Level III. Later meetings with Level II teams resulted in the realization that this had been only the tip of the iceberg.

Phase 5 Achievement: an internal mapping process to gather the required information

All the members of the interdepartmental group (numbering about 200) were assembled on a predetermined date, with prior instructions that a detailed list of inputs into their functional areas and outputs to adjacent functional areas be produced for a large display. The flow of each project from start to finish would be explained. This all-day meeting was a complex discussion of detailed inputs and outputs, function-by-function, area-by-area, until at the end of the day complex projects extending over five years were detailed. The group could see each project from beginning to end. Looking at the mass of information which occupied three of the four walls of a large auditorium, the group became aware of the incredible complexity – well over 1200 hand-offs of technical material of engineering design, blueprints, equipment, requests or other significant pieces of data which were required in the process of each project.

At this preliminary stage the group was distinctively aware of the fact that there were two different kinds of projects, and separated one – an upgrade and renewal project – from the second – the installation of an entirely new channel of communication from point A to point B. This analysis and one of the other problem points, namely useless information being prepared for reports which were no longer required due to changes in governmental regulations, proved significant. This attention to significant irritants was the investment of the subordinate team, who now clearly saw gains from the change process and bought into it. The recognition of 'useless information' turned out to be a second-order learning moment. In the shift from microwave technology broadcasted from tower to tower to optic fibre technology with no broadcasting, these reports were no longer needed and resources for their preparation could be used elsewhere.

Change of vice-president

The V-P for Engineering, who had started this whole process, graduated from the school which had triggered the consulting relationship. He left the company to become president of another communications company operating on the West Coast. Immediately a process to select a successor was initiated within the local company. The person appointed was an engineer by background, had worked in another division of the organization and therefore had not been privy to the ongoing change process conducted in this area into which he was now entering. He met the group and consultant and discussed the change project and whether its continuation was warranted. He also joined the same executive MBA programme in which his predecessor had participated and was exposed to the construct of levels in the classroom discussions. After a lapse of about two months the inter-departmental group was re-assembled and the change process refocused on two types of projects – an upgrade renewal project and a new communications channel installation project. These two projects would serve as examples of the remainder of the processes within his division and therefore would be fully mapped.

Internal mapping with all the interdepartmental group members

The new V-P brought the group together to begin the internal mapping process with two simplified versions of the project which had been delineated at the previous meetings. Once again, a large auditorium with more than 200 people was filled and the process began with input-output maps of each area and each division being juxtaposed with each other area or division in which there were hand-offs. Lines were drawn from one chart to another and the quality of the input-output transactions was discussed. This process took two complete days. A third day was set aside for a discussion on the type of action that would be needed and requirements for its implementation.

Phase 6 Follow-through: setting flags and forming correction teams

The action phase took the complex data of the large system and all its interfaces, as played in the mapping function and began defining problem areas, thus enabling change to take place. After significant discussion with the consultant the group concluded that it needed a way to deal with how certain points seemed more critical than others to some people. A system was set up whereby 'flags' – sets of highlighted markers – could be placed anywhere on the displayed project scheme. When a flag was placed, the person who felt that this was a problem presented the issue to the entire group. The group listening to the detailed explanation either agreed or rejected that this was a problem and clarified the issues at stake. Once a flag was placed and the group admitted that this was a true dysfunctional point, a fixing team was set up. Any person who had a stake in what was going to be changed in the process of fixing this problem was included on the team. A process flag team leader led the team and a flag solver – the person who had originally placed the flag or had the best description of the dysfunction – was named. It was the flag solver's judgement which would be required for the elimination of the flag. At the end of the third working day, 23 significant flags were located and change teams set up.

Over the next four-month period, flag meetings were held regularly, some weekly and others on a three-weekly basis. Members of these change teams were at different levels of the organization's echelon. If a flag was significant enough to cause real disruption in the projects, the change team leader might well have been a vice-president. Others were within functional areas in a division with a group manager leading the team.

At the end of each three-week period an update on the progress of each of the flags was prepared and sent out in written form to the entire group. Top management met weekly and reviewed what was happening in the organization, how the change was progressing and how the change teams were working. Everyone agreed that the process was having a good effect and that change was taking place. In many instances before flags were completed, people realized what was going wrong, came up with detailed solutions and solved the problem without waiting for the entire organization and the next flag meeting.

Phase 7 Sustaining: burning the flags

At the end of the first four-month period a flag burning ceremony was held at an assembly of the entire group. Any flag which had been brought to completion was detailed as to how the solution had been found and what action was being taken. The group response was to accept or reject that the flag had been solved. When all parties agreed that a flag was completed a small paper flag was placed in a fire-proof container and burned. The group cheered that change had come into the system.

Overloading

Early on in the change teams it was found that other issues seemed to require attention and were afforded problem-solving time and energy. People saw the opportunity to change the organization and suddenly the change teams found themselves burdened with issues other than the flags on which they were working. Sometimes it was management that added new issues; sometimes it was individuals within the teams. These extraneous, additional incremental-type change processes had to be nipped in the bud and were declared to be outside the realm of the change process.

The sustaining phase of a learning organization was not realized. The organization was restructured and the teams broken up before ongoing learning processes were in place. Later discussions, after several years had passed, revealed that individuals had taken aspects of the flag process into new restructured parts of the organization to overcome problems they found there. The learning that had occurred had indeed been by individuals who then transferred their experiences to other parts of the organization.

Questions for reflection and discussion

1. How did the change in the case involve all four levels?
2. The project involved face-to-face team interaction in problem identification and solution generation – do you think this changed team behaviour in other functions?
3. The major thrust for change came through the Level III assemblies, where the systemic picture of the projects was displayed in a manner which enabled the different functional teams and areas to grasp the overall picture and understand the linkages between one area and another. What made this effective?
4. The case emphasizes how in a complex change process people are exposed to the change question at different stages and typically respond initially in a denial and dodging mode. Did some of the denial and dodging occur around the consultant?

References

Christensen, C. (1997) *The Innovator's Dilemma: When New Technologies Cause Great Firms to Fail.* Boston, MA: Harvard Business School Press.

Christensen, C. (2003) *The Innovator's Solution: Creating and Sustaining Successful Growth.* Boston, MA: Harvard Business School Press.

Crossan, M., Lane, H. and White, R. (1999) An organizational learning framework: From intuiting to institution. *Academy of Management Review*, 24(3), 522–537.

Lawrence, T.B., Mauws, M.K., Dyck, B. and Kleysen, R.F. (2005) The politics of organizational learning: Integrating power in the 4 I framework. *Academy of Management Review*, 30(1), 180–191.

Rashford, N.S. and Coghlan, D. (1994) *The Dynamics of Organizational Levels: A Change Framework for Managers and Consultants.* Reading, MA: Addison-Wesley.

PART III

The strategizing process through interlevel change

In Part II we explored how large-scale, large system changing comprises individual change which contributes to team changing (and vice versa), which contributes to interdepartmental group changing (and vice versa), with the result that the entire organizational system changes. In Part III we consider large-scale organizational changing with strategic intent. Strategic management encompasses strategy formulation and actualization (a top-down approach by organizational leaders) as well as strategy emergence resulting from behaviour and actions of members of the organization at every level. Part III introduces and describes an approach to help effect sound intentional strategic influencing on an organization and is composed of an introductory chapter and five additional chapters, each of which addresses one of five fundamental elements in strategic intent. As such, each chapter offers a different lens, examining the respective fundamental strategic element in light of content, process, roles of different stakeholders, and selected interlevel issues. This intentional change can be operational (doing better what has been done in the past or is being done now) or involve the organization's reason for being (doing something completely different, up to and including a change in its very identity and composition) but in every case the interlevel dynamics described in Parts I and II of this book are central processes to achieve desired strategic change.

8

INTRODUCING STRATEGY AND THE FIVE STRATEGIC FOCI

We have grounded our understanding of organizing in a framework of systemic health, which we described as having a sense of identity and purpose, the capacity to adapt to changing external and internal circumstances, the capacity to perceive and test reality and the internal integration of systems and subsystems. In enacting systemic health, organizations engage in cycles of continuous coping and adaptation as they take in information, process it and transform it into outputs. The adaptive coping cycle undertaken as an expression of systemic health is what is usually called strategizing. Broadly envisioned, strategy is akin to the soul of the organization, the expression of its systemic health. Organizing a complex system made up of sub-systems achieves synchronized integration at all levels towards a common goal defined by its strategic intent. Understanding and influencing an organization's strategy therefore is not solely the domain of senior members of an organization, but rather the prerogative of every member.

Strategizing and the use of the five strategic foci

Why do some organizations perform so much better than others? The answer, in great part, is in their strategies. Leaders of established businesses, whether start-up entrepreneurs or CEOs of organizations with tens of thousands of employees, attempt to develop strategies to seize opportunities in the marketplace in ways that other companies have difficulty matching. This is not just sheer luck as the use of strategic planning is visible in the success and failure of organizations.

Strategizing is the recognition of opportunity and a plan for seizing it, but it also recognizes and deals with threats to the organization. These opportunities and threats come from external forces – changes in customers' preferences, competitors' actions, technological breakthroughs, government actions such as deregulation, geopolitical shifts, trends in fashions and many other unexpected occurrences.

Opportunities also arise from an organization leader's convictions, personal values, or a flash of insight on changing times.

We have broken down strategic thinking and acting into five components called foci (Figure 8.1). The term *focus* implies the clarity and attention that must be given to each of these components in the systematic interaction required to generate and implement a complex and functional strategic plan. Focus is defined as the utilization of all resources both internal and external of the organization to develop a key fundamental element or component of the formulation and actualization processes.

The term *focus* is used in photography to mean the ability to bring an image into clarity. The photographer accomplishes this by adjusting the lens to obtain the greatest clarity in that part of the image that is the centre of interest. The use of focus is a technique that draws the viewer to the key points of interest in the subject of the photograph as determined by the photographer. In photography there are three primary 'grounds,' namely foreground, middle ground, and background. In strategic thinking and acting a focus occurs when a portion of the whole is clarified in order to attend to it while keeping the other elements of the whole in perspective. The map of the whole inter-related strategic elements is a

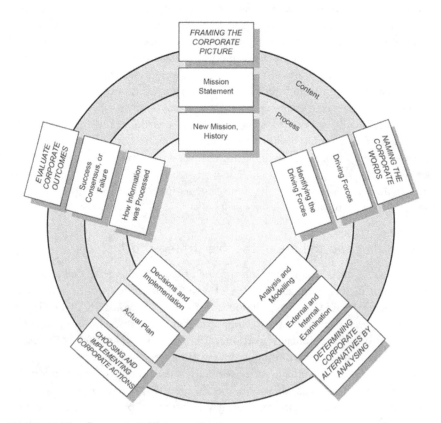

FIGURE 8.1 The five strategic foci

non-linear system comparable to a large and detailed photograph of a complex subject. A focus is a clarified segment or portion that can be attended to in perspective of the whole. The five foci are the counterpart to the three photographic 'grounds' in strategic thinking.

The purpose of the five strategic foci framework is to define the space in formulating and actualizing strategic plans in a complex world by complex organizations as they enact the adaptive coping cycle. We referred to these spaces as foci not because they are steps in a process but rather five ongoing systematic elements of interaction: content, process and culture components which exist within a context in the determination of strategic formulation and actualization. Part IV spells out the interaction among the five foci in light of the concepts discussed in Parts I through III.

The complex process of generating strategic thinking and acting evolves through the following five foci:

- Framing the corporate picture
- Naming the corporate words
- Determining corporate alternatives by analysing
- Choosing and implementing corporate actions
- Evaluating corporate outcomes

We apply the template that we introduced in Part I to each focus. Each focus can be dissected in terms of six components. The content component addresses the tasks and relational issues to be addressed. The process component examines how task and relational issues are implemented. Culture explores the hidden collective assumptions that underpin the action of each focus and is affected by content and process: in each focus the culture component is the residual, i.e. what is left over as a result of the choice of content addressed and the choice of process which occurred.

The first focus, *framing the corporate picture*, refers to the key individuals and the history of the organization as it comes to affect strategy. The contents of this focus are the core mission and the characteristics of the organization as affected by its key players. The process aspect focuses on the construction and involvement of different members and processes, and on putting together and embracing the corporate mission and its statement.

The second focus, *naming the corporate words*, refers to operations or functions that have become the lead operations or functions over time, some of which are core capabilities or competencies. These are also referred to as driving forces and become the articulation, or lived-out mission statement of the organization. The process focus of naming the corporate words deals with the power aspects and conflicts as well as successes and burdens that come from being a lead function or operation.

The third focus *determining corporate alternatives by analysing* deals with obtaining critical information and preparing data into a comprehensive scenario or modelling of alternatives for the organization. The process aspect of determining corporate alternatives by analysing considers whether bias or contamination is introduced into the strategic planning process during this information-gathering focus, if a comprehensive group of the organization is involved, and if the proper questions are being asked. The analytic process acknowledges the appropriate connectedness of this focus to the focus of mission in framing the corporate picture and to the focus of choosing and implementing corporate actions which will of necessity follow.

The fourth focus, *choosing and implementing corporate actions*, refers to the selection and structured implementation of a strategic plan of action with its dependent components. The process aspect, of choosing and implementing corporate actions, refers to the bias and influence on the selection process that comes from sources other than the analysis focus.

The fifth focus, *evaluating corporate outcomes*, refers to the acceptance of the choice of criteria in the appropriate review and evaluation of the resulting state of the organization. The process aspect of evaluating corporate outcomes looks at the appropriate and fair evaluation of outcomes: it centres on avoiding selective or biased evaluation of outcome states. This refers to all possible strategic actions, including changes in the mission statement, new driving forces, and new methods of analysis in the formulation of ongoing strategies. Evaluation must be unbiased as some changes can be such that a new organizational identity results, occasionally so radically different that the new would not be recognizable from the old.

These fundamental elements are called foci (focus in the singular) in order to avoid the misconception that they are sequential steps in a linear process to formulate strategic objectives and actualize them. The complex processes required to respond to quickly changing environmental issues demands that the flexible organization attend to several foci simultaneously. The overall strategic process is systemic and dynamic. The model of a thinking living organism comes to mind, being both multi-tasking and responsive. This is in contrast with trying to come to awareness of the whole all at once or in linear steps. We think there are five distinct points of focus in this reality. The skills required for application of the five foci framework in academic and professional environments can be developed through a pedagogical process described in Rashford and Neiva de Figueiredo (2011). Figure 8.2 depicts the five foci with their components, offering a more detailed illustration of the process.

The strategic foci are one part of the picture. The other part of the picture describes how the enactment of the strategic foci link integrally to the interlevel dynamics of intentional strategic change. In the following chapters we describe each strategic focus individually and then in Part IV show how they are integrated and interdependent. Throughout Chapters 9 through 13 we use selected vignettes to illustrate how the strategic foci are applied in action. End-chapter cases provide further illustration.

Reference

Rashford, N.S. and Neiva de Figueiredo, J. (2011) The live in-class CEO intervention: A capstone experiential technique for leadership development. *Journal of Management Education*, 35(5), 620–647.

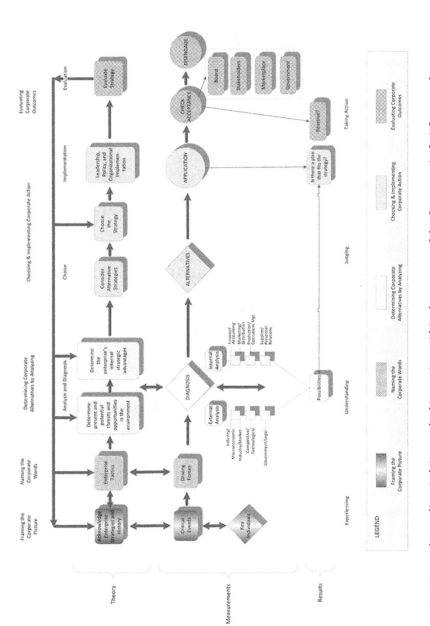

FIGURE 8.2 Experiencing, understanding, judging, and taking action within the context of the five strategic foci framework

9

FRAMING THE CORPORATE PICTURE

Framing the corporate picture lays out the heart of an organization. It is the internal reference for organization members to understand and incorporate what they are about and why the organization exists. It is also the external reference for the market to know with whom it is dealing and for society to understand whom the organization serves and how. Figure 9.1 summarizes the *framing the corporate picture* focus.

The content of framing the corporate picture

The corporate picture is a composite of the history of an organization, its mission, the vision of its senior managers, as well as the perceptions of its board of directors and the entities framing what it is and what it does. Every organization, no matter how large, has at its root, a basic, defined template from which it started. In long-standing organizations this originating corporate picture may have developed and changed over time. Wal-Mart is an example of permanence. The original corporate picture endures to the present day in spite of the tremendous growth and development. The Wal-Mart chain, now one of the largest in the world, had as its start a single store with a single owner, Sam Walton, and a basic purpose. Walton's single-minded purpose was to bring to small towns a selection of goods at a reasonable price in one location, but even this was subject to adaptation as seen in the company's long history.

The corporate picture is the basic identity of an organization. It is based on at least two major building blocks: the original objective of the enterprise and its historical transition over time and the stories and the components provided by the organization's present-day key stakeholders. These building blocks are based on the ethical imperative to be socially responsible and are what give the organization a reason to exist, a distinct culture and a defined direction. This sense of direction is the organizational purpose or mission.

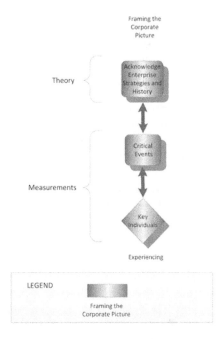

FIGURE 9.1 Framing the corporate picture

The fundamental question, 'What business are we in or what service do we provide?' focuses on the basic identity of an organization. This identity is summarized in the organization's mission statement. The mission statement is a fixed set of expressions, which attempts to convey an organization's spirit, task and vision in a brief and concise way. It is fixed in that it represents the best expressions in the present time. The critical corporate picture that gives the organization life resides in the minds of the senior executives and shareholder groups with a significant stake in the organization. The actual history and the interpreted history of the organization serve as a benchmark for plotting new directions and extending old goals for the people making decisions for the future of the organization. The underlying assumptions about the identity of the organization as developed in its tradition are critical and powerful forces. These traditions are built on the personalities and successes of the past. Sometimes they are so embedded in the organization that they cannot be seen until some process brings them to light. This is very true in large organizations and in those with high turnover. Sometimes the corporate picture includes the way these traditions govern how the organization operates or whom the organization perceives to be the valued customers. In sharp contrast to Wal-Mart is the history of the Wawa company, whose traditions also are deeply rooted in meeting customer needs, but which changed throughout its history. Originally Wawa was an iron foundry, then a dairy, then a convenience store chain, one that more recently has taken the lead in adding auto servicing to its offerings. The contrast to the Wal-Mart example is the evolution over time in the types of businesses Wawa was involved in. Wal-Mart did not change its main business focus, it just grew in size, while Wawa changed its business model and vision (it reframed its corporate picture) throughout its more than two centuries of existence.

Founded in 1803 in New Jersey as an iron foundry (Wawa, homepage – accessed May 25, 2015 www.wawa.com/About.aspx) and later a textile company, the Wawa Company moved into the dairy industry in the early twentieth century with the installation of a small processing plant in Wawa, PA, in 1902. The milk business thrived throughout the first half of the last century based first on dairy product quality, and later on both product quality and the reliability of Wawa's daily bottled milk delivery system. Home delivery of milk declined in the early 1960s so the company again sought ways to adapt to changing customer tastes. The first Wawa convenience store opened in Folsom, Pennsylvania, in 1964, and the company began expanding into new geographic territories and experimenting with several new offerings, including fresh meat, two fast-food stores, and even hydroponic tomatoes. The chain grew at a fast pace and shortly after the turn of the century operated more than 530 stores in five northeastern states of the US employing over 13,000 associates. At that point in time a different corporate picture was being considered, namely the systematic addition of gasoline retailing to the company's convenience stores as an add-on to an already well-functioning convenience retail system under the rationale of offering the consumer scale economies in time and savings – true one-stop shopping. This would represent a new picture and would require capital and expanded operating procedures.

Wawa's business had been built on a foundation of trust and strong corporate values, and had always been led by a management team dedicated to the consumer, focused on people, and unrelenting in its approach to service. Dick Wood, the company's president and chief executive officer, spoke passionately about the need to make consumers think of Wawa as their store of choice. This commitment to the consumer was reflected in a company statement (Wawa will stop at nothing to deliver the best in the industry, which brings our customers back to visit us day after day) and in its then stated core purpose (to simplify customers' daily lives) and core values (value people, delight customers, embrace change, do the right thing, do things right, have a passion for winning). This basic vision is the point of continuity from the original iron foundry organization through the dairy to the convenience store chain of today.

Wawa sat at a crossroads in the company's history. The opportunity to go public to raise capital was a viable business alternative, especially if the company decided to pursue a path as a gasoline retailer. The ability to expand through the acquisition of existing assets or the construction of new gas stations would be greatly aided by a public offering to raise capital. This would necessitate a new corporate picture for the privately held company that had been with the same family since the nineteenth century and had always been completely focused on the long term. Wawa was indeed able to finance the heavy investments needed for gasoline retailing primarily from strong operational cash flows, i.e. with means other than the public equity markets. Despite not having gone public, the company's basic business vision changed yet again, as the stated core purpose was updated to 'fulfilling lives, every day' to reflect the addition of gasoline. However, none of the six 'core values' were altered.

Today Wawa is the customers' 'all day, every day' stop, with over 22,000 associates, 645 convenience retail stores (over 365 offering gasoline), and a wide range of services at any time structured for those 'on the go'. Examples of products and services provided are built-to-order foods, beverages, surcharge-free ATMs, and fuel services. The company is also testing the waters beyond its core Middle Atlantic geographic region, having opened stores in central Florida. With a Forbes-estimated annual revenue of more than $9 billion, Wawa, which regularly showed up in the top third of the magazine's annual 500 Top Private Companies feature, was ranked 38th in 2014 (Forbes. America's Largest Private Companies, 2014, accessed May 25, 2015, www.forbes.com/largest-priva te-companies/list). The dairy business itself still generates sales of more than $70 million a year, and processes more than 100 million fluid quarts annually. Wawa is an example of a company that has repeatedly been able to reframe its corporate picture to adapt to changing environments throughout its history.

An organization's culture is partially shaped by the persuasive power that mission statements may or may not have. When the mission statement clearly articulates the commonly held perception of an organization's core mission, members feel involved and important. This is vital in forming an accepted corporate culture. When mission statements are posted around an organization and are perceived by staff to be largely untrue or distant from reality (what we refer to as espoused strategy), this creates a corporate picture (a strategy-in-use) which differs from the one created by senior management and which may contribute to an adverse corporate culture.

The process of framing the corporate picture

The process whereby identity is articulated normally comes through a study of the history of the organization and the formulation of its contemporary mission statement. Framing the corporate picture can be achieved through two approaches. The first approach deals with a review of the historic timeline of the organization where leaders and members are involved in a process to discern elements that have endured. These consist of values, beliefs and practices that have remained for the organization over time and in changing circumstances. This approach can be used either to produce a new corporate picture or to reinforce a present identity. The second approach, detailed in the A&P case in Chapter 15, deals with the formation of a corporate picture in which there was involvement of senior leaders only. Although this leads to a speedier process in framing the corporate picture, the process of communicating the corporate picture to the organization's membership is much more difficult, and therefore widespread buy-in could be compromised. The choice between these approaches is based on the need for involvement and ownership. High involvement to embrace the mission and carry it out requires early involvement in framing the corporate picture.

The key process is reaching consensus between constituent groups as to how the corporate picture is framed and the mission perceived. An organization's board, chief executive, senior management group, and members are the central stakeholders in formulating organizational identity and mission. Several methods to achieve this consensus have been developed and tested, some based on Richard Beckhard's (1969) suggested use of behavioural science techniques for planned interventions to achieve change within the organization. One example is the selection of the following four activities from a collection of process designs by Napier et al. (1999), which are very well suited to help frame a corporate picture:

- **Shared history exercise.** This activity creates a common ground experience for participants regarding their organization's history. A large sheet of paper on a wall is utilized in this exercise. A timeline is drawn reflecting the significant events in the history of the organization. Participants share their perspectives and insights regarding their history. This enables everyone to see the significant choices that have been made and reveals the values the organization has held over time, helping develop a shared perspective and deep appreciation of the uniqueness of the organization. As a result, participants tend to forge new directions and create enthusiasm for tackling the future. The historical values that are revealed contribute to the corporate picture.

- **Stargazing exercise.** The key to this design is to select a quality group of 'stargazers' as panel members whose purpose is to help participants broaden their perspective, deepen their knowledge, and stimulate their thinking. Stargazers are individuals who tend to have a future focus, a broad perspective, or a deep knowledge about a particular subject. They should be individuals who have credibility and a reputation for creativity, clear thinking and autonomy. The panel members can be individuals within the organization, complete outsiders, or a combination of both. After opening remarks, each panel member meets with small groups of participants (10–20 people). They spend some time in each group sharing their expertise and answering questions. Every 20 minutes, the panel members rotate to a new group and the process continues until they have interacted with all the small groups. It creates energy, enthusiasm and real participation of all who are involved. After the small groups have interacted with the panel members, they organize themselves and make recommendations that help form the corporate picture.

- **Heroic journey.** In some sense the strategic planning process is a journey into the unknown. It takes real courage and discipline to ask the tough questions, define the core principles of an organization, and take risks in the decisions that are made. The participants are asked to reflect on heroic experiences in their own life. These are shared with the group. The participants then develop a heroic code for the organization. Participants find three of the heroic statements that they can all agree upon. The summary of these statements becomes a basis for the values or principles to guide the organization. They provide the heroic vision of the corporate picture.
- **Creating a vision statement.** The purpose of this activity is to create a shared picture of the future for an organization or group. The design starts with each individual taking 10–15 minutes to write five or six statements that best describe what he or she would like to see in the vision statement of the organization. These individual statements are then shared in small groups (four–eight people). Each group seeks common ground first, around the strategic themes for the future. After common ground has been established, groups can include 'gentle agreement' statements. These are individual statements that each group member can agree to because they are worthy of their commitment. The ultimate goal is to have a 50–75 word statement written on a flipchart that is the formation of a vision statement or corporate picture.

The contrast to the formal and large organization approach to framing the corporate picture is the new entrepreneurial organization where the founder brings the vision and forms the corporate picture.

VerticalNet had its origins in 1995 when Mike McNulty, the trade publishing salesman for trade journals came up with the idea that the time had come to move trade publishing to the Internet for industries such as those selling pumps and valves. Mike Hagan, college roommate at Saint Joseph's University left Merrill Lynch and joined him in this new venture. The initial momentum was helped when they raised 7 million dollars of new capital from the Internet capital group of Wayne, PA and another 9 million dollars from other firms. With this financing McNulty and Hagan set up offices in Horsham, PA. The location was chosen because it was close to b2b publications that were based in Philadelphia, New York and Boston. They started putting together sites on the web for the industrial communities in so-called 'vertical' markets, which surrounded particular industries with focused interest.

In the early days at VerticalNet very little time was spent in formulating a mission statement, but a corporate picture emerged. The picture, which was clear enough to attract investors, was based on the clear vision of the purpose of VerticalNet shared by the two founders. The focus was on the users in the formation of vertical communities on the Internet and the uniqueness came from a different approach. While most Internet entrepreneurs had heretofore attempted to use the web to replace a traditional marketplace with their proposed Internet marketplace, McNulty, who knew the industrial trade sector of the market as a salesman, had the vision to realize that purchasing agents were part of a community in which everybody knew one another, developing and maintaining relationships through trade shows and business dealings. McNulty saw it as a world in which they needed to supplement these relationships and not try to replace them. VerticalNet became a member of this marketplace and did not try to replace it.

The corporate picture framed by VerticalNet was unique and was developed somewhat intuitively and organically given the founders' prior experience. Since McNulty knew the environment very well from his previous work it was easy to adapt to customer needs and since Hagan had financial expertise they were able to differentiate the company in the marketplace: the understanding of who the company was and whom it served made a difference to their early success versus those Internet companies that failed in the early years of the Internet. However, it is very difficult to sustain the corporate picture in a fast-changing environment when it has been developed intuitively and organically. Given the intensity of the early Internet days and the upheaval that followed the dotcom bubble in the early part of the century, it is possible that VerticalNet could have benefited from a more structured process of framing the corporate picture, enabling it to respond even more effectively to the rapidly shifting environment.

Roles in framing the corporate picture

We now introduce how framing the corporate picture relates to different perspectives regarding what is happening in the organization: that of the leader, that of a member of the organization, and that of the OD consultant.

The leader's role in framing the corporate picture

The role of the leader, and of all senior leadership for that matter, is to own and embrace the process of developing and framing the corporate picture. Without this top-level interest and involvement, no approach can work well. Conversely, experience shows that lack of vision and committed leadership in the process by the leader dooms the framing of the corporate picture to failure. Concomitant with this vision is the leader's ethical stance. Leadership on social responsibility as well as personal and corporate ethics are major factors in how the organization's members act and are important components of the corporate picture.

A CEO's job experience is a crucial component of the process. For example, each CEO will have come to the chief executive role from within an interdepartmental group, either within the same organization or from another organization. Return on investment will be a key driving force for a CEO whose background is finance. Similarly design will be key for a CEO from an engineering background, production for a CEO from manufacturing and so on. This will be especially true with new or young entrepreneurs who have designed the business and been involved in all aspects. Howard Head is a good example of this involvement. He was a design engineer and production specialist, and when he tried to run the company he could not move away from his own expertise. This made it especially hard for him to let others run these aspects of the ski company (Rashford and Coghlan, 1994). This impact of the leader and his or her experience is sometimes not conscious, as exemplified by the Head vignette.

Donald Hambrick and Gregory Fukutomi (1991) of Columbia University have studied the seasons of CEOs and their life-cycles. The first phase begins as *a response to a mandate*. This occurs when the new CEO embarks on his or her tenure with a commitment to a particular paradigm – a model based on personal assumptions about how the organization ought to be structured and managed. This model is fuelled, of course, by the CEO's toolkit – the knowledge base and experience that he or she brings to the job. If the paradigm proposed by the CEO is rejected by the organization, most often a career setback ensues.

Next is *the experimentation phase* where the CEO's commitment to his or her original paradigm varies depending on success or failure in the initial stage. This is when the CEO's knowledge of his/her task required by the job is moderate, interest is high, and power is somewhat increased. The CEO's information continues to flow from numerous sources, but becomes increasingly filtered by the time it reaches him or her. If the CEO fails to observe this filtering and its consequences, his or her life-cycle could have a short timespan.

The third phase, to a great extent, is the CEO's *defining phase*. It is characterized by the CEO's level of commitment to his/her paradigm. At this point, the CEO's task knowledge is stronger, rate of learning declines, interest remains moderately high, and information comes from fewer and somewhat filtered sources. Here, the CEO's power is moderate and continues to grow. Survival of the CEO through this third phase is most commonly observed.

The fourth is a *convergence phase* as a CEO pursues a series of incremental actions to reinforce the major changes that have resulted from his/her commitment to a certain paradigm. By this time, a strong task knowledge has grown, interest is starting to diminish, and information is highly filtered, arriving from even fewer sources. The CEO's power is strong and increasing. When this phase ends, it may involve a confrontation between the board and the CEO as he or she gradually loses touch.

In the final stage, which is defined as *dysfunction*, the CEO's effectiveness is seriously diminishing. The CEO's commitment to a given paradigm is hardened, which seriously weakens any interest in experimentation. As specific tasks become habitual, the CEO's interest in them wanes considerably. At this stage, the CEO depends only on a very few, highly filtered sources of information. As the CEO's interest ebbs, his/her energy for risk and dramatic changes all but vanishes. Paradoxically the CEO's power and ability to lead are at an all-time high. This phase may come to a close when within the organization there is a growing awareness of the need for a new strategic paradigm.

The member's role in framing the corporate picture

The role of the member should also not be underestimated in the effective framing of the corporate picture. The involvement of members in carrying out the mission is much less likely without their participation in framing the corporate picture. Participation for a member consists of sharing individual historical anecdotes relating to the corporate history. The members' contribution to the debate in the formation of the statement used to frame the corporate picture is equally important. Unfortunately the need for member input is often forgotten in many organizations. To miss this is to risk misunderstanding the essence of the organization.

OD consultant's role in framing the corporate picture

OD consultants are useful in helping organizations frame their corporate picture. With their skill at process they can facilitate the dialogue needed to articulate a meaningful mission. The OD consultant works with the organization at the request of top management or the board of directors and, as an outsider, has a facilitating role. The most important group in ratifying the mission of an organization is the board of directors. How the board performs this task is critical to its success. Sometimes the board accepts and ratifies the mission statement prepared by the organization. Other times, the board places its imprint on the mission statement by adding components of its own. This is a legitimate role of the board, which has policy responsibility for an organization. Even though the board provides important input, this must not be done at the cost of suppressing input from the rest of the organization.

OD consultants need to remind themselves that their main function is to facilitate the process and not affect the content. Their role is to help the organization find its soul and its mission, not to generate it. One example of a method to facilitate the process of reaching consensus towards the mission under the guidance of an OD consultant was mentioned earlier in this chapter.

Selected interlevel dynamics issues in framing the corporate picture

Framing the corporate picture is an ongoing process which is required by changing environmental conditions, by changing strategic advantages, by changing expectations of outside stakeholder groups, and by interactions among the key participants within the organization. The process of changing an organization's corporate picture requires a clear sense of the reasons for change, an idealized visualization of the new corporate picture, and strong support for change throughout the transition from the old to the new one (Nadler, 1998). Changing the corporate picture is a large-scale change as described by Mohrman et al. (1989), as it constitutes a deep change which entails shifts in members' basic beliefs and values in the way the organization is understood.

Listed below are seven interaction scenarios, which can challenge an organization's current corporate picture:

1. The interaction between the leader and an external information source.
2. The leader with the senior management group.
3. Relations of both the leader and senior management group with the interdepartmental group level.
4. The circumstance when no single leader exists and the mission comes from multiple sources.
5. The context of a merger or acquisition when all parties are required to understand and manage new relationships on the occasion of the total organization being merged into or acquired by another.
6. The integration of the board's changes to the corporate picture with the leader and senior management.
7. The integration of outside influences such as financial analysts with the CEO and CFO.

The leader and external information sources

The leader and external information sources deal with the interactions that occur when a leader meets other leaders or information sources at trade or professional organizations or another such institutional forum. This may be where the sensing step of the adaptive coping cycle begins. A leader's relationships with these competing organizations and trade groups or associations are key to finding information on benchmarks, industry trends, or economic conditions that are in play at any time. The leader should also be attuned to issues relating to corporate social responsibility which may surface through external relationships.

The leader is often the conduit of disconfirming information. It is difficult to accept and process information within an organization when it comes from outside. This occurs through the previously mentioned association with other CEOs, in relations with customers, in the application of intuitive dreaming of the next plateau, or in contact with other organizations like we saw previously in VerticalNet. In the process of examining and evaluating new information or ideas, the leader moves a stage ahead of everyone else in the organization. This is when the loneliness of being at the top becomes clear. He or she is past denial of disconfirming information and is ready to begin an organizational change process. The converse is also true. When senior members of the organization bring disconfirming information to the leader and he or she is in denial of it and is not ready for change, the messenger suffers the brunt of the loneliness. In both of these situations, the process questions become: how are the information, the time for reflection, and ownership handled?

As the information that is sensed is brought into the organization and as the new information and the conclusions drawn from it are thrust on the organization or the leader, little reaction may be observed and a large effect can be set in motion to deny later participation because of the lack of ownership in the early definitional stage. Any negative information that disconfirms a central belief of an organization will produce denial when it is first presented. This was explained in Chapter 7 when we discussed how change moves through an organization. Disconfirming information may either contribute to a corporate picture that has no reality or to a hung process that will not frame a corporate picture that can provide an energizing mission statement.

The leader with the senior management group

The leader with the senior management group is the next interlevel relationship for the process of framing the corporate picture. Here the critical issue deals with how the senior team processes the elements of the new corporate picture. Each senior manager leading a functional area looks at these elements as representing different degrees of threat. The threat comes from having to embrace change in his/her functional area. The reverse is also true. A senior management group with new ideas can threaten the leader who does not want the organization to change. The amount of threat is related to the amount of change required in accepting and implementing the new corporate picture. As new ideas are used to frame a new corporate picture, they are being assessed by the interdepartmental leaders on the effects that the change will have for their members. In this scenario, individual issues deal with the change in role and identity of the team members as well as the leader him or herself. As a new corporate picture emerges, individual roles change and some are eliminated. Team issues relate to the new determination of priorities and task assignments. A new corporate picture forces the senior management group to set new priorities and allocate work to the divisions and departments in a different way. Interdepartmental issues centre on the new allocation of resources and information flow required in carrying out the new corporate picture. The leader should also inquire into and receive reports on issues that reflect corporate social responsibility, particularly to be able to recognize unethical behaviour that may be occurring across the organization.

The senior management group is quite different from other face-to-face working teams and plays the pivotal role in this dealing with framing the corporate picture. In the prevalent working team, each member participates in a role for and by him or herself to accomplish team and organizational goals. In the senior management group each line member represents a functioning interdepartmental group; hence the actions of the group affect the entire organization. When in the interdepartmental group a function is threatened, the respective officer-team member acts many times in a defensive way on behalf of his or her own functional area constituency. As mentioned before, the reverse can be true when a CEO is threatened by change suggested by his/her management group.

Relations of both the leader and senior management group with the interdepartmental group level

These relations involve the process behaviour around the corporate picture between the Level II senior management group and the Level III interdepartmental group. This aspect is most often overlooked because many senior managers believe that working groups do not need to be brought into the discussion until it is time to implement the new corporate picture. This, however, is too late in the process if participation and commitment are needed. The Level III interactions with Level I produce a most challenging task if an organization is to be successful in achieving its goal of enabling divisional human capital in the organization. When people are changed in function or role, this affects their Level I matching needs with an organization. The interdepartmental functional change (Level III) produces an effect in Level I with a new required role or functional change for the individuals within the functional area. The challenge comes from the need to work with both individuals (Level I) and teams (Level II) in the allocation of work and priorities generated through the new or changed mission within the interdepartmental groups (Level III). The need to accept change comes from the shift in resource reallocation and the adoption of new information systems required for the new or changed mission. Also implicit is the effect on individuals (Level I) if the new mission brings about a change in self-esteem, job design or internal motivation. While the completion of this complex interaction in working out a new corporate picture with its resultant required behavioural changes occurs throughout all of the foci in the strategy/change process, it is here that perceptions of the organization are formed. Perceptions last a long time.

The circumstance when no leader exists and the mission comes from other sources

This is the fourth scenario for interlevel relationships. Sometimes in not-for-profit organizations, the response to multiple boards of directors and complex relations with sponsoring organizations makes the precise framing of the corporate picture very difficult. The following case of Wills Eye Hospital is an example of such an occurrence.

Wills Eye Hospital is an institution of national renown in the field of ophthalmology. Established in 1832 in Philadelphia, it is the oldest eye-care hospital in continuous operation in the United States and is regularly ranked among the top three ophthalmology centres in the country. The entity has a unique governance structure as the founder, James Wills, stipulated that either the Mayor of Philadelphia or representatives would participate in managing the hospital. As a result, the administration of the institution to this day comprises three constituencies, the Board of Directors of City Trusts, the Wills Eye management and the medical staff.

In 1972 Wills Eye affiliated with Thomas Jefferson University and since then has trained that institution's physicians-to-be in ophthalmology. During the 1980s and 1990s, after expansion into a new facility, creative innovations by Wills management allowed the hospital to consistently maintain an operating profit through programmes of diversification into other medical specialties. In addition to ophthalmology, Wills moved into the areas of hand surgery, geriatric psychiatry, and neurosurgery. The general philosophy was to bring more patients to the hospital on an inpatient basis to increase revenues. However, this coincided with a period of great changes in healthcare, including the beginnings of a gradual and continual move to outpatient care, which reduced the need for inpatient care. An aggressive policy of increasing inpatient care was therefore swimming against the tide.

With this in mind, Wills' core mission could have moved in several directions. First, it could have pursued aggressive programmes specifically designed to elevate the reputation of Wills stature as the premier ophthalmology programme in the United States. Second, it could have pursued an outpatient surgery network. Third, it could have continued to diversify into other medical specialties in order 'not to put all of one's eggs into one basket'.

Since three constituent groups with competing interests administered Wills Eye Hospital, it was extremely difficult to find agreement on a mission statement. The first group, composed of the Board of City Trusts, desired above all to be true to the intent of the original financial gift which was service to the 'indigent, the blind, and the lame', as specifically stated in the original bequest. The second group, the management group, desired to ensure they operated a financially viable institution. The third group, the medical staff, had as its primary objective the continuation of the centre's reputation for world-renowned ophthalmology. These three groups, by nature, were at odds to accomplish a single purpose, as top priorities and orders of prioritization were very different. The interests of the initial charter, financial savings, and excellent patient care and research (which led to increased spending) competed against one another. In addition, there were no physicians on the Board of City Trusts and no one person as overall CEO.

In 2002, Wills Eye Hospital sold its major facility to another medical institute and, thereby, relinquished its inpatient business. It has moved to a central facility that enables outpatient work, fosters a research environment, and provides a place to train residents. It continues to build a network of outlying centres as well. The new situation does not require maintaining the overhead of eight floors of a hospital. Nor do other specialties come into play in the new situation. This is an example of a successful, albeit lengthy path towards framing the corporate picture through the gradual evolution of three constituencies' mutual understanding in the face of a changing external environment.

The Wills Eye Hospital case illustrates the point that mission statements are not necessarily the first element in proposing a new strategy, although they most often are. Circumstances, the environment and history influence the mission statement. The case also illustrates the difficulty in achieving total organizational buy-in to a complex mission statement when different segments have different missions. Framing the corporate picture proved very difficult when no one could get the groups to work together to frame a single mission statement. This example also illustrates the non-sequential nature of the five foci, with each one potentially providing an information feedback loop to all the others.

Mergers and acquisitions

Intercompany transactions comprise the fifth scenario which is likely to impact the focus of framing the corporate picture. In any acquisition or merger many adaptations occur, most often due to the need to capitalize on synergies, which usually involves eliminating redundancies. It is necessary for members of an acquired organization to understand and adapt to a new corporate picture. When organizations merge or have been sold off, it is difficult to reconstruct the corporate picture of these divested major parts that are now in a new environment. It can be just as difficult for the acquiring organization or the acquired subdivisions to determine the key characteristics that are still important. In one possible scenario, what was at one time a Level IV organization may become a Level III interdepartmental group in a larger organization. This is a demotion in emotional terms from the point of view of the merged organization . What appeals to the large conglomerate, e.g. profitability, may not have been part of the corporate picture of the acquired organization in its former independent state. However removed, these corporate pictures from the early starting points in an organization's history are important to work out. If these are not acknowledged, they remain as pervasive hidden elements which may compete with the new strategic processes.

Throughout its existence, Cisco Systems has been able to successfully ride sequential waves of technological innovation through both internal R&D and an intentional mergers and acquisitions strategy. Cisco's approach has been based on a clear strategic vision and on two core competencies: sound analysis of most promising emerging technologies in the marketplace and an effective M&A implementation process. Between 1993 and December 2011 Cisco acquired roughly 150 companies while maintaining a strong in-house R&D capability. The company achieved competitive advantages by identifying and analysing promising technologies, developing them either in-house or through successful acquisitions, and introducing them to the market with precise timing. During this period, the firm maintained strong growth and generated high returns to shareholders. A very emblematic example of Cisco's highly effective acquisition expertise occurred in the residential networking market. At the turn of the millennium, the main challenge for technology providers was the 'last mile' to consumers' homes and to small businesses, as providers sought to increase transmission speeds from massive backbone networks to customer premises by improving the capabilities of local customer network access. Cisco launched a line of upstream Cable Modem Termination System (CMTS) products, which were highly successful and dominated the market. The company acquired a series of R&D-intensive firms that possessed knowledge complementing its own, and used these acquired capabilities to develop significant competitive advantage in the nascent market. A clear strategic vision was a necessary condition for Cisco to repeatedly succeed in absorbing companies throughout its history, and to do so in different niche markets. Just as important was the ability to successfully absorb different types of smaller entrepreneurial companies that brought different skills, often highly specific to a given function, technology or sector, in an eloquent example of Level III and Level IV integration.

Cisco Systems developed a company-wide approach to integrating acquired businesses which is a source of pride to the company (Cisco, 2007). From the point of view of the acquired companies, which were mostly small and highly specialized in a specific technological niche and therefore needed to make the transition from Level IV stand-alone identity to Level III component of a larger whole, tradeoffs needed to be worth it. Cisco's global marketing and distribution allowed for much quicker market access, and in a fast-moving technological innovation environment in which scale and speed were (and still are) necessities the challenges of becoming a small part of a large entity seemed indeed worthwhile. These advantages carry down to Level II (teams) as there is a higher likelihood of project success given Cisco's broad scope and ample resources as well as Level I (the individual) as opportunities are broadened. The sheer number of successful Cisco acquisitions over the years is evidence of the advantages the acquired companies perceive because any news of dissatisfaction would have travelled quickly in the market, eroding the integration reputation Cisco is so proud of, and leading to fewer such deals closed.

Integration of the board's changes to the corporate picture with the leader and senior management

The board of directors, the board of management, or the board of trustees is the group that has the power of authority in most organizations. In dealing with mission statements or corporate pictures, most boards let management construct the statement and then ratify it. In those cases in which the board takes an active role in the design of the mission statement, this input tends to happen after the members and senior management group have generated a statement. In discussing the statement for approval at the board meeting it is tempting to adapt or change phrases or words. This can often be done without the benefit of a facilitator or reflection on the part of the board. The rewritten mission statement is then approved. When this happens the changes have to be processed by the leader, who can otherwise feel undercut in the process, and by the senior management group who must explain the changes to people who had contributed to the original statement and now see a different one coming from the board. The board also has the responsibility for ensuring the organization's ethical behaviour in the market-place. The better approach with a board in framing the corporate picture is to open the organization's process to board members and have them experience the dialogue and the interaction with the organization's members. When they are part of the process and understand the deliberation that has gone into it they will have less will to change it later on when it is their duty to ratify it.

The integration of outside influences, e.g. financial analysts, with the CEO and the CFO

This integration is also necessary for a comprehensive corporate picture. External groups and organizations have input that needs to be integrated into framing the corporate picture. Financial analysts may seek definitive statements in the corporate picture, such as levels of profitability or particular markets. While these do not have direct input, what is excluded from a mission statement may raise serious questions. Private universities in the United States cannot be controlled by external groups and still receive federal funding. Yet the corporate picture can be representative of the values and beliefs of the founding institution. In other types of organizations, such as public trusts, donor requests must be accounted for in the corporate picture for legal reasons.

Conclusions

In this chapter we have described the focus *framing the corporate picture*, as the activity that grounds the organization's identity, and have shown how it comes to affect strategy formulation and actualization and how it relates to the key individuals and the history of the organization. The content aspects of this focus are the core mission and its statement of the organization as well as the characteristics of the key players. The process aspect focuses on the engagement and involvement of different members and the construction of processes to effectively put together and embrace the corporate mission and its statement. Table 9.1 summarizes the task and relational issues regarding the framing the corporate picture focus.

TABLE 9.1 Assessment and action template for framing the corporate picture

	TASK	*RELATIONAL*
Content	What business are we in? Core mission Corporate social responsibility	Differing view of key strategists and stakeholders
Process	History search Examine mission statement Stargazing	Building consensus Agreeing to differ
Culture	Traditions of the organization Build ethical culture	Power of key statements

The perspective of organizational leaders, whether the CEO, board of directors, members of a senior management group, or divisional heads, is that the corporate picture enables an organization to move in a proactive, ethical, and adaptive manner to meet future challenges. The perspective of an organization's members is whether or not they fit into the corporate picture and whether their role is well defined and relevant. The OD consultant's perspective is whether the organization has a clear and jointly owned picture of itself. The outcome of framing the corporate picture is that the organization has a distinct identity to present to the external world: a picture which is clear and owned within the organization, and which enhances and energizes the other four strategic foci.

Figure 9.2 depicts the loop model structure for inquiring into when and how the corporate picture is framed. The three inquiry loops depicted begin from different possible desired and observed outcomes in framing the corporate picture, which are represented by questions in Figure 9.2. The three loops represent inquiring about appropriateness of actions taken (single loop), about suitability of goals set (double loop), and about desirability of ultimate purpose (triple loop). Illustrative questions regarding each of these loops as applied to framing the corporate picture are included in the box below the figure. Please note that each loop has two illustrative questions, with the first representing a content inquiry and the second representing a process inquiry. The level of complexity in organizational change rises exponentially from single to double loop inquiry and from double to

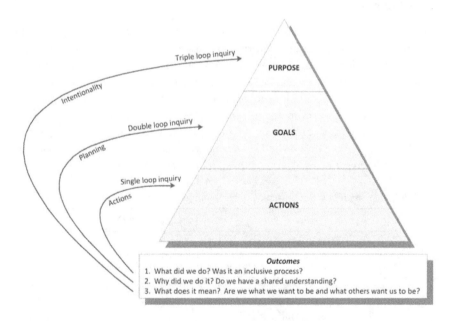

FIGURE 9.2. Single, double and triple loop inquiry when framing the corporate picture

triple loop inquiry. The timeframe for introduction of organizational change related to each level of inquiry loop likewise will increase. For single loop change this timeframe is usually measured in months, for double loop change it is usually measured in up to two years, and is higher than that for triple loop change.

Reflexive engagement activity 9.1

Below you will find a blank Table 9.2. In relation to an organization with which you are familiar, fill in the boxes with what you see as the important content, process and cultural issues in task and relational terms in framing the corporate picture. Discuss this with your team, or better still, copy the blank form and invite each team member to fill in the blanks prior to your discussion. In terms of $L=P+Q$, what P of framing the corporate picture is being challenged by your experience?

Reflexive engagement activity 9.2

Adopting the clinical approach, review the focus of framing the corporate picture from the four perspectives.

	TASK	RELATIONAL
Content		
Process		
Culture		

TABLE 9.2. Refelxive activity

Leaders

Corporate leaders, whether the CEO or members of senior management group or divisional heads may consider the following questions:

- Given the goals and modicum of excellence that we have achieved, how do we now get to the next level of goals and excellence?
- How do we enrol others in partnership to achieve this?
- What is our shared history? What does it tell us?
- Who are the stargazers that can give us input for a new future?
- What are our criteria and standards of corporate social responsibility?

Organizational members

Organizational members may ask the following questions:

- Do I know what the organization's mission is?
- Does the stated mission fit my experience of working in this organization?
- How can I adapt my work to fit the mission?
- Can I take the risk required to trust in a new future?

OD consultants

OD consultants may pose the following questions.

- Does the organization have a clear picture of itself?
- Is this picture jointly owned?
- What group experience designs can I use to help in the determination of the corporate picture?

Outcomes

Taking $L=P+Q$, what P from framing the corporate picture is challenged from your experience of the outcomes in your organization?

- Does the stated corporate picture reflect the reality of the key activities of the organization?
- Were there any parts of the mission statement disregarded or set aside in the final assembly of the statement itself?
- Were there previous corporate pictures, such as those of subdivisions that were purchased, not taken into account in the final corporate picture?
- Does the organization exhibit ethical behaviour?

Case: Saint Joseph's University

Continuing the case of Saint Joseph's University from Part II, in 1986 the higher education competitive environment in the tri-state area surrounding Philadelphia was extremely competitive. As mentioned in Chapter 6, there were almost 70 higher education institutions in that region and although Saint Joseph's had developed a very strong local reputation as the only Jesuit university in the area, there were ten other Catholic ones. The strong undergraduate liberal education had been the backbone of its success and the main focus of the administration for decades. In addition, the Pennsylvania Association of Colleges and Universities was beginning to show signs of lack of unity (which later led to the break-away of the independent colleges), the GI bill was in its final years and Pell grants were coming in, all of which contributed to a perception of increased uncertainty. The state of higher education was such that at that juncture it would be highly beneficial to Saint Joseph's University to raise its regional and national profile.

The new president arriving on the July 1, 1986 started to work away at changing the corporate picture by making the graduate and evening programmes part of the mainstream university. This second stream of the university had been taught up to this time primarily by part-time faculty, and responsibility for the credibility of the programmes resided with the evening division coordinator. Full-time faculty had no sense of ownership of the graduate programme and in truth many did not want to teach in it.

Additionally, full-time faculty by and large had a perception that decisions were made in a top-down command-and-control fashion, in a process with little input from various stakeholders – including faculty themselves – so challenges to the new status were perceived as rebuffed. A group of the faculty met with staff and formed a committee to confront the situation. Its suggestion was that an external OD consultant might be helpful to the process. Several consultants were interviewed. One consultant team with acceptable stature for both faculty and administration was found to work with them to resolve the impasse. The president and the senior management group had agreed with the plan to obtain an outside consultant team and jointly participated with the consultant team in the four-day off-site retreat meeting described in the Chapter 5 case. Gradually, a vision statement was developed through a shared scenario exercise, which was very helpful to arrive at a collective understanding of the issues, but the process was not easy, nor smooth. Eventually a new corporate picture was framed.

Questions for reflection and discussion

1. Can you discern from the case any elements that may have helped trigger the change in Saint Joseph's University's corporate picture?
2. How was the process for framing a new corporate picture structured?
3. How do organizational levels and interlevel dynamics help understand what took place and why?

4. What levels were evident in the four-day retreat meeting?
5. What role would you think the OD consultants played?

References

Beckhard, R. (1969) *Organization Development: Strategies and Models*. Reading, MA: Addison-Wesley.

Cisco (2007) How Cisco Applies Companywide Expertise for Integrating Acquired Companies. Cisco Systems website, accessed July 6, 2015, www.cisco.com/web/about/ciscoitatwork/downloads/ciscoitatwork/pdf/Cisco_IT_Case_Study_Acquisition_Integration.pdf.

Hambrick, D. and Fukutomi, G. (1991) The seasons of a CEO's tenure. *Academy of Management Review*, 16(4), 719–742.

Mohrman, A., Mohrman, S., Ledford, G., Cummings, T., Lawler, E.E. and Associates (1989) *Large Scale Organizational Change*. San Francisco, CA: Jossey-Bass.

Nadler, D. A. (1998) *Champion of Change*. San Francisco, CA: Jossey-Bass.

Napier, R., Sidle, C. and Sanaghan, P. (1999) *High Impact Tools and Activities for Strategic Planning*. New York: McGraw-Hill.

Rashford, N.S. and Coghlan, D. (1994) *The Dynamics of Organizational Levels: A Change Framework for Managers and Consultants*. Reading, MA: Addison-Wesley.

10

NAMING THE CORPORATE WORDS

Naming corporate words is the strategic focus that explicitly states the character-istics that allow the organization to succeed in a complex ever-changing (chaotic) environment. This focus strengthens the sense of identity of an organization. These are the driving forces, the core capabilities, and the core competencies that result in sustained competitive advantage. Corporate words in this context are different from the 'words' used in the mission statement. The mission statement, while it uses words, is a fixed set of expressions that attempts to contain the spirit or mission of an organization in a brief, concise way. The concept of corporate words compris-ing this second focus has a more dynamic nature. It is the tactical application of the mission statement. Corporate words represent the forces and drivers that interpret and actualize the mission statement, i.e. the elements that permit the corporate picture to become reality. Figure 10.1 summarizes the *naming the corporate words* focus and its relationship with the *framing the corporate picture* focus.

The content of naming the corporate words

An organization's effort is directed toward the efficient use of resources to deliver products and services to different geographic markets, market segments, and cus-tomer groups. In order to do so successfully over time, organizations need to offer something unique to customers on an ongoing basis. An organization's structure, resources, capabilities, plans, decision-making and problem-solving are ultimately directed toward providing products or services for diverse markets. Corporate words represent the most impactful ways in which each organization uses its strengths to seize opportunities to provide those products and services and to overcome threats to its success. Over the past 50 years, the search to understand and improve the process of strategy formulation has focused on the examination of opportunities and threats in the environment, and of strengths and weaknesses

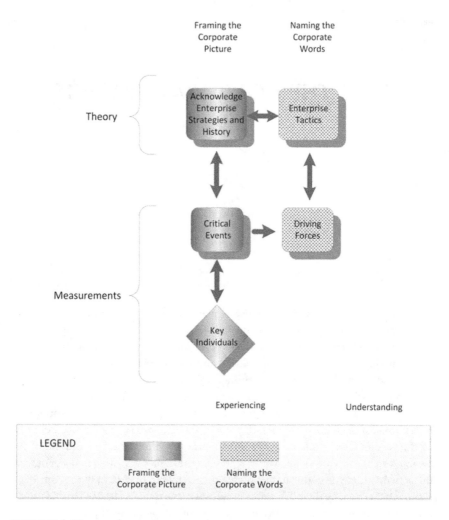

FIGURE 10.1 Naming the corporate words

within the organization. Every organization faces a unique combination of con-textual conditions and company characteristics which may lead to the prominence of specific and unique corporate words, representing the combination of what it does best as an organization and what is most effective in the marketplace. In fact, it is the organization's skill-set that allows it to also affect the environment and change the marketplace. As an example, it was this level of self-knowledge that allowed Nutrisystem to change the weight-loss competitive marketplace in 2004 from a stand-alone support group weight-loss model towards an integrated e-marketing and telemarketing approach.

Over the past 50 years strategy academicians developed a consistent theoretical body of knowledge to help organizations identify and develop resources and capabilities that would result in uniquely suited drivers of success in the market-place. Andrews (1971) advocated leveraging corporate strengths to follow a delib-erately chosen direction. Tregoe and Zimmerman (1980) established categories to characterize an organization's most relevant driving force, according to them the primary determinant of the scope of future products, services and markets. They postulated that organizations had only one driving force, holding this to be the case because it was considered the precondition or assumption underlying the formula-tion of the corporate strategy and the actualization of the corporate plan. Since then academicians and practitioners alike have agreed that driving forces leading to competitive advantage can and do coexist under the right conditions. Porter (1985) developed the Value Chain to identify activities within the firm which contribute most to add value as measured by the difference between each activity's cost and its contribution to customers' willingness to pay. Prahalad and Hamel (1990) intro-duced the idea of core competencies as intangible knowledge-based and difficult-to-imitate characteristics. The resource-based view of the firm developed by Barney (1991), Petaraf (1993), and Wernerfelt (1984) among others, focused on the individual characteristics and idiosyncrasies of the firm, which set it apart from competitors and which were both valued by the customer and difficult for rivals to imitate. By the turn of the millennium this view had established itself as an alter-native to the so-called industry-based view, pioneered by Porter (1980), and based on external industrial organization analyses of contextual factors as much as indi-vidual firm characteristics. Naming the corporate words is a look inside the orga-nization to identify, understand and explicitly articulate the main characteristics that allow it to succeed, and without which it would lose its soul: it bridges the framing the corporate picture focus with the strategic analyses described in this paragraph to identify the key factors of corporate success.

The articulation of the organization's corporate words goes to the heart of asking the question, 'What ultimately drives the organization?'. Is it engineering? Is it sales? Is it marketing? Is it the organization's distribution system? It is not always easy to sort out the corporate words and more than one driving force can propel an organization towards its mission. The identification of a driving force is intimately linked to Level III, i.e. to the functional or departmental level within the organization because a driving force is inextricably linked to flawless execution.

Mosaico S.A. is a company established in Chile in 1990, devoted to the pro-duction and commercialization of plumbing products. Mosaico has its head-quarters in Santiago and its production operations in China, with over 200 employees, who manufacture more than 800 products under two brands for different markets.

The CEO, Horacio Pavez, says that in the beginning, he started his opera-tions with sales of wooden toys made in China. Through this he developed contacts in China, for production and importation of toys for the Chilean market. Later on, with these established contacts and having experience in the processes and regulations affecting offshore businesses, he decided to evolve the business toward plumbing products, a more lucrative business which benefited from distribution through the same hardware channels as the toys.

After being a sales and marketing company in the wooden toy import business, Mosaico needed a shift in its corporate words. Seeing the possibilities and advantages of a global operation, Pavez decided in 1994 to change the business by developing his own production and assembly of plumbing products in China. The plumbing fixture market in Chile was dominated by a Chilean company that manufactured locally. In order to overtake his competitor Pavez would have to have a better and cheaper product. To this end he established his own production operations in Hong Kong through a branch company called Plumbtech Industries Limited, with a manufacturing plant in Guangzhou, China, taking advantage of that country's export-oriented development model as well as the low cost and production expertise in the area.

Pavez previously focused mainly on a sales and marketing driving force and added a production driving force. He did this through a distinct shift in thinking and approach. He hired engineers and plant managers. He added skills not present in the company before. He determined that by doing this he could move to the top market share position in Chile and successfully overtake a major Chilean company with its production in Chile. He focused the company on quality production run by managers and engineers from Chile in China. This shift in driving forces achieved two ends: it left Mosaico as the leader in the marketplace in Chile, moving it to expand in other Latin American markets. In addition, it completely changed the plumbing/fixture market from median quality in-country production to higher quality/lower cost sourcing from China.

The process of naming the corporate words

An organization's driving force is identified and evolves through the examination of the organization's traditional strengths and functions. The manner in which the inputs of key stakeholder groups are received and processed, in which decisions are made, and in which conflict is managed, all are added to become an extension of the driving forces. The process itself helps solidify the corporate words and is critical in the evolution of the driving forces. The power and priorities of stakeholder groups in the evolution of a driving force are significant. When a driving force favours one part of the organization because of its functional strength or customer perceptions, this can cause friction with other functional units. A common example occurs where engineering, or production, or sales, or any other function is 'king' in a functionally driven organization. At Hallmark Cards, quality is the driving force. The corporate slogan 'if you care enough to send the very best' stressed quality. The founder, J.C. Hall had himself been a printer. He would only place his mark on quality work, hence the name of the organization, Hallmark. In most people's eyes at Hallmark, production was 'king' as the quality of the printing was synonymous with quality products. In discussions on artistic merit, if the card could not be printed in a quality manner as designed, quite often a change in artistic layout occurred. This is not to say that there was no artistic component, nor even that it was not strong, but how the product was made, that is, how it was printed was the major perceived contributor to its quality.

The relative power derived from occasionally conflicting driving forces may be formal or informal: formal in that there is a clear articulated hierarchy of functions within the organization and informal in that individuals or functions may manage to build powerful positions which are resented and not discussed explicitly. These forces are a combination of characteristics which are developed with top-down intentionality and other characteristics which evolve in a bottom-up organic way from within the complex adaptable system which is the organization. The interplay between these forces results in the articulation of corporate words which make explicit the organization's main drivers. Naming the corporate words therefore is simultaneously a conscious process both of identifying the leader-encouraged intended drivers and of recognizing the potential emergence of non-intended drivers from within the organization. Because drivers may change over time through organic bottom-up influences within the organization, deep awareness of its inner workings is necessary. The ongoing process of naming the corporate words requires an emotional and economic commitment and helps provide the organization with elements of competitive advantage which can be difficult to replicate.

Founded in 1983, Team Clean, Inc. is a commercial janitorial services company in Philadelphia that enjoyed huge growth in its first two decades of existence mainly due to the service focus and vision of its founder, Donna Allie. By 1999 the company was the fourth-largest woman-owned business in Philadelphia and had been identified by the Wharton Small Business Development Center as one of the fastest growing small businesses in that metropolitan area. Having recently obtained her BA in sociology but unable to fulfil her dream of working in her chosen field, and finding herself as a single mother who needed to provide for her child and herself, she discovered the potential of cleaning houses on Philadelphia's Main Line by answering newspaper advertisements requesting that service. She then developed the business by hiring and training women and sending them in pairs to clean houses. With a strong emphasis on quality and reliability, Team Clean's reputation grew and in 1985 the company signed its first contract for commercial cleaning.

An inspiring and engaging leader, the social mission front of the company is front and centre in her vision – upon meeting her one gets the impression that she will never forget how difficult her early days were, and that she wants to do everything she can to help other minority women overcome obstacles and realize their dreams. Once, after a long shift cleaning a stadium, she was giving a ride to an employee who was carrying a bag. When she said they could leave the bag in the dumpster, the employee said that although its contents had been left for trash, she was taking it home for her family because she would put the discarded materials to use. Perhaps the ever-present reminder that one person's trash is another person's treasure has been the main factor that kept Donna's focus on quality and reliability of service as driving forces which supported the realization of the vision; they were the named words that enabled the corporate picture.

Today Team Clean still is the Philadelphia region's largest minority-owned business, with over 700 employees and over 10 million square feet of office and industrial space under contract. However, over 30 years since the company's foundation, the company has been growing at a much slower pace as there is a need to address succession and to reduce operating costs. Over the years some employees have risen in the organization and have eventually left to start competing businesses, therefore altering the competitive landscape. Because identifying and developing the drivers, i.e. naming the words, is an ongoing process, the driving forces need to reside within the organization, impregnating it. The process never stops.

Roles in naming the corporate words

We now describe how naming the corporate words relates to different perspectives regarding what is happening in the organization: the leader's, the members' and the OD consultant's.

The leader's role in naming the corporate words

In discussing main driving forces, the leader's role is very important. Although occasionally organizations do not deliberately choose one or more main driving forces, it is helpful to be explicit about them. In organizations in which driving forces are left implicit, they often are the past functional role of the chief executive or even the founder, because this past role will colour the leader's perception of critical events affecting the organization. Triggering events that may start a change in driving forces that can occur from critical events that arise and face every leader. They are the recent issues, most often in the form of threats that need solutions and that require the leader's time and attention. When these events arise, such as tight capital markets, new competitive products, or customer-driven change, they need to be addressed decisively. Most leaders react by using the greatest strengths in an organization to address unforeseen issues. If the necessary attributes to react do not exist in the organization, they must be developed from within or hired/outsourced from outside to counter a threat or capitalize on an opportunity. This can cause a change in the organization's drivers.

As discussed in Chapter 9, the moment in the life-cycle of the CEO is an important consideration. In the first phase of the CEO's life-cycle, *response to a mandate*, the driving forces often are directly linked to his or her prior experience.

In internally focused organizations it is the functional role that the CEO knows best and most likely the reason for his or her choice as CEO. This may provide an opportunity to change the entire marketplace. Nutrisystem in 2003 is again an example of seizing such an opportunity. In results-directed organizations with profitability as a driving force, this criterion is likely to be a strong argument for selecting a CEO with financial experience. In phase two of the CEO life-cycle, *the experimentation phase*, his or her vision is often reformulated. CEOs with operations-related skill-sets can shift to profitability as a main driver. Likewise, CEOs with financial skill-sets may also shift towards operations drivers. This shift in CEO sponsorship for driving forces may also occur in phase three, *the defining phase*. In phase four, *the convergence phase*, or in phase five, *dysfunction*, there normally is no change in driving force characteristics.

The perspective of an organizational leader on naming the corporate words is that the driving force be the appropriate one, that it represent balance and functionality within the organization and that it enable the organization to fulfil the vision and mission, i.e. that it be consistent with the corporate picture.

The members' role in naming the corporate words

In most organizations, the members' role in naming the corporate words will be inconsequential unless change starts to occur. If an organization faces change it needs to evaluate its driving forces, to evaluate what is done successfully. Lobbies for the driving force role, subtle or not, may then be observed. Each Level III group or interdepartmental unit wants to take the lead. If not addressed it remains as a subtle force pushing behind the scenes. The concept of driving forces, i.e. the naming of corporate words, often is difficult for members of the organization to clearly conceive for two main reasons. First, this lack of recognition may happen because these forces may be so embedded in the fabric of the organization that they are considered too normal or too obvious to even state explicitly. Second, the lack of recognition may happen because members are so deeply involved in their own functional specialties that they may miss linkages with the whole until they are challenged to do so. This is most apparent in organizations that are internally focused due to the perceived strengths of the respective key functions. If on the other hand the organization is externally driven or results driven there is less appeal for Level III groups to jockey for power. The perspective of members is to want to be part of the mainstream of the organization and to contribute to the organization's thrust. If particular members are not part of the driving force then they need to know how they relate and contribute directly to it.

OD consultant's role in naming the corporate words

There are consultants that work with organizations to help them determine, understand and/or improve their driving forces. They are content specialists. Some focus on operations and the improvement of specific driving forces. Examples include Six-Sigma consultants who improve process quality, organizational consultants who work on management processes, and systems consultants who work on improving efficiencies. Other consultants focus on strategy with the objective of identifying driving forces and examining whether there are opportunities to expand the role of a particular driving force. Historic examples include the use of the experience curve decades ago, the various mechanisms to identify core capabilities, and the use of strategic frameworks to understand whether the organization's strategy and its main driving force are aligned. There also is a role for OD consultants as they can be useful in the emergent driving force situation where perceived power is lost by one functional group and won by another. For example, when an organization moves from an engineering driving force to a sales driving force, information and resource flows change. If this is missed and not reflected upon, dysfunction will follow. OD consultants can work with the manager to address the Level III issues of information flow and inter-group politics. The OD consultant keeps an eye on whether there is congruence between the organization's espoused driving force(s) and the one(s) that actually has (have or should have) priority. Furthermore, OD consultants can help assess whether the driving force(s) that is (are) espoused within the organization is (are) the same one(s) that is (are) perceived externally by customers and other stakeholders.

The process of fine-tuning Team Clean's corporate words involved all three constituencies mentioned above. OD consultants were able to provide a dispassionate outsider's view and pinpoint areas that needed attention, such as grooming for succession and improving operational efficiencies. The CEO, Donna Allie, added a communication element to her role as a hands-on motivating leader to make sure her leadership by example was accompanied by a clear articulation of goals and systems, and operational procedures which supported those goals. Long-standing members of the organization were able to articulate their views and perceptions of the evolving nature of service in a changing environment, as not only the competitive landscape was altered, but also customer needs, which became more linked to the need for sound sustainability practices. The participation of the three constituencies helped provide Team Clean with a clear sense of the evolution of the corporate words. The participation of three constituencies, namely the leader, selected members, and a third party (here embodied by the OD consultants) provided Donna Allie the opportunity to further articulate and fine-tune Team Clean's driving forces.

Selected interlevel issues in naming the corporate words

Naming the corporate words is a process dictated by changing environmental conditions, changing strategic advantages, changing functional priorities which may result from mergers or acquisitions by outside shareholder groups, and interactions or changes among the key participants within the organization. The process of changing an organization's corporate words requires a clear sense of why change is needed, a formulation of what the new corporate picture would ideally look like, and strong support for change through the transition from the old to the new. Altering the corporate words is a large-scale change as described by Mohrman et al. (1989), as it often leads to shifts in members' basic beliefs and in the way the organization is understood, therefore effecting pervasive change throughout the organization.

Listed below are four interaction scenarios, which can challenge an organization's current corporate words:

- Interdepartmental nature of a driving force.
- Key individuals and their respective interdepartmental groups.
- Team issues in the senior management group with an origin in the driving force choice.
- Level IV or organizational issues around naming the driving force.

Interdepartmental nature of a driving force

Driving forces are by their nature interdepartmental. If the driving force in an organization is designated as engineering then the key interdepartmental group is engineering. In the same way if design and production are the key words of the organization then the interdepartmental group which has priority is production. Therefore driving forces are directed at the key interdepartmental group and give it priority within the organization.

Senior individuals and their respective interdepartmental group

In understanding the interdepartmental group (Level III), relationships and the functional teams' level (Level II), and the senior individuals (Level I) who lead these teams, the driving forces provide the *raison d'être* for each team's existence. As was pointed out earlier, the discipline or field in the career path of the CEO can provide an additional bias toward one discipline as a driving force. This becomes especially critical with change of CEOs coming from different disciplines.

Team issues in the senior management group with an origin in the driving force choice

Team level issues within the senior management group are sources of conflict as senior management group members represent the different constituencies within the organization, which are potentially vying to be the organization's driving force. The tension arises when team members are caught between supporting the team effort of the company and representing the needs of their functioning group. Most often this comes into the forefront when there is a redefinition of the key driving force and a restatement of the corporate words.

Level IV or organizational issues around naming and changing the driving force.

The subtlest interlevel conflicts arise between Level III and Level IV around naming the corporate words. The change of a lead group or function provides a shift in perceived power or influence. In this shift there are winners and losers. This changes the overall organization climate when some people no longer feel appreciated and others feel more important. The rest of the organization gets uncomfortable with this submerged conflict. The best way to address the issue is to discuss the change, the reasons for it, and the natural resentment which can arise. It is also an occasion to stress the importance of supporting people within the organization.

Conclusions

In this chapter we have described the second focus, *naming the corporate words*, and how it relates to those operations or functions that had become lead organizational drivers over time. These are most often referred to as driving forces and become the articulation, or lived-out mission statement of the organization. The content of naming the corporate words deals with the identification and development of these driving forces. The process of naming the corporate words deals with the power aspects and conflicts as well as successes that come from the lead function or operation. As described previously, the culture elements of naming the corporate words are the unseen traditions, conventions, and expectations in the organization and how they are altered by the second focus. Table 10.1 outlines the task and relational issues of naming the corporate words.

The most favourable outcome of the process of naming the corporate words is that the corporate words be congruent with the corporate picture, i.e. that the driving force(s) be completely aligned with the corporate vision goals in a mutually reinforcing way. The main driver(s) need to support the mission and be nourished by it. Importantly, the driving force(s) cannot be perceived as a force that excludes people and functions within the organization, but as one that enhances participation and contribution rather than curtailing it.

Figure 10.2 portrays the loops model seeking to clarify how the outcome of naming corporate words influences strategic direction. The single loop inquiry

TABLE 10.1 Assessment and action template for naming the corporate words

	TASK	RELATIONAL
Content	Driving force CEO life-cycles	Priority of functions Are we marketing or engineering or...?
Process	Look at past and present decision processes	Stakeholder input both internal and external
Culture	Unexamined driving forces	Relative power of stakeholder groups

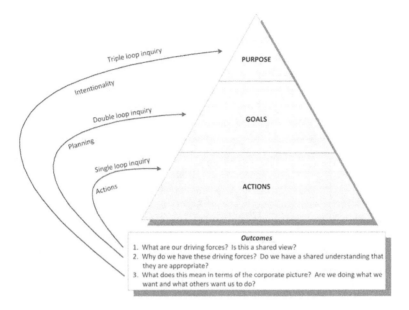

FIGURE 10.2 Single, double and triple loop inquiry when naming the corporate words

relates to the identification of a driving force and to the prevalence of its impact. The double loop inquiry refers to the appropriateness and reasons for existence of the driving force(s) as well as the shared understanding of its appropriateness. The triple loop examines the tightness of the linkages between driving force(s) and the corporate picture. Notice that if the triple loop inquiry requires reformulation, it might be necessary to rethink the corporate picture. Illustrative questions regarding each of these loops as applied to framing the corporate picture are included in the box below the figure. Please note that each loop has two illustrative questions, with the first representing a content inquiry and the second representing a process inquiry.

Reflexive engagement activity 10.1

Below you will find a blank Table 10.2. In relation to an organization with which you are familiar, fill in the boxes with what you see as the important content, process and cultural issues in task and relational terms for your organization with regard to naming the corporate words. Discuss this with your team, or better still, copy the blank form and invite them to fill in the blanks prior to your discussion.

Reflexive engagement activity 10.2

Adopting the clinical approach, review the focus of naming the corporate words from the four perspectives. In relation to an organization with which you are familiar, reflect on the following perspectives and try to answer the questions.

	TASK	RELATIONAL
Content		
Process		
Culture		

TABLE 10.2. Reflexive activity

Leaders

Senior organizational leaders may pose the following questions:

- Given the corporate picture we have selected, is the driving force correct and appropriate?
- How do we in the senior management group work together to select and implement the driving force?

Members

Non-executive members may pose the following questions:

- How do I relate to the driving force of the organization?
- Do I agree with it and am I part of it or in support of it?

OD Consultants

OD consultants may pose the following questions:

- Is there congruence between the espoused driving force and the one which actually operates?

- How does the senior management group process work to be an effective working team on selecting and working the driving force?
- How does the organization as a whole manage inter-functional cooperation and rivalry and conflict?

Outcomes

In terms of $L=P+Q$, what P from naming the corporate words is challenged from your experience of the outcomes in your organization?

- Does naming the corporate words enhance the productivity of the organization?
- Does the process of naming the corporate words get in the way or help organization productivity?

Case: Diaz Steel Group

The Diaz Group, Inc. (DGI) was a privately owned holding company with several subsidiaries, one of which was ABC Tolerance Rings. ABC Tolerance Rings also served a number of industries as a marketing arm of British Tolerance Rings, a UK engineering company. Each of these two companies had a long, rich history and a strong footing in South America through Chile.

ABC Tolerance Rings was in the business of selling tolerance rings, which are corrugated metal strips that act as frictional fasteners that are pressed between two mated circular or cylindrical components for tight fit. Tolerance ring technology competes favourably with other methods of fastening, including epoxy and set screws. Customers for tolerance rings are precision manufacturers in many sectors, including automobiles, home appliances, power tools, electric motors, and computer disk drives, as well as many other mechanical products. The tolerance ring is a versatile item since it is both tough and delicate. For example, a tolerance ring can be used as an anti-theft device on a steering column in an automobile, or as a miniature ball bearing in a computer disk drive.

The company had been in business since 1961 and was optimistic about growth potential because there were proven applications for markets that had not yet been fully tapped. The challenge for ABC Tolerance Rings in the early 2000s was to double sales in the ensuing five years. The company primarily marketed and sold products manufactured by the UK-based British Tolerance Rings, although alternative ways could be used to both produce and/or source items, i.e. there was no exclusivity in place. With expertise in engineering, British Tolerance Rings was well suited to address engineering issues while ABC Tolerance Rings focused on market expansion in Latin America. Chile was an effective base of operations because of its recent macroeconomic stability.

At that time the company's main driving force was in technical areas of engineering, and not in marketing and/or sales. The organization's history was one of having ABC design an engineering solution and either finding a manufacturer for the customers' specifications or manufacturing the component itself. In the day-to-day work of the organization such a technically motivated driving force no longer was the best fit with market requirements.

Mr. Diaz, the CEO, therefore guided ABC Tolerance Rings towards functioning exclusively as a marketing arm of British Tolerance Rings. Mr. Diaz also explained that his employees had, for years, devoted the majority of their time to providing engineering solutions. The sales personnel, engineers by profession, did not share Mr. Diaz's view and in fact many had openly said they were not marketing or sales people but engineering people. Through a process of recruiting, training, skill development, and persuasion, the CEO was able to successfully include marketing and sales as driving forces in addition to offering the best engineering solution. This was made possible because customer needs were often highly technical and the marketing and sales functions also needed specialized engineering expertise to provide the best service to customers.

Questions for reflection and discussion

1. Where does the need for this change arise?
2. What needs to happen to enable this change in driving force to take place?
3. What are the interlevels issues and how would you contribute to enabling this change to take place?

References

Andrews, K.J. (1971) *The Concept of Corporate Strategy.* Homewood, IL: Irwin.

Barney, J. (1991) Firm resources and sustained competitive advantage. *Journal of Management,* 17(1), 99–120.

Mohrman, A., Mohrman, S., Ledford, G., Cummings, T., Lawler, E.E. and Associates (1989) *Large Scale Organizational Change.* San Francisco, CA: Jossey-Bass.

Petaraf, M. (1993) The cornerstones of competitive advantage: A resource-based view. *Strategic Management Journal,* 14(3), 179–191.

Porter, M. (1980) *Competitive Strategy: Techniques for Analyzing Industries and Competitors.* New York: Free Press.

Porter, M. (1985) *Competitive Advantage: Creating and Sustaining Superior Performance.* New York: Free Press.

Prahalad, C.K. and Hamel, G. (1990) The core competence of the corporation. *Harvard Business Review,* 68(3), 79–91.

Tregoe, B. and Zimmerman, J. (1980) *Top Management Strategy.* New York: Simon and Schuster.

Wernerfelt, B. (1984) A resource-based view of the firm. *Strategic Management Journal,* 5(2), 171–180.

11

DETERMINING CORPORATE ALTERNATIVES BY ANALYSING

This strategic focus, determining corporate alternatives by analysing, is the foundation for the focus described in Chapter 12, the choice and implementation of the best courses of action and, in double and triple loop learning situations, it can also be the foundation for framing the corporate picture as well as naming the corporate words because it can help identify opportunities and strengths, and therefore discern important driving forces for the organization. This focus, determining corporate alternatives by analysing, involves the generation of actionable alternatives and possible scenarios, and therefore provides direction: it is not itself the choice. It frames the stages in the adaptive coping cycle where the sensed information is exposed to rigorous analysis. Figure 11.1 summarizes the *determining corporate alternatives by analysing* focus.

This is a critical stage in strategy formulation. The methods chosen to do the analysis help determine the structure of the answers and therefore affect outcomes. In relational terms across the four levels, the task of doing analysis involves the complex involvement of senior management and organizational members in technical analytic activities that also may become highly political. In this chapter we first describe the technical content of analysing. We then explore the organizational processes through which analysis is conducted. Third, we examine roles in determining corporate alternatives by analysing and we conclude by discussing selected interlevel dynamics issues when conducting corporate analysis.

The content of determining corporate alternatives by analysing

The analysis focus of the strategic management framework presented in this book is one that has received increased attention in recent decades. Indeed, over the past half-century the study of business strategy formulation and execution has increased in depth, breadth, sophistication, and number of tools. This significant deepening

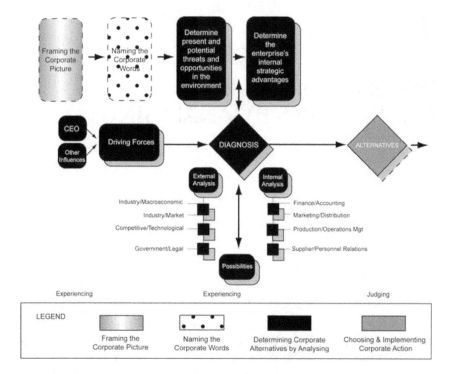

FIGURE 11.1 Determining corporate alternatives by analyzing

in the understanding and the implications of strategic management has sometimes led to the belief that this analysis phase is more important than others, a notion with which we strongly disagree: as described throughout Part III of this book, all five foci are fed by and in turn feed each one of the others and as such, they are all equally prominent and important. Because of the extensive literature on the content of business strategy analysis, with several streams of academic thought, including the resource-based view of the firm and the industry-based view of the firm, in this section we will succinctly describe the content framework of corporate analysis.

Corporate strategic decisions usually are either related to strategy formulation or strategy execution. Strategy formulation involves the fine-tuning of goals and objectives and the establishment of a reliable roadmap to achieve them, which includes the translation from strategic goals to tactical objectives to operational tasks. Strategy execution involves the ongoing comparison between the formulated strategies and the emergent strategies, i.e. the constant examination of signals that are being received by the organization from various stakeholders, be they customers, employees, suppliers or the community, regarding unforeseen opportunities or threats. The organization needs to have a clear understanding of the top-down formulated strategy and also needs to be able to stimulate the emergence of alternative bottom-up strategies in order to incorporate on an incremental basis those that are promising and had not been considered beforehand. Most often these emergent strategies imply some degree of incremental change in the organization. In an unforgiving and unpredictable world, events often lead to a formulated strategy requiring radical change, and sometimes a first sign of possible need for more significant change can be difficulty in implementing incremental change, something which is often only recognized during the focus described in the next chapter covering choice and execution. This focus, determining corporate alternatives by analysing, is therefore an integral part of strategy formulation in addition to its role in examining emergent strategies on an ongoing basis. As a result, determining corporate alternatives should be a continuous effort throughout the corporation and the influences of this focus and effects on it from the other four foci should be attentively followed not only during times of strategy formulation, but also during the ongoing normal course of business.

Scope of analysis

The starting point of any strategic analysis is the issue to be addressed, namely the issue to be analysed. This issue can be part of strategy formulation and extremely broad (What should be the strategic direction of the corporation over the ensuing 10 years?) or highly specific (Given that we want to produce this number of widgets, where is the best place to do so?). If the issue results from an emergent strategy opportunity or threat, likewise it can be extremely broad (Our subsidiary in country X has successfully built a business applying our product to a completely different industry: what do we do now?) or highly specific (Our customer is asking for this innovation in our service operations – should we do it?). Framing the corporate picture and naming the corporate words as well as the implementation and evaluation foci help the process of identifying relevant questions: as described for each respective focus, findings may lead to revisiting the picture, the words, the analysis, the implementation, or the evaluation, and in some cases, as a result, may lead to rephrasing the question, the issue to be addressed. In strategic analysis, often the most difficult task is not to answer a question appropriately, but rather to ask the right question to begin with.

After a strategic issue has been enunciated and the corporation's purpose and drivers clearly articulated, the next step is to determine whether the strategic scope is at the corporate level (What businesses should we be in and how?), the business level (How can we attain competitive advantage in this particular line of business?), or functional level (How can manufacturing help us sustain our competitive advantage?). Yet another possible scope of analysis involves cross-border strategies in an increasingly globalized world (Whether and how should we attempt to produce or sell in a given region or country?). More often than not, analysing to resolve a given corporate issue will lead one through more than one of the aforementioned scopes of analysis. As an example, the decision of whether to diversify into another industry abroad (corporate-level strategy) may also entail determining how the corporation can succeed in that industry (business-level strategy) and whether it has or must develop the operational capabilities to succeed (functional-level strategy), let alone understanding how to compete in a different institutional and cultural environment. Despite the occasional scope overlap, it is necessary for the analyst to clearly understand the question being asked at each point in time. The analysis to be done depends on the main issue to be resolved, and it is not uncommon for the choice among the different possible scopes of analysis to be ill thought through, leading to misguided decisions.

Corporate-level strategizing involves decisions regarding which industries to compete in given the opportunities available and the company's current portfolio of businesses. This involves considering the possibility and likelihood of sharing resources and capabilities and/or transferring competencies across businesses when considering diversification, whether horizontal or vertical. Leaders often over-estimate the benefit of utilizing organizational competencies in different businesses and may extend themselves in unrelated diversification exploits. Furthermore, it is necessary to understand the point from an industry and/or product life-cycle per-spective before attempting to engage in either a related or unrelated diversification effort.

Business-level strategy analysis involves determining the best way to compete given the company's characteristics and environmental conditions. Two basic ways to compete are either through differentiation (by providing a product that always will be preferable to competitors if sold at the same price, i.e. that is perceived as better by customers, therefore allowing the company to charge a higher price and profit on larger margins) or through low-cost offerings (by providing a product at a lower price than competitors and therefore giving the costumer the option of paying less for the same result). Any organization should provide as much value as possible to all relevant stakeholders because its sustained success in society is dependent upon it. From a purely economic starting point, the value the organi-zation is able to provide to a given customer is the difference between the utility or satisfaction the customer obtains from (his or her *willingness-to-pay* for) a product and its price. Companies which follow a differentiation strategy try to provide products which will augment potential buyers' willingness to pay through product attributes that enhance uniqueness and appeal to specific needs, and therefore hope to succeed in charging a higher price. Companies which follow a low-cost strategy hope to produce with very high efficiency levels so they can offer products at prices lower than their competitors making up in volume the lower margins per unit sold. There are variations of these two broad themes, such as the use of a focus strategy when targeting a specific consumer segment, or the uncommon situation in which both objectives, i.e. low-cost and differentiation, can be achieved simul-taneously. In following either of these two generic strategies or any combination of them for a broad or limited target consumer base, it is necessary to have a clear understanding of the external environment (opportunities and threats) as well as the internal characteristics of the firm (strengths and weaknesses). The essence of the business-level strategy is how to outflank competitors in a given business.

Lastly, functional-level strategies involve tailoring the company's functions to the needs of the corporate- and business-level strategies to achieve superior performance. This may involve achieving increased efficiency in operations, quicker innovation in product development, more reliability in deliveries, or achieving a level of excellence in some element of importance to consumers. It goes without saying that whatever the scope of strategic analysis being considered, a clear understanding of the environmental conditions as well as the company's characteristics is necessary. For this reason the content of the third focus includes analyses both internal and external to the firm. However, before going into the specific analyses, it is important to identify decision-making criteria.

Nature of the issue and criteria for decision-making

Once the issue to be resolved is clearly articulated, in any analysis it is necessary to understand the nature of the problem and the criteria which will be used for decision-making. Some types of issues are such that different rational agents, when thinking about them and applying adequate tools to address them, will always find the same result (which in mathematical terms might be called the optimal result). These types of issues in the business world are mostly operational (such as: What is the ideal programme for a manufacturing run with given characteristics? or What is the ideal routing for a UPS delivery truck given the expected stops for the day?) and have straightforward solutions obtainable through mathematical modelling. They usually have one main objective, i.e. one criterion which will guide decision-making, such as minimizing costs or maximizing a benefit, and usually are amenable to precise modelling, meaning that models of the issue tend to reflect nearly perfectly what is observed in the real world. The analysis of these types of issues uses codified knowledge and logical reasoning and therefore lends itself to a high degree of automated support.

At the opposite extreme are issues (some of which may also be operational) which are of a very different nature: different rational agents, when thinking about them will find very different answers despite using the same (and adequate) tools to provide decision support. These types of issues do not have straightforward solutions and are not amenable to mathematical modelling. In fact, one could argue that there are several different solutions for an issue of this nature, all of them correct. Consider publishing decisions (What cover should our newsweekly have this week? or What should be the headline of our blog today?) for which crowdsourcing can be helpful, but doesn't really offer a solution because it depends on the targeted audience in each case. Issues of this nature usually have more than one main objective, i.e. there are several criteria which should guide decision-making. These issues usually present the additional difficulty that each of these criteria may be of difficult modelling, i.e. models will not reflect perfectly what is observed in the real world. The result is that different and very experienced professionals may come up with very different decisions. The analysis of issues of this nature uses tacit knowledge and intuitive reasoning. It therefore does not lend itself to a high degree of automated support. Sometimes the critical factor in marketing a product or service might involve altering the business model in a way that defies established codified knowledge. Such a critical factor is often reminiscent of Schumpeter's creative destruction paradigm, namely the process of continuous evolution through technological and organizational innovations that lead to new business models, altering economic structures from within and causing the replacement of industry leaders. One example of this is Nutrisystem in 2003, which reframed the weight-loss industry by replacing group support and group weigh-ins with an online support model and home-delivered food products.

Strategic analysis decisions run the gamut from one extreme to the other and nearly always incorporate elements of both. Because there is such a strong component of so-called softer elements which defy precise codification in many strategic decisions, the process of determining corporate alternatives by analysing, including building buy-in for subsequent implementation, becomes very important (more on this in the process section below). For these and other reasons, it is necessary to have and share a clear understanding of the criteria which will guide decision-making, as these criteria will necessarily guide the analysis. This understanding of the nature of the analysis and of the criteria to be used for fine-tuning strategic alternatives by necessity involves the use of both types of analytical thought, namely logical and intuitive reasoning, and involves both levels of knowledge, codified and tacit. When to use each depends on the nature of the issue to be addressed and the judgement of the decision-maker, which in turn depend on the precise specification of the decision at hand as well as the criteria to be considered in analysis.

Regarding criteria, it is helpful to begin with the *framing the corporate picture* focus and the *naming the corporate words* focus. Several questions might be useful, such as: what is the company's vision and purpose, what are the company's goals, how has the company been able to reach them in the past, what have been the main drivers of this success (of reaching these goals) in the past, and are these drivers the ones that will sustain success in the forecasted external environment? Most decisions will require trading off some cost with some benefit. It is necessary therefore to have the criteria for analysis very clear.

Criteria will necessarily depend on the scope of the analysis and differ from case to case. For example, in an analysis of corporate-level strategy scope, the possibility of synergies across perhaps unrelated businesses is important and therefore organizational structure, transfer pricing, and other cross-company systems may be paramount, as well as understanding whether and how competitors are succeeding. In an analysis of business-level strategy scope the main effort should be either to lower the company's costs (to increase the probability of becoming a price-leader and low-cost provider) or to raise customers' willingness-to-pay (to increase the probability of becoming a significant differentiator). In an analysis of functional-level strategy scope, functional objectives and efficiencies as well as inter-functional linkages including make-buy choices potentially involving outsourcing need to be taken into account. The leader needs to translate corporate objectives into more-easily-understood concrete objective measures which serve as criteria for analysis and later for evaluation. One tool to achieve this is the Balanced Scorecard, which will be briefly described in the process section below.

External analysis

External analysis involves a deep understanding of the environment within which the organization operates. This includes an examination of the institutions which affect its actions, the macroeconomic environment, an analysis of the industries under consideration, the expected market evolution and competitive landscape within each of these industries, and technology and innovation expectations affecting the sectors in which the organization expects to compete. The literature on strategy formulation and execution is an extensive source of tools to help in each of these analyses, which by definition are interdisciplinary, involving knowledge of several business areas as well as economics, political science and sociology, in addition to disciplines specific to the industry being targeted.

The external analysis begins with understanding the relevant industry structure (including a five forces analysis – Porter [1980]) as well as basic supply and demand characteristics expected in the time horizon being considered. Porter's five forces are a time-tested tool to estimate the potential attractiveness of an industry because it considers the threat of new entrants, the rivalry in the industry, the power of buyers and suppliers, and the threat of substitutes. It also can provide insights into opportunities for altering the structure of an industry in a way that favours the organization as its use should not be limited to a static snapshot approach but rather the examination of dynamics occurring in the industry which may expose hidden opportunities. An estimation of future demand includes an examination of potential market growth as well as expected price behaviour as industries evolve through well-studied life-cycles. The survival of a firm depends on understanding the expected behaviour of consumers' willingness-to-pay which is directly linked to evolving tastes and preferences, and provides insights into future price and volume dynamics in the market. It is also necessary to study the supply environment in the industry, which by necessity includes looking at competitors to build supply curves and determine component costs and prices that likely will be observed at different market levels. Implicit in the analyses discussed in this section is determining which players in a given industry are appropriating the lion's share of value created.

Internal analysis

Internal analysis involves developing a deep understanding of the organization itself, its strengths and weaknesses, which builds upon insights gleaned from *framing the corporate picture* and *naming the corporate words*. For example, if a given function is believed to be a main driver of the organization, analysis needs to support this belief. The literature on strategy formulation and execution provides an extensive source of tools to help identify and quantify internal strengths and weaknesses, and over the decades, different techniques have fallen in and out of favour with strategy practitioners and theoreticians. The resource-based view of the firm has classified resources or capabilities into those which are valuable (leading to competitive parity), unique (leading to temporary competitive advantage), or of very difficult imitation (leading to sustained competitive advantage).

The internal analysis begins with understanding what makes the organization special and how these characteristics are translated into the company's competitive position relative to the issue at hand. Porter's Value Chain analysis (1985), McKinsey's Seven-S framework, Barney's VRIO methodology (1991), and Prahalad and Hamel's (1990) core competencies construct are an integral part of internal analysis. The objective is to build as accurate as possible an image of the organization's internal characteristics relative to the issue being addressed. Part of the internal analysis is to determine the company's cost position relative to that of competitors, a necessary condition to understand the organization's competitive position and to predict the evolution of competitive dynamics within the sectors being examined, which we will examine next, in the section on the process of analysing.

The importance of sound analysis is illustrated by the recent history of Petroleum Products Corporation, a Pennsylvania company that adapted its business model to a changing environment several times since its foundation in 1924. Originally conceived as an anthracite coal supply company, it introduced smokeless semi-bituminous coal shortly thereafter due to anthracite coal miner strikes. After the depression the company added coal stoker and heating equipment installation services, expanding to oil burner installation and conversion in the late 1940s. In 1953 the company entered the fuel oil distribution business, finally closing the coal portion of the business during the 1970s. This series of transitions from coal supply to heating services to fuel oil distribution was accomplished in a gradual and deliberate fashion under the stewardship of three generations of the founding family who consistently maintained the strong values of the business, namely hard work, thoughtful planning, customer focus, teamwork with strong respect for the individual, self-initiative, and a willingness to make long-term bets.

In the late 1980s the company continued to develop retail and wholesale fuel distribution services in a business environment in which both categories were becoming increasingly commoditized resulting in a sector-wide margin squeeze. What followed in the early 1990s was a period of deep analysis of industry trends, macroeconomic conditions, and sources of competitive advantage. The fourth generation family member who was transitioning to leadership enrolled several members of management in a one-week intensive seminar on business strategy at a major east coast university during which the team spent every evening adapting the lessons of the day to their own unique situation. This continuous exercise of external and internal analysis was the foundation for a new strategic direction, namely to target fuel wholesale at a time when most competitors were favouring retail operations and to do so by gradually locking in storage and pipeline assets in the company's geographic area. Several years later, in 1999, the retail operation was sold, allowing the company to focus solely on the wholesale business.

As of 2014 the company owned storage tanks to store and pipelines to distribute diesel fuel, heating oil, gasoline and other oil derivatives, including 14 pipeline terminals serving the Pennsylvania, Virginia, West Virginia, Maryland, Ohio and New York state markets. On April 15, 2015, ArcLight, a private equity firm specializing on energy assets announced that it had acquired the company (*ArcLight, 2015*). Both buyer and seller were private companies, so the purchase price was not disclosed, but industry reports and local press estimated the transaction as including more than 4 million barrels of fuel storage tanks, a company with an annual EBITDA of approximately US$100 million and an aggregate consideration estimated at above US$1 billion (*Central Penn Business Journal, 2015*). The main architect of the executed strategy and the successful sale of the business attributes the extremely positive outcome to two basic factors: the careful formulation of a viable strategy to secure first-mover advantages in acquiring non-substitutable assets; and the careful and deliberate implementation of the strategy over the ensuing 20 years.

The process of determining corporate alternatives by analysing

The process of analysing covers an examination of the external environment and of the internal characteristics of the organization. Practitioners traditionally have given different names to each of these labour-intensive tasks. The examination of conditions external to the firm is often called an external audit and leads to a deep understanding of the threats and opportunities in the environment. The deep understanding of a company's internal characteristics leads to the articulation of its main strengths and weaknesses, including the knowledge of which positive factors are sustainable in the long term. Herein we call these steps respectively external and internal analyses, as described in the previous section covering the content of determining corporate alternatives by analysing. The process doesn't stop there though, as it is necessary to augment the analysing with intelligence on competitors, determining the competitive situation at a given point in time (competitive positioning) as well as its expected future evolution given the internal and external analyses conducted (competitive dynamics).

The essential technical tasks in determining corporate alternatives by analysing can thus be subdivided into three steps:

1. the external analysis;
2. the internal analysis; and
3. the competitive positioning and competitive dynamics analysis.

External analytic process

The elements of this approach to analysis are illustrated in Figure 11.1 under the 'External Analysis' box. These factors are components of external analysis. They are: industry-related, macroeconomic, government and legal, market-related, competitive, supplier and technological.

The first, the industry structure and economic factors, represent the overall milieu in which the organization is functioning. Industry structure analysis involves examining the targeted industry as described in the previous section. The economic analysis includes but is not limited to such things as growth of the economy, consumers' ability to afford products and services, exchange rates in international organizations, economic constraints on consumers or suppliers, the cost of borrowing money, equity returns against savings returns, etc. A component of the economic factors is the government and legal environment. This category includes things such as laws that govern operations and products, international trade agreements, tariffs and other restricting devices, requirements for services provided, service and product liability questions, issues concerning patents and equality employment legislation, etc.; e-business and new approaches to commerce are impacted by these regulations as well as government regulations of equity and fixed income capital markets.

The next factors involve the market and competition. This is consideration of the competing products and how they affect results. Market share by product or service, product innovation, product packaging, market presentation, and advertising are analysed at this stage. Important to this type of analysis is the trend over time, i.e. are the market and the share declining or growing? This is analysed by each product or service in isolation and then in the aggregate. The organizational life-cycle should be a background to the alternatives that are developed at this stage. The presence of the organization in its external environment and its ability to be a player are accounted for in this phase of the analysis.

The next factors deal with the suppliers and technological changes in the environment or on the horizon that could affect production. This would seem at first to apply only to a production organization where the technological know-how and source of materials are essential. The aircraft, auto, and electronic components in the computer industry are classic examples where this information and analysis are critical. Yet the supply chain affects every organization. Medical supplies to hospitals, books and food service to universities are but two examples. Critical cost changes can produce dramatic effects on service pricing. In some situations the supplier has a great hold over the end producer of the products or services. Sometimes the reverse is true when one end producer is the sole buyer of the supplier's product.

Suppliers are not alone in having effects on service organizations. Technological factors can also have a strong effect. Medical organizations are a good example where new technology is an advantage in gaining patients and providing better care. This is very true with new imaging procedures. Each hospital or clinic needs to have the latest MRI to serve patients. Hospitals also have learned how important the physician supply of patient referrals is to their census. This has caused new hospital–physician alliances and has introduced competition in medical care in both the USA and Europe.

When Christian Haub became president of A&P and had total control he began the process of analysing to determine where the company was and where it should go. As Haub describes, 'the team sat down in April and May and set out criteria for the analysis. The auditors provided the results of their internal audit and we put together analysis for the external environment. In order to enhance the outside information we engaged investment bankers to help us get competitive data, most of which was publicly available, to determine the critical benchmarks in terms of sales, growth, profitability, return on capital, financial comparisons and market share.'

It is interesting to note reliance on outside analysts, because Haub felt the internal people were too close to the issue to be able to clearly and accurately do the analysis that was required. The result of the analysis made it clear that the company had to fundamentally change. It was mostly Haub's own vision that provided the clarity to see that present methods would not work. The end product of the analysis was to begin forming a new corporate picture. Chapter 15 includes an extensive development of this case.

Internal analytic process

The analysis focus now turns inward and deals with the internal analysis, located under the 'Internal Analysis' box on the right side of Figure 11.1. Some of the internal factors have a counterpart in the external analysis with a resultant relationship. Economic condition relates to finance and supplier/technological relates to production. These relationships should be kept in mind. The factors involved in this internal analysis are: finance and accounting, marketing and distribution, production and operations management, personnel and labour relations, and corporate resources. Corporate resources is the catch-all of other factors that should be looked at and analysed but do not have a specific category.

The first factors are the finance and accounting factors. Here consideration is made of the major financial ratios. Some financial ratios to be considered are rate of return, debt to equity, inventory turnover, sales turnover, equity to sales, and sustainable growth rate. The comparison to industry norms on earnings, net worth, and inventory turns is also critical. Cash management and other financial procedures are processed in this analysis. Sustainable growth rate is also a crucial analysis tool for new or smaller organizations. This ratio determines if a firm can continue to finance growth through its ability to generate profits and keep adding equity in order to increase production. This ratio is most important to small organizations that may be under-capitalized. Acquiring external equity funds in small firms dilutes the ownership, which most entrepreneurs do not want. The accounting analysis consists in determining if there is an effective budget and plans in place and whether suitable controls are used in the implementation of the budget. The accounting report, 10K, etc. are all part of the analysis at this point.

The next part of the analysing is marketing and distribution. The key questions here deal with market share. How firm is the current share? Is the share diversified between different product offerings? What is happening to prices and margins in the markets? Grid analysis for products is a useful analytical tool, if appropriate. The distribution system, which can be a driving force as we have already seen, is a part of the analysis of an organization's efficiencies. The type of distribution systems used can directly affect the success of an organization. Many firms use the distribution system as their critical advantage. One such company is Wal-Mart. Wal-Mart is highly efficient and effective in getting large amounts of goods sent from its manufacturers to its outlets/distribution sites. In doing 'just in time' distribution to the point-of-sale Wal-Mart achieves significant cost advantages.

Analyzing production and operations management provides new processes, savings, and faster production, yet is often overlooked in importance in the analysis focus. This is an opportunity to analyse whether the production process is correct and whether it offers any strategic advantages by using the power alley concept found in manufacturing. The power alley concept maintains that the more common processes that can be found and maximized, the greater the cost savings will be. Market advantage can be gained, as seen in the example of the Black and Decker company. It did not invent the weed-eater but by analysis of available processes and building a product with no unexpected production or engineering costs, Black and Decker introduced the Weed Wacker. This product competed and won against a new product from a new company. Having the production capabilities required for the new product and using its own distribution system to sell this product allowed Black and Decker to roll out nationally and win on price. Additional savings were obtained because the company did no marketing. Through these savings, and because of its strong name and distribution, Black and Decker was able to profitably produce and sell more product than its competitor, quickly going up the product's experience curve. When customers came to buy a Weed Eater, Black and Decker with a better name had its Weed Wacker on sale at a lesser price.

The production and control analysis can provide other sources of advantage. Take for example, the Hallmark Card organization, which through large-scale printing and a high quality control, can produce high quality products at low cost. This enables Hallmark to price in a higher margin or compete on cost. It does both under different names with quality under the Hallmark label and cost under the Ambassador line. Included in the analysis are personnel and labour relations. It is at this point that the amount of turnover among employees and senior executives is analysed and is compared to the rest of the industry. Also the labour relations climate in which the firm or organization operates is analysed.

Corporate resources and other factors need to be considered when conducting internal analysis. An organization has a life-cycle and a place within an industry dating back to its birth. It is important to note the critical people who founded and influenced the organization. The development of the goals and products over the years and the resulting organizational learning are vital as well. The manner in which an organization has gone through past changes is indicative of its ability to undergo future changes. The organizational life-cycle examination in this instance is internal-looking and deals with the ability of an organization to manage change. This analysis is used in the case of acquisitions, to determine the price paid for goodwill, which is the intangible value a long-standing organization may be able to obtain for its ability to provide products and services.

A critical aspect in today's organization is the determination of the quality of the management information systems (MIS) or information and communication technology (ICT) aspects of the firm or organization. The information systems and the technology required to operate at a high level are critical to real-time understanding of the factors affecting an organization. This analysis aims to determine whether the information systems are providing all the value expected and whether they are doing what they were designed to do. The questions are threefold: first, is the necessary information an accurate reflection of the existing situation; second, is this information available to decision-makers in usable format in a timely manner; and third, is information being used appropriately in decision-making processes?

The Balanced Scorecard approach to strategic management by Robert Kaplan and David Norton (1996) can be a powerful tool to support the process of analysing and is an implicit support tool for the five foci approach used here. The Balanced Scorecard uses four perspectives to cover four areas of measurement for successful strategic management:

- customer perspective
- financial perspective
- internal business process perspective
- the learning and growth perspective

Each of these perspectives has four components: objectives, measures, targets, and initiatives. The basic assumption is nothing that can't be measured is valid for making a difference in the greater strategic picture. While all four perspectives taken together provide a complete view and allow visualization of the company as a whole, it is interesting to note that the customer perspective is linked to external analysis while the financial perspective is linked to internal analysis. The internal and business process perspective is intimately linked with the implementation focus while the learning and growth perspective is fed by the evaluation focus.

Competitive positioning and competitive dynamics

Senior individuals many times play on both sides of the line as they move from one organization in the same industry to another. Trade shows and industry or sector associations are venues in which the strategic players become known to each other and learn how each one will act in competitive situations. Organizations want to analyse the uncertainty of a wider environment, and then with such knowledge, situate their own plans with those of the competition (Figure 11.2). Understanding the company's competitive position is an integral part of determining corporate alternatives by analysing. For this it is necessary to estimate the company's cost advantage (and/or disadvantage) relative to various competitors in the market and to probe deeper to investigate potential causes for these cost differences. On the demand side it is also necessary to understand whether and how competitors are able to benefit from a willingness of customers to pay a price premium. Competitive benchmarking can be extremely helpful to answer these questions.

It is not enough to understand the position of a company vis-à-vis competitors because of the changing nature of business – the only certainty is constant change as no competitor is standing still. It is necessary to carefully study potential competitor reactions to any move a company is considering. Understanding the likely reaction of a competitor if an organization plans to pursue an aggressive move such as entering a new market or launching a competitor product head-on is a necessity. Game theory and decision trees can be extremely useful tools when analysing the likelihood of different outcomes.

This process of action and reaction between major players may even become somewhat of a closed system when organizations within the same industry closely interact with one another. Mutual knowledge is effectively built among organizations and critical moves of dominant players in an industry can be readily

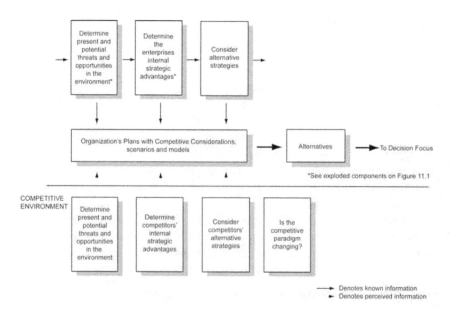

FIGURE 11.2 Representation of the analytic process stressing the competition and the dynamic external environment

anticipated. The input required to achieve this degree of mutual knowledge is intelligence on competitors, which can be of two kinds. The first kind is common knowledge obtained from public documents on competitors and general overall figures for an industry. The second kind is good intuitive approximations from past experience extrapolated into the future. Likely scenarios of retaliation or accommodation are created through a wide range of inputs from everyone with knowledge of the competitors or the industry from within the organization. Models projecting company performance into the future are then enriched with several tools, such as careful consideration of the economics of likely retaliatory or accommodating reactions from competitors. Often certain events lead to a sequence of consecutive actions, each of which has a different probability of occurring, leading to the need to use game trees and a clear understanding of payoffs under different scenarios of outcomes. Once these projections are developed, sensitivity analyses should be conducted.

Building a simulation model of the organization in its environment provides the opportunity for sensitivity analyses, done continuously in real time. By running 'what if' scenarios, with win and lose outcomes and respective probabilities attached, impact to the bottom line in different situations is examined. While initially, the perceived information from the competitors is unclear or uncertain because the information is perceptual, over time, as experience grows, a firm's process of guessing what will occur checked against the reality of what did occur can permit learning, which allows estimates to increasingly approximate reality.

A large university in the northeast part of the United States began a process of modelling in 1985. The key variables, such as enrolment, departmental budgets, charges for depreciation, potential tuition increases, and myriad other important data points were put together in the model. The model continued to be used over the next 15 years and with each annual iteration the model became more accurate and had more numerous applications. When the question arose to self-operate the telephone system or submit it out for bid, the model showed self-operation integrated with information technology would not only save money but make money. If the decision was made with confidence, it was due to the model. The predicted result was met within one percent. Other significant issues provided the same economies using the model.

In this vignette the organization was ahead of its competition and had flexibility and confidence in the decisions made in a highly competitive environment. The models take time to work and are of value, providing better understanding of alternatives considered.

To summarize, the process steps are a sequence of internal and external analyses including careful consideration of the competitive position and competitive dynamics. Each organization runs this task process in its own unique way. Most common is the practice of an organization to use internal and external audits to make minor corrections and to engage in continuous competitive dynamics analysis in search of early warning signals.

Roles in determining corporate alternatives by analysing

We now describe how determining corporate alternatives by analysing relates to different perspectives regarding what is happening in the organization: the CEO's, the members', and the OD consultants'.

Leader and senior management roles in determining corporate alternatives by analysing

The role of the leader in the process of determining corporate alternatives by analysing begins by identifying issues, setting up criteria for analysis, and establishing clear ownership of the process. Showing strong interest is important for the outcome. An additional role of the leader is to be open to the results of the analysis focus. This means putting aside preconceived notions of what 'should' be the output of the analysis. Corporate analysis is an ongoing process: the difficulty that a leader needs to avoid is losing interest in routine outputs, which may result in missing an otherwise telling discontinuity. Corporate leaders, whether the CEO or members of the senior management group or divisional heads, are constantly monitoring whether accurate and useful information is being gathered and whether its assessment is intuitively right. They are comparing the organization's analysis with industry results and competitors' benchmarks. The leaders' perspectives on the activity of determining the corporate direction through analysis focuses on: a) the quality, comprehensiveness and relevance of the information gathered; b) whether it appears to be intuitively right; and c) whether benchmarks with competitors can be made.

In terms of a broader picture, senior management needs to come to the analysis focus aware of the possibility that discontinuous change could be needed. This openness to the possibility of discontinuous change means accepting that it often occurs without direct information that can be tested for accuracy. It is possible that critical information for a decision on discontinuous change is unclear or even absent. An intuitive guess opens the door for research and the manner in which analysis is performed affects outcome. The dynamics of the committees and task forces, which execute the external analyses, the internal analyses, and the competitive positioning and dynamics analyses, are critical for the organization to formulate proposals for strategic direction or pass the information to the senior managers who do select alternative scenarios. On the other hand, the leader also needs to ensure that a process for developing alternatives through analysis is institutionalized so that periodically the organization goes through the analytical process. These two approaches were seen in the case of Saint Joseph's University's new president.

The joint development of a new corporate picture and the consensus process that was followed by the new president upon arrival at Saint Joseph's University helped disseminate clarity of purpose. Organization members bought into a broader corporate picture of discontinuous change which included graduate education as a priority. For example, because the new president had had prior experience in Executive Business Education, he had an intuitive feeling that such an initiative could be successful at Saint Joseph's. External analysis was performed to verify this hypothesis, confirming that an Executive MBA Programme would fill a market need in the Philadelphia metropolitan area. Internal analysis confirmed that certain university characteristics such as long-standing relationship with the tri-state business community and strong Marketing and Accounting departments made it uniquely qualified to offer such a programme. Several alternatives of next steps were developed and an Executive MBA Programme was established.

One role of the leader and the senior management group regarding the analysis focus is to continuously be aware of potential changes in the environment and ask questions which may lead the institution to capitalize on opportunities or avoid threats, such as the EMBA example above. Through membership and participation in the National Association of Independent Colleges and Universities and the Independent Colleges Association of Pennsylvania, the president was continuously informed of evolving conditions in the external environment. Through these associations, the president also became aware of and in some cases initiated potential cost-saving and revenue-generating alternatives such as common procurement, common insurance and common telecommunications services.

Another very important leadership role is that of embedding the practice of analysis in the organization. Once the senior management group became cohesive in a new vision for Saint Joseph's University, an effort to institutionalize the process of analysis began. The president and the senior management group encouraged increased ongoing awareness of changes in the external environment which could present opportunities or pose threats. Likewise, an increased awareness of the university's strengths and weaknesses evolved from the more participative culture that replaced the previous top-down environment.

Leadership next instituted periodic examination of the external and internal environments to ensure recurrent analysis and to generate well-thought-through alternative courses of action, both proactively in anticipation of change and reactively in response to change. The first step in this direction was restructuring the budgeting process to be more inclusive and realistic. This was achieved through the Budget Advisory Committee (BAC) which started meeting more frequently throughout the year. Annually the subsequent year's budget was prepared by the BAC, then challenged and supported by the cabinet, and finally approved by the president. In addition, among the various obligations of the BAC was to meet annually to evaluate execution of the budget of the prior year. Simultaneously a performance review process was institutionalized throughout the administration from the presidential level (evaluated by the Board of Trustees) to the cabinet, director and supervisor levels, a step which increased the scope of internal analysis. The third step was to institutionalize detailed strategic plans which were developed at intervals and reviewed on a sliding-window schedule. These were five-year plans in which years in the immediate future had considerably more detail than those farther out. Several other initiatives to institutionalize the continuous examination and analysis of both the external and internal environments were undertaken under the president's leadership.

The member's role in determining corporate alternatives by analysing

Members have multiple roles in this focus as they need to be involved in different aspects of internal, external and competitive analysis as well as in model-building, if one is used. The choice of criteria and measurements that reflect the reality in each aspect of the organization's functions falls on members throughout the organization. Furthermore, the critical testing of reliability and validity of the research analysis from different points of view also falls on members, which in and of itself is a reason for inclusion. The role of organizational members is sometimes underestimated but, because they are guardians of accuracy and timeliness, their roles are extremely important. Members are concerned with why they are doing the analysis, what its relevance is and how it is congruent with their own understanding of the situation. A process concern is the role of disagreement and whether members feel free to challenge the analysis.

OD consultant's role in determining corporate alternatives by analysing

OD consultants perform a dual role in this focus. They ensure that the technicalities are performed accurately by asking questions: Is there completeness in data gathering? Is information openly shared and jointly owned? What happens to negative feedback? Is process critiqued and reviewed? These are the difficult questions for organizations to ask themselves, providing a valuable role for the OD consultant. In the heat of the discussion on alternative potential outcomes quite often the process issues get lost. OD consultants focus on the completeness of the data gathering and whether it is openly shared and jointly owned, and whether alternative views and negative feedback are encouraged. They work at enabling review and critiques of process and at facilitating shared understanding of the workflow process across the multiple functions of the interdepartmental group. Without an OD consultant, less invested in the outcome, these questions often do not get asked. Another valuable role of the OD consultants is to provide a process for developing scenarios. Additionally, they ensure that the interlevel dynamics which we will discuss in the following section are being managed properly.

Selected interlevel dynamics issues in determining corporate alternatives by analysing

Determining corporate alternatives by analysing is a process necessitated by changing internal or external conditions, by the need to obtain strategic advantages, by changing functions from mergers or acquisitions by outside shareholder groups, and by decisions of or changes among the senior leaders within the organization. Listed below are four interaction scenarios, which can challenge how the organization does its analysis.

- Cultural issues in how the analysis is performed: interdepartmental group roles.
- Disagreement within the senior management group in facing discontinuous change.
- Level of interdepartmental group conflict resulting from degree of change.
- Potential interlevel conflict resulting from modelling choices.

Cultural issues in how the analysis is performed: interdepartmental group roles

There are cultural issues in how an organization engages in analysis. Each functional area has to examine its own analysis and process its own functionality as well as how the interdepartmental group's function affects and is affected by others. Each functional area has its own sub-culture, where functional groups have developed their own traditions, language and basic assumptions, characteristics of a self-contained subsystem. The ability to self-correct and to hear critical comments forces new relations from this 'content' area. So each functional level is offering its view of the whole from the perspective of its own sub-culture in the interdepartmental group activity. How these analyses or 'views' inter-relate, are accepted or are rejected, is critical as most often in integrating multiple functions, the cross-links between functions are potential sources of trouble. The analysis within functions is most often correct but the workflow or process flow between functions is one possible source of confusion. As a result, interlevel aspects of this focus are complex as each unit in the interdepartmental group normally has some specific analytic expertise. The finance department also plays a central role, as financial data are critical for analysis. There are also contributions from the information technology area that must be considered.

Disagreement within the senior management group in facing discontinuous change

The senior management group usually does the determination of potential threats and opportunities in the environment. In its work with counterparts or even competitors at national meetings, intuitive insights give the group a starting point for this analysis. Whenever intuition comes into play it is easy for disagreement to arise. The leader may see it one way and others may see it quite differently. The resolution of these conflicts is then dependent on analysis conducted by the research team. Due to internal competition between functional areas, the senior management group may well be in conflict as well, an undesirable situation which needs to be resolved.

Level of interdepartmental group conflict resulting from degree of change

The amount of interlevel conflict will be directly related to the degree of change required by the organization. In those changes which are incremental, conflict may be minimal, and disagreements may revolve solely around performance. In those changes that are revolutionary, the disagreement about a new environment can be quite severe. These conflicts are between Level II and Level III, and between Level I and Level II and Level III.

Potential interlevel conflicts resulting from modelling choices

Whenever financial projections and other complex dynamic models are used in determining the corporate direction, this whole process becomes more complex and the possibility of interlevel conflict becomes more apparent because accurate modelling requires multiple inputs. In forming a model, the cooperation of all parties needs to occur. There must be a common view of the operation of the organization both internally and externally for any modelling effort to be useful, including the need for continuous adjustments as new information comes in. This requires cooperation between Level I in the leader, Level II in the senior management group and Level III in the interdepartmental group.

Conclusions

Determining corporate alternatives by analysing is the activity in the adaptive coping cycle where sensed information is subjected to rigorous scrutiny and analysis so as to consolidate the basis for judgements and decisions. The analysis on which the strategic plan rests is its foundation. If the foundation is poor, the resulting strategy likewise will be poor. The focus on determining corporate alternatives by analysing is an intricate mix of task and relational, and content and process elements, all operating together to open the organization's leadership to new possibilities, even discontinuous ones. For organizations to respond quickly this analysis focus must be second nature and habitual. In most environments, quick, efficient, inclusive and responsive analysis is critical. Intuition comes into play in how the choices are made and in what to analyse. Table 11.1 outlines the task and relational issues of determining corporate alternatives by analysing.

The outcome of determining corporate alternatives by analysing is that there is organizational learning about what needs to be changed in the organization.

TABLE 11.1 Assessment and action template for determining corporate alternatives by analyzing

	TASK	RELATIONAL
Content	Internal and external analyses Virtual plan	Link (or not) those analyzed with those doing the analysis
Process	Analysis Modelling Intuition	How planning committees and task forces are chosen and their effect on outcome
Culture	Sense of confidence in the analysis; either true or false way of proceeding	Divisional cultures, market segments or operations as a whole

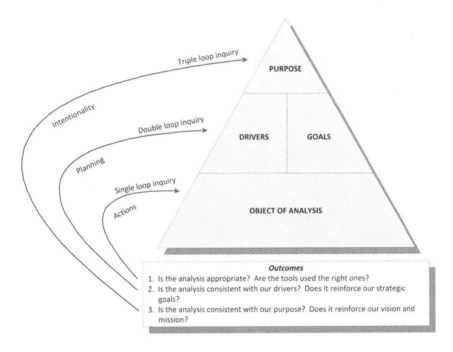

FIGURE 11.3 Single, double and triple loop inquiries when determining corporate alternatives by analyzing

Figure 11.3 provides a structure for inquiring into the outcome of determining corporate alternatives by analysing. The three inquiry loops begin from the outcomes of determining corporate alternatives by analysing and lead to reflection regarding results from each of the other foci. The three inquiry loops represent appropriateness of analysis done and analytical tools used (single loop), consistency with goals and drivers (double loop), and support and coherence with stated purpose (triple loop).

Reflexive engagement activity 11.1

Below you will find a blank Table 11.2. In relation to an organization with which you are familiar, fill in the boxes with what you see as the important content, process and cultural issues in task and relational terms for your organization with regard to determining the corporate direction through analysis. Discuss this with your team, or better still, copy the blank form and invite them to fill in the blanks prior to your discussion.

Reflexive engagement activity 11.2

Adopting the clinical approach, review the focus of determining corporate alternatives by analysing from the four perspectives. In relation to an organization with which you are familiar, reflect on the following perspectives and try to answer the questions.

Leaders

Leaders may pose the following questions:

- Is the proper information being gathered?
- Is assessment of the information intuitively right?

	TASK	RELATIONAL
Content		
Process		
Culture		

TABLE 11.2. Reflexive activity

- Are there benchmarks available?
- What are our competitors' benchmarks?

Organizational members

Non-executive members may pose the following questions:

- What are the reasons for doing the analysis?
- How does my part of the analysis fit?
- How do I relate to other areas or people to make a complete analysis of my area?
- Will this information change my work situation?

OD consultants

OD consultants may pose the following questions:

- Is there completeness in data gathering?
- Is information openly shared and jointly owned?
- What happens to negative feedback?
- Is process critiqued and reviewed?

Outcomes

In terms of $L=P+Q$, what P from determining corporate alternatives by analysing is challenged from your experience of the outcomes in your organization?

- Is the analysis authentic?
- Are there flaws in the information?
- Does the analysis show up an agenda for change?

Case: VerticalNet

VerticalNet is an example of the use of a standard analytic process with competitors. This process utilizes the internal and analytic process on itself and on the competitor and then makes a decision on an acquisition. This comparison is centred on the question of compatibility. VerticalNet, a dotcom company, found itself in this situation in the 1999–2000 timeframe. Just as important as internal organic growth, VerticalNet was extremely aggressive in terms of external growth through acquisitions. Extremely high company valuations in the early days of the Internet allowed the CEO to acknowledge that VerticalNet 'used stock as a (strategic) weapon' in acquisitions. In analysing the competition, stock prices were compared and became a factor in choosing which organizations to acquire. Among VerticalNet's key acquisitions were: Safety On-Line – online occupational health and safety community, ElectricNet – online electric power industry. Lab X.com – scientific laboratory equipment e-commerce site and Real World Electronics – electronics exchange.

VerticalNet's model sought to provide richness within a specific industry and achieved reach through the expansion of the industries which it served. As such, each of VerticalNet's communities featured its own version of distinctive branding, lending to the air of focus that was necessary to achieve the trust of the individuals within the respective industry the site served. This approach was validated by industry experts as well as by the influx of capital to fund new competitors, such as Fobchemicals.com and Promedix.com.

VerticalNet's formula for successful online communities included the analysis of 'content, community, and commerce'. The content factor was achieved by offering a variety of news and other information, including white papers, coordinated by respected industry insiders that served as managing editors, not unlike a standard print trade publication. Each acquisition was analysed for the content it could provide. The community analysis involved a number of beneficial components including discussion fora, career information, and events. This analysis scaled each acquisition target for its contributions area and added this to the contribution the acquisition made to VerticalNet. Commerce factor analysis included online auctions and transactions and it too was scaled and combined with the other factors, in order to make the final decision on acquisition. Like many new media companies, VerticalNet's primary revenue source was advertising, including the development of storefronts, or web pages within the vertical trade communities that highlighted the advertiser and provided links to the advertiser's website.

VerticalNet's valuation, however, like that of other b2b Internet companies, was based less on the current revenue mix and more on the expectation that the company would deliver enormous transaction-related revenue in the future. This drove the analysis towards potential growth rather than present revenue. It also provided a challenge of how to structure these acquisitions.

The structural design of these acquired companies was consistent with VerticalNet's main purposes. It resembled a network with different hubs all apparently operating by themselves, but every one of them interconnected to the total system, and all of them operationally self-sufficient and simultaneously able to leverage connections through mutual information dependence.

Questions for reflection and discussion

1. Through your analysis, which acquired companies seem more congruent with VerticalNet's culture and corporate self-image?
2. In the simplest definition of their business, VerticalNet sees itself as a 'market maker' that links buyers and sellers. Is it a natural evolution for it to increase its transactional revenue, moving away from its reliance on advertising into more of an e-commerce revenue model?
3. How do interlevels affect an understanding of this case?

References

Arclight (2015) ArcLight website, accessed May 27, 2015, www.arclightcapital.com/documents/FG/arclight/news/358645_Pyramid_-_PPC_-_Press_Release__FINAL__4-15-15.pdf.

Barney, J. (1991) Firm resources and sustained competitive advantage. *Journal of Management*, 17(1), 99–120.

Central Penn Business Journal (2015) Central Penn Business Journal website, accessed May 27, 2015, www.cpbj.com/article/20150316/CPBJ01/150319808/report-bostonbased-private-equity-firm-acquires-pennsylvania-fuel-terminal-network.

Kaplan, R. and Norton, D. (1996) *The Balanced Scorecard*. Boston, MA: Harvard Business School Press.

McKinsey (2008) Enduring Ideas: The 7-S Framework. *McKinsey Quarterly*, March, accessed on October 21, 2015 www.mckinsey.com/insights/strategy/enduring_ideas_the_7-s_framework.

Porter, M. (1980) *Competitive Strategy: Techniques for Analyzing Industries and Competitors*. New York: Free Press.

Porter, M. (1985) *Competitive Advantage: Creating and Sustaining Superior Performance*. New York: Free Press.

Prahalad, C.K. and Hamel, G. (1990) The core competence of the corporation. *Harvard Business Review*, 68(3), 79–91.

12

CHOOSING AND IMPLEMENTING CORPORATE ACTIONS

Choosing and implementing corporate actions is the strategic focus that marks the third and fourth steps of the adaptive coping cycle, where pursuant to a choice changes are made in the production or conversion processes and new products or services offered are in line with the perceived need for change. The issues requiring a decision by an organization can arise from three sources. First, they are prior outcomes, different scenarios, or the various pending decisions resulting from the previous focus, determining the corporate direction through analysing (Chapter 11). Second, they arise from critical events that require decision responses occurring on a regular basis in most organizations. Third, they come from the need to respond to situations of significant threat that face the organization, which by definition do not occur on a regular basis. In the case of critical events occurring in the regular course of business or of the need to respond to significant unforeseen threats, when time permits, they are analysed in the previous focus with a set of alternatives and then are processed in this focus. Decisions and implementation need to comply with the organization's cultural and ethical norms for corporate social responsibility. In this chapter, the decision-making and implementation content is examined first. This is followed by an examination of the process: first, the decision process, both who and how, and then the implementation process are presented and followed by discussions of roles and interlevel interactions. Figure 12.1 summarizes the *choosing and implementing corporate actions* focus.

The content of choosing and implementing corporate actions

The content of this focus, as we have stated, includes at least five components: a set of outcome scenarios deriving from the available alternatives and uncontrollable external conditions, the alternatives themselves, the decision (or choice) to be made, the ethical and cultural norms guiding the choice, and actionable steps

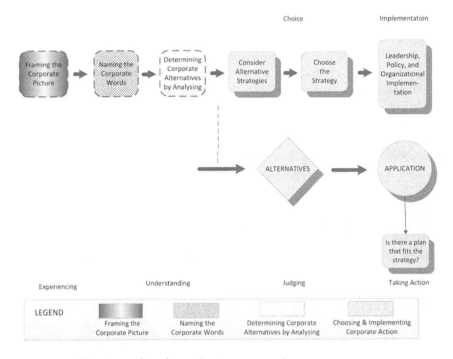

FIGURE 12.1 Choosing and implementing corporate actions

necessary to implement alternatives. Each component is critical for the selection and implementation of corporate actions. Each of these components, the possible outcomes, the set of alternatives, the decision process, the guiding ethical norms, and the implementation directive forms a part of the whole. It is necessary to pare down the alternatives available, resulting in the actual number of alternatives from which to choose. If only one remains, revisiting the analysis focus is recommended because only one alternative precludes choice: if there is only one alternative, then there is no choice to be had and one decision results by default. On the other hand, too many alternatives are not desirable either as this may signify that the analysis focus used criteria which were not stringent enough. Neither of these conditions, namely one choice or too many choices, is desirable.

Implementation has two major aspects. They are: setting implementation criteria and delineating implementation processes. Criteria are necessarily tied to the goals and objectives being pursued, they are a function of what is being optimized in the decision. Criteria result from the analysis focus and need to be agreed upon by the leader, the senior management, and ideally also accepted more broadly by members of the organization. The criteria resulting from the analysis focus may be such things as: the financial ratios, the level of anticipated success, turnover, ethics, and/or other elements anticipated in the analysis phase that must be stated as goals that can be measured. Additional criteria can come from benchmarking comparable organizations or even from industry-measured averages. It is important to tie criteria to precise goals with a clear agreement of what constitutes success as this sets up the stage for the focus described in Chapter 13, evaluating corporate outcomes. The leader is critical in setting up these criteria because of his/her interaction with counterpart leaders who may provide a good sense of the competition. Organizations that are innovators have to determine these criteria internally. The senior management group also has their outside sources. Members of this group tend to be narrower in their approach because their vision is usually coloured by technical expertise in functional areas and also by some degree of turf concern. As a result it is important to take the senior management group's opinions into consideration with perhaps some degree of caution in order to avoid overemphasis.

Implementation steps depend directly on the type of decision and the resulting order of change, as depicted in Figure 12.2 at the end of the chapter. Implementation of a new corporate picture requires a new organization. Development of a new organizational driver requires some level of restructuring. Other more basic changes, i.e. new products or services, will require new goals and new criteria. The implementation directive, i.e. the detail of how to implement, is often neglected in the name of speedy decisions. Implementation details are necessary for the completion of this focus. The complexity of these details varies directly with the type and level of change that has been decided upon. Incremental change by its nature requires no adaptation in basic approaches or in execution philosophy. For example, in a production system taking up slack, incremental change occurs until new processes are required. On the other hand, discontinuous third-order loop change can require restructuring or reformulating the organization together with cultural shifts, an ambitious implementation agenda which requires great detail as well as large-scale change (Chapter 7).

In 2012 the commercial pharmaceutical packaging operations of a northeastern drug development and supply company were purchased by a private equity firm specializing in healthcare. The objective was to expand the scope of the original commercial pharmaceutical packaging operations to include other healthcare packaging services. Although there was a clearly formulated strategy to expand into other areas of health-related packaging services, the whole plan depended on precise execution in expanding into clinical trial packaging, laboratory packaging, and later into contract manufacturing support services. While the company's main drivers are flawless customer service and technical knowledge to develop top quality in both contract manufacturing and award-winning proprietary packaging solutions, the strategy depended on successful execution of a series of company acquisitions. The company leadership had previous experience on both ends of dozens of mergers and acquisitions, which allowed for the successful incorporation of operations and consequent growth of the company. The content of the implementation in this situation included not only the clear formulation of the strategy but also the requisite skills in merging companies. This need for implementation expertise in mergers is not uncommon. Some technology companies, exemplified by Cisco Systems, have over the decades developed significant core capabilities in identifying companies with special synergies and in integrating acquired companies in a very efficient manner. Indeed, the stated strategy of selected private equity funds is to use a management team's acquisition expertise to execute 'roll-ups' in specific sectors and/or geographic areas.

Any strategic option will carry some implementation detail from the analysis performed in the third focus. Some evaluation goals are brought forward from that focus as well. Who decides and who is involved in the role of decision-making discussed above becomes critical in the implementation. If people do not own a part in the decision, they will not own a part in the implementation. The internal business perspective of Kaplan and Norton's (1996) Balanced Scorecard approach mentioned in Chapter 11 is embedded in this focus. A major part of the implementation aspect of this focus is encompassed by the processes and measures required.

The process of choosing and implementing corporate actions

The outcome scenarios and action alternatives derived in focus three, *determining corporate alternatives by analysing*, can carry a bias with them. When the leader or senior management group is invested in the analysis process, this can have both a positive and negative effect. It is positive in so far as it helps in the selection and implementation process because of prior engagement in the analysis. It is negative in so far as it pre-empts their freedom to choose equally among all alternatives, especially those still not fully understood because of imperfect information. When a significant investment of monies and time has been spent on analysis, it is very clear that a decision of some sort is required to complete the process. In this situation, not to decide and implement is not acceptable because of the level of investment made in the analysis.

The decision-making process

The few issues that require a decision without analysis come to the leader with a critical time limitation. Some of these are decided in combination with the senior management group while the leader alone decides others. These issues arise from changes in existing plans, unforeseen changes in the environment or customer base, or threatening elements from within or outside the organization. One such example is the Wawa case when Dick Woods had set a goal for margin of profitability on gasoline. The change in the world oil marketplace, causing the changing prices at the retail level, made it impossible to achieve this margin. To accept this as a loss just to encourage customers to come to the stores was not enough. He wanted to determine what approach would return the margin to its original goal. Then he had to decide how to do it. This is an example of a critical event triggering a new round of analysis and decision-making.

Some alternative strategic options should ideally be reduced to two choices in order to expedite and facilitate decision-making and implementation. The process in which this reduction is accomplished can implicitly help determine the choice. A quick reduction of alternatives to one favourite alternative result entails the flawed consequence that no decision is a real choice. It lacks the comparison of a pro-con tradeoff examination between two good choices. Yet, this is a common enough default process often used and often resulting in no one feeling good about the decision. The more people who are tied to a particular alternative in the decision process, the more difficult it is to pare down the alternative matrix. When the leader is engaged in this by him or herself, intuition and a gut sense may form a big part of the selection process. Analogously, when the senior management group works together to pare down the decision matrix some members find it difficult to resist the temptation to protect their own turf. This influences the decision choices they would like to keep on the table. Is also illustrates the driving force effect on the reduction of alternatives (Chapter 10).

The reduction of alternatives has a direct connection with the corporate picture (Chapter 9). How does each alternative fit the corporate picture? Some alternatives may be eliminated because they do not fit within the corporate picture. The corporate words have an impact as well. Does one alternative fit the driving force of the organization better than any other? The remaining criteria tend to be outcome oriented. Which one will increase market share? Which one increases return on investment? Which one meets shareholder acceptance? Which one fits customer needs the best? Sometimes a decision tree is constructed with each path given a value on a set of criteria. The process works best if it is selected before the decision point. How the decision is made can and does have outcome implications.

There are several mental processes normally being used in complex decision-making. One of these might be described as a purely rational and analytical process sometimes referred to as playing it by the numbers. This process can be linked to a deductive approach in which pros and cons, costs and benefits are examined using codified knowledge, time-tested analytical techniques, and sound reasoning in light of the objectives to be pursued. Another might be described as a more intuitive approach, referred to as using a gut feeling or the sensing activity that opens up an agenda for change. Although later verifiable through judgement, this process can be linked to a more inductive approach in which experience plays a major role, tacit knowledge gains stronger weight, and unknowns are taken into account in subjective ways. These and other approaches can be used on their own but often are used together. Christian Haub at A&P can be seen to have used both. He had a good gut feeling of what could be transplanted from Canada to the USA and then ran the numbers to assure himself and the board that his intuitive perception was supported by unbiased examination of the data and that the strategy would work. Of course decision-making may also be governed by interlevel political processes as discussed later in this chapter, and by the tacit defensive routines inhibiting learning discussed in Chapter 5. Analysis after intuition is the decision process that uses intuition to set the stage and analysis to work out the details. The advantage of this approach is a reduction in work because only the most promising choices are processed. Using analysis alone has the disadvantage of too much detail work and lack of focus (analysis paralysis). Intuition alone has the advantage of being quick, but the disadvantage of not having good detail and of possibly being wrong because something important is missed. Probably the most common approach is the use of intuition after the analysis has been done. The decision is not made on the basis of the numbers alone, but by using intuition to consider the best fit for the organization, the situation, and the organization's ability to implement. Decision speed is important when contextual conditions affecting a whole industry sector are faced by individual organizations. How these organizations react can provide a distinct, if often temporary, competitive advantage. The CEO who is quick to react to a situation that affects the total industry is the one who stands to gain the most in the case of a correct decision. One main objective of using this focus in this way is to provide a quick and decisive response.

The implementation process

Once the strategic decision has been made, leadership, policy and organizational implementation follow. The second step in this focus is the directive of implementation and the preliminary setting of evaluation criteria. Once the decision is made, leadership implementation consists of putting together a brief on why and how the decision was made and the steps needed to implement the decision. This is usually provided to anyone needed in implementation. Work commences on policies and plans on what needs to be done. This has traditionally been a motivational component of getting the chosen strategy to be accepted.

Implementation of decisions has traditionally been a group of action policies and procedures that breaks down the strategy into tactical and operational elements and goals which, when accomplished, provide a path for the organization to achieve the end determined as correct by the strategy. This is the Taylor-like process of dividing the overall work into smaller pieces of work. When they are integrated, those elements, united with other elements, form a coherent set of actionable strategic objectives for the organization. Sophisticated information systems control these interactions and relationships in large organizations. The extent of the decision drives the organization to be restructured if need be. A major change in a large organization requires extensive work to identify changes in job flows, in locations, and, in some cases, changes in organizational purpose to enable implementation of the decision. By the time an organization has been reorganized, it will have moved into the evaluation focus of the strategic plan. The more encompassing the change that is required to enable new functions, the greater the need for restructuring will be.

Financial services firms focusing on retail investment advisory and brokerage have faced a dynamic competitive landscape in recent decades due to the proliferation of online investment support tools and the transaction disintermediation effect of the Internet, which allows for direct trading and streamlines transactions. One important challenge these companies face is the consequent change in investor preferences, as according to a McKinsey report affluent investors under 40 years old are three times more likely to apply for new investment accounts on line and as much as 50 per cent more amenable to interacting with financial advisors via virtual meetings. Implicit in this statement is the need for financial services advisories to find the middle ground between the 'do-it-yourself' model and the 'full support' financial advisor that had previously been the norm. What needs to be accomplished is clear, namely to provide financial support that addresses the needs of a younger, technology-savvy generation and spread resources efficiently. Mobile technology allows for better understanding of individual consumer preferences in a wide range of services, such as entertainment, retail and gastronomy, for example, and financial advisors know they need to understand the individual characteristics of each potential investor. They know 'what' is necessary, but the 'how', i.e. the implementation, has been elusive. The process of implementation involves identifying how strategic action will be executed.

Roles in choosing and implementing corporate actions

Who makes the decision? Who owns it? These questions are at the heart of strategic choice. The variations of decisions are not as straightforward as we might want to believe. Furthermore, the way in which the process is perceived by members of the organization will most often have important outcome effects. We now examine the different perspectives on choosing and implementing corporate actions.

The role of the leader when taking sole decision-making responsibility

It is quite common in start-up organizations, family-owned companies, or in organizations facing a crucial life or death situation to observe the leader making decisions alone. The obvious advantage is that the process is quick. On the other hand, alternative points of view are not considered as there will be no input other than that developed by one individual. The risk and the reward are concentrated in one person and the responsibility for the decision is unquestioned.

The leader making the decision with consensus of the senior management team, but still keeping sole responsibility, is an approach seen in larger more complex organizations with senior management that works well as a team and have multiple interdependencies. The advantage is that the approach can be carried out quickly and has more input than that of the leader alone. Yet, the risk and reward are still concentrated in one person and responsibility for the decision is focused. Wawa is a good example of this approach. Dick Woods made the decision after general agreement was reached in the senior management group. He discussed the issues and wanted to be sure to get all of the input before making the decision. This action reinforced the core mission of the organization, to care for the customer, because the leader cared to hear the senior management group's input and take it into account in his own decision-making.

In large organizations with strong CEOs typically what is observed is the CEO making the decision with consultation. This consultation can be either internal or external and sometimes involves both. This approach is quick in that the CEO controls timing and desired input is selected by expertise. This expert input can be in terms of decision content or, alternatively, can involve the process. The disadvantage is that the decision can be perceived as a 'fiat' from on high and support from the organization may not be forthcoming in carrying out the decision.

The role of the senior management group when sharing responsibility with the leader in deciding

In larger organizations with strong senior management groups a sharing of the decision-making responsibility between the leader and the senior management group is often observed. While this is not the quickest approach, it has the distinct merit of ensuring support from the functional areas of the organization which have taken part in the decision, as they will be more inclined to execute the decision. A variation of this approach is open discussion of all decision matters with senior management. The discussion is held openly until dissent is removed and then the decision is made by the functional member of senior management when the decision is in their own area. This does delay decisions and needs a process facilitator to make sure the senior group does not prevaricate with decisions postponed. The Saint Joseph's University senior management group, during the time of the case presented in Chapters 5 and 6, was functioning with shared responsibility. The senior management group heard input from all others in the group before making the decisions that affected their functional area. This flowed from a larger inclusive planning process by the university's constituent groups. By sharing the discussion, senior management could convey to the constituent groups why and how the decision was made.

Senior management making the decision after consultation is most often used in large organizations with strong senior management groups: input is sought from those with expertise. This input can be from internal sources, for example in the form of details of the analysis focus by the members who performed it. The input can also be from external sources, such as in the use of consultants in setting the context and process for a complex decision. The advantage in the use of multiple inputs is the resulting wide perspective. However, the process can also be time-consuming and somewhat frustrating if the analysis is too far removed from the decision, allowing things to change in the interval. VerticalNet used this approach for acquisition decisions. Senior managers in each vertical network were involved in deciding who could be purchased and who could add overall strength to each area of the company business.

The senior management group making the decision with consensus is the most highly process-oriented decision methodology. It is most often seen in large organizations with a strong tradition of and desire to involve members in the analysis and decision-making. Such organizations are often involved in high technology, aerospace, or other technical and scientific fields in which highly specialized knowledge, whether codified or tacit, can make or break a decision. The distinct advantage of this type of decision-making is the commitment of each member of the organization involved in execution of the decision. The disadvantage is that a consensus is difficult to achieve in a short period of time, and may even require an internal process consultant. Organizational examples of this decision-making process are rare.

The role of the board of directors

The CEO may have closure and final say in most organizations, but major decisions are subject to ratification by the board of directors. Normal procedures involve operating responsibility for the CEO and senior management, and policy responsibility for the board of directors. This interaction can be easy or difficult depending on the personalities, temperament, and career history of the participants. When the board becomes an operating board there is a distinct role change by members. They become a second senior management group. The career backgrounds and the expertise brought to the board become the board members' portfolios, e.g. the bankers may become finance officers, the accountants may become controllers, the leaders of other organizations may become alternative CEOs, while board members with marketing experience may take on marketing and sales roles. In these situations the board may act like a competing senior management group.

The role of the OD consultant

The role of OD consultant in this focus is mostly a process role, rather than a content one. To engage in content at this point would be to have direct input in the decision, which is rarely called for. The appropriate process role of an OD consultant is to keep the process on track, free from bias, to engage the proper people and to avoid getting involved in the actual decision. The OD consultant's role at Saint Joseph's University was of this nature. Hired to start an inclusive planning process, the OD consultant remained involved in the evolution of the process through decision-making and implementation. Sometimes, the OD consultant's role may be assigned to a member of the organization. While this is a difficult role to perform from within, it can be very helpful when done in an unbiased and effective way because the internal member has so much knowledge of the organization itself. When the OD consultant loses focus on process and drifts into content, he or she may be triggering his or her own demise.

Selected interlevel dynamics issues in choosing and implementing corporate actions

As decision-making lies with senior management, the interlevel dynamics of this focus concentrates mostly on the leader and the senior management group, organization members are also involved.

A central aspect of the interlevel dynamics in the *choosing and implementing corporate actions* focus is the political and competitive dynamics in the interdepartmental groups because different alternatives may have very different functions as supporters. There is likely to be a perceived winners and losers outcome. Hence an important covert agenda is the extent to which individuals' and teams' attitudes and inferences are privately held, with the possible result that issues pertaining to the planning process, which certain factions believe to be incorrect, are never surfaced or discussed (Argyris, 1985). This becomes the hidden area of what is not chosen or discussed openly within the organization.

Interlevel dynamics issues involving the leader

As seen in the previous section, the leader is the final decision-maker. Most leaders bring an outside perspective, in the form of a gatekeeper role, by looking at the competition through exchanges with other leaders. The CEO also is most often the one to see problem areas that are internal to the organization when they are cross-functional. This comes from having an overall view of the organization. Both of these characteristics give the leader a unique perspective in decision-making but also have interlevel dynamics implications.

Level I aspects of these two perspectives are profound. Leaders bring their beliefs, experience, career paths, and anchors with them. These factors provide team members, board members, and OD consultants with insights into the leader. There is a clear relationship between anchors, decision-making processes, career paths, and the perspective taken in a gatekeeper role.

The leader also is responsible for closure in the decision process. In most organizations, the leader is expected to have the final word. Expectations are such that there is the perception that a decision is not final until the leader has acted on it. CEOs who like to take risks often reject closure on the grounds of wanting to wait to find a better solution. CEOs who like closure can often be rushed to conclusions in order to be finished with the decision. Leaders in their decision role continuously interface with senior management groups and when this interface is prolonged and the differences between alternatives ambiguous at best, the leader can get trapped into deciding along the lines of his or her own past career experience.

Sometimes when the leader makes the decision alone, his or her involvement in the previous focus, i.e. in the analysis phase, becomes important and highly desirable. When he/she is required to make a final decision on a process of which they have not been part, the outcome can be unexpected, resulting in negative interlevel consequences as different functions and members will react differently to an unforeseen result.

Interlevel dynamics issues involving the senior management group

Senior management group members have different levels of involvement in different scenarios or in different alternatives sets. With the responsibility for functional areas, senior team members can find it difficult to separate the corporate good from their functional perspectives. The role of being defender of a particular function, when that function is under attack or is up for change, conflicts with the role of being open to the greater good. Often, conversations on quality of analysis will have occurred with some of their subordinates who have worked on the analysis phase, including scenario and alternative selection. In critical events, sometimes the solution comes to the leader from one of the senior group members because the solutions that solve the problem lie within that senior member's area.

Interlevel dynamics issues involving the organization's members

The role of the members of the organization varies greatly by type of decision, time allotted for making the decision, and magnitude and degree of importance of the decision. In general most members do not have a role in the analysis or the decision. Some members of the organization do have a role in the analysis, but not in the decision. In some more complex organizations, those who worked on the analysis phase are given the chance to provide input into the final decision.

Interlevel dynamics are/can be affected by the level of member involvement in the decision process. Members can be aware of decision processes going on in the organization, but not be involved at all. They can be involved in one phase of analysis, but not involved in decisions. They can be involved in the analysis and the decision. Lastly, a member can also not be involved or even be aware that a decision process is going on. The issue of member involvement is important because of implementation consequences: the more collaboration that occurs in the decision, the more involved participation will be in implementation. Repeated non-involvement will generate a culture of defensive routines. On the other hand, the higher the number of people collaborating with the choice process, the more difficult it will be to limit the number and scope of alternatives. Over time this generates an open, non-defensive routine culture in an organization. Yet the external analysis, which often does not include most members, must weigh heavily in the choice process. Customers, clients, financial markets, macroeconomic conditions, and institutional changes are factors in the external environment that help decide whether the organization will succeed or fail and therefore need to be taken into consideration and shared with members if they are to fully support an unexpected decision.

Conclusions

In this chapter we have described the focus *choosing and implementing corporate actions*, which deals with the selection and structured implementation of a strategic plan of action with its concurrent tactical and operational plans. The content of this focus involves understanding and incorporating the factors resulting from the analytical focus, as well as the others, into the choice and execution of a selected strategic direction and set of related activities and structural changes. The process aspect, namely that of choosing and implementing corporate actions, looks at the bias and influence on the selection process that comes from sources other than the analysis focus. Table 12.1 outlines the task and relational issues in choosing and implementing corporate actions.

The leader's perspective on choosing and implementing corporate action is that the action desired and planned takes place and that there is congruence between the corporate picture, the corporate words, the analysis and the action. Members need to know how their own micro-level action contributes to the macro-level objectives, outlook and situation, and whether senior management even cares about their contribution. OD consultants look for a basic honesty in evaluating action options, and for minimal defensive routines deriving from turf-related issues for example. They watch for continuing resistance and dysfunction. The outcomes of choosing and implementing corporate actions are coherent, coordinated and owned actions that are congruent with the corporate picture, the corporate words and the analysis through which long-term survival and productivity are achieved.

Figure 12.2 depicts the triple loop inquiring model as applied to choice selection and implementation issues, i.e. how the outcome of this focus can influence strategic direction. Each loop has two questions, the first pertaining to content in choosing and implementing corporate actions, and the second pertaining to process. The single loop inquiry reflects the possibility that the choice or implementation might have been based on flawed analysis. The double loop inquiry reflects the possibility that the decision and/or implementation failed to take into account the specifics of the driving forces, perhaps including the need to adapt or change one. Lastly, the triple loop inquiry examines the closeness of fit between the choice and implementation and the prevailing corporate picture. As in each previous focus, a single loop inquiry correction might require revisiting the analysis focus. A double loop inquiry correction might mean re-examining the corporate words. Likewise, a need to address a triple loop inquiry inaccuracy would signal the desirability of again reflecting on the corporate picture including the mission and vision of the organization.

TABLE 12.1 Assessment and action template for choosing and implementing corporate actions

	TASK	*RELATIONAL*
Content	Actual plan alternatives	Ownership of plans
Process	Decision-making Implementation processes	Political dynamics of choice and implementation
Culture	Meaning of plans to organization	Defensive and non-defensive routines

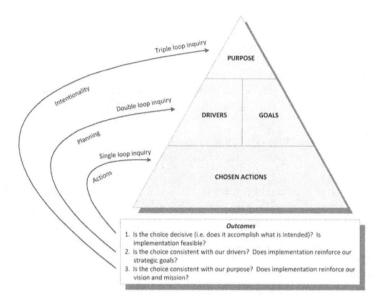

FIGURE 12.2 Single, double and triple loop inquiries when choosing and implementing corporate actions

Reflexive engagement activity 12.1

Below you will find a blank Table 12.2. In relation to an organization with which you are familiar, fill in the boxes with what you see as the important content, process and cultural issues in task and relational terms for that organization in choosing and implementing corporate outcomes. Discuss this with your team, or better still, copy the blank form and invite them to fill in the blanks prior to your discussion.

Reflexive engagement activity 12.2

Adopting the clinical approach, reflect on choosing and implementing corporate outcomes from the four perspectives. In relation to an organization with which you are familiar, reflect on the following perspectives and try to answer the questions.

Leaders

Corporate leaders, whether the CEO or members of senior management group or divisional heads may consider the following questions:

- Is the planned and desired action taking place?
- Is the action ensuring the organization's survival?
- What has slipped between the picture, the words, the analysis and the action?
- Are the actions ethical?

	TASK	*RELATIONAL*
Content		
Process		
Culture		

TABLE 12.2. Reflexive activity

Members

Non-executive members may consider the following questions:

- Are the actions realistic?
- Do I feel part of the decision?
- Do I feel part of the change?

OD consultants

OD consultants may pose the following questions:

- Is there consistency of effort across the organization?
- Is there dysfunction in the action?
- Are there people distressed and fighting the action?

Outcomes

In terms of $L=P+Q$, what P from choosing and implementing corporate outcomes is challenged from your experience of the outcomes in your organization?

- Is there a plan for implementation?
- Are there criteria for evaluation?
- Is the implementation sufficient to accomplish actions needed?

Case: Saint Joseph's University

Saint Joseph's University's first strategic plan was concluded in 1996 and covered five years, and the process was repeated in 2000, but faculty wanted a stronger voice. In 2004, the Institutional Planning Committee (IPC) issued a progress report to inform the university community about the status of its efforts to draft a new strategic plan for Saint Joseph's. What follows is a description of the process then instituted for development of the strategic plan and its supplemental documents for all divisions to better participate in long-term strategic planning and projected changes in the annual budgeting cycle.

During the latter part of the spring semester and early summer, the IPC engaged various constituencies at the university in discussing the seven initiatives which would constitute the heart of the new strategic plan, dubbed the 2010 plan. The seven initiatives were originally forwarded to the IPC by the president after consultation with the senior management group. During June and July the IPC Drafting Committee reviewed input gathered at these community sessions, incorporating contributions into further revisions of the initiatives and other sections of the projected plan. The Drafting Committee had also been reviewing recommendations developed through the Middle States process (the university's accreditation agency) to ensure that all were represented in the new plan. Additionally, the committee reviewed and revised the SWOT analysis and reviewed other strategic tools which were included in the plan. Finally, the enrolment profile discussed by the community earlier in the spring went through yet another revision and provided the basis for a five-year enrolment management plan.

The strategic plan was supported with more detailed six-year plans designed to make the goals of the overall strategic plan operational. The following six targeted corollary plans were put in place: a capital plan, an enrolment management plan, a financial plan, a comprehensive campaign plan, a diversity plan, and an assessment plan. A draft of a capital plan was completed by the vice presidents and senior management group. The enrolment management plan was drafted and reviewed by a new enrolment management task force when it was completed. The Budget Advisory Committee (BAC) worked on the financial plan. The Development Office drafted the comprehensive fund-raising plan linked to strategic goals and the IPC Drafting Committee put together the diversity plan based on the Report of the Diversity Commission in 2000 and the International Education Task Force Report of 2003. An assessment plan for the university was developed. A subsequent step in the new planning process was the creation of five-year plans for all divisions of the university. In Academic Affairs, for example, this meant that each of the colleges would have its own five-year plan, based on the broader strategic plan and its corollary documents. Next, each department would draft a multi-year plan (three- or five-year) based on both the university's strategic plan and the respective college plan. These plans would then be the basis for requests for resources from the Budget Advisory Committee for each ensuing fiscal year.

This institutionalization of the strategic plan process underwent a few changes in the ensuing years under a new president. First, the duration of strategic plans was extended to cover a decade. Second, detailed three-year plans were instituted on a rolling basis. Third, the main characteristic of the process, namely broad constituent participation and support continued. The financial crisis of 2008 coupled with the evolving demographics of the country resulted in pressures on Higher Education and a 2020 plan was developed under these challenging conditions. In many institutions of higher learning in the US, the period from 2008 onward was indeed characterized by budgetary pressures, leading to erosion of goodwill on the part of the faculty and to a gradual drift towards a more hands-on role on the part of the Boards of Trustees.

It is interesting to note the cyclical nature of organizations. Saint Joseph's University was in 2015 in a much stronger position than it had been 30 years earlier, having become a prestigious regional institution, with AACSB accreditation, strong Phi Beta Kappa participation, high ranking departments, and other noteworthy indicators of academic recognition and success. On the other hand, recent years of difficulty balancing budgets coupled with strong Board of Trustees emphasis on business aspects had resulted in decreased faculty confidence. Therefore, as of 2015 the new president of Saint Joseph's University is facing challenges not dissimilar to those of 30 years before.

Questions for reflection and discussion

1. What insights have you about how organizational levels and interlevel dynamics frame your understanding of how Saint Joseph's University went about choosing and implementing its corporate actions? Where's your evidence in the case as described?
2. What insights have you about the quality of engagement in the choosing and implementing process? Where's your evidence in the case as described?
3. Would other organizations have the time required to approach the implementation process in this manner?
4. What insights from this case might you bring to other organizational settings?

References

Argyris, C. (1985) *Strategy, Change and Defensive Routines*. Marshfield, MA: Pitman.
Kaplan, R. and Norton, D. (1996) *The Balanced Scorecard*. Boston, MA: Harvard Business School Press.

13

EVALUATING CORPORATE OUTCOMES

Evaluating measured outcomes of corporate actions is the strategic focus linked to the final step of the adaptive coping cycle, in which feedback enables the exploitation of learning to take place and provides the foundations for a new adaptive coping cycle. This functional focus is concerned with the evaluation and organizational learning components of strategic management. As we have done with the other foci, we examine sequentially the content of evaluating corporate outcomes, the process of this focus, the roles of different stakeholders, and selected issues in the interlevel dynamics. Furthermore, contingency planning should also be made an explicit result of this focus, in order to prepare for and avoid several potential pitfalls in case events do not occur as planned. As mentioned in Chapter 8, and as detailed in Part IV, the use of each focus is not sequential as when probing each focus, the degree of examination and the loop of inquiry becomes explicit, shedding light on which focus should be reviewed next. That having been said, a simplifying temporal analogy could help clarify each focus and sharpen its emphasis. *Framing the corporate picture* and *naming the corporate words* deal respectively with foundations and drivers, *determining corporate alternatives by analysing* looks at the future through analysis, and *choosing and implementing corporate actions* mainly visualizes the present through implementation. This focus, *evaluating corporate outcomes*, is a past-perfect endeavour, attempting to understand whether actions taken are consistent with the other four foci. Figure 13.1 summarizes the *evaluating corporate outcomes* focus.

The content of evaluating corporate outcomes

The evaluation methodology starts with a set of prior expectations and assumptions about the then-future goals and structure of the organization. Key questions on the content are straightforward such as: Have we achieved the preset targets? Have we

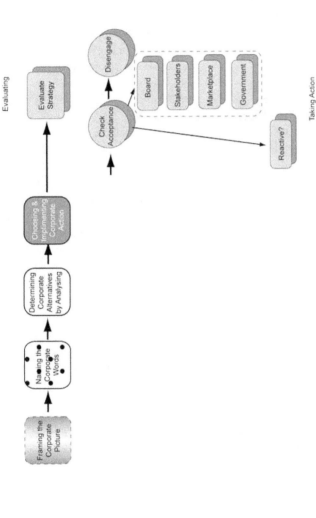

FIGURE 13.1 Evaluating corporate outcomes

made our marketing goals? The evaluation takes place through a careful review of the set goals over a set timeframe. Incremental deviations are evaluated for impact and meaning. Large deviations are studied for their relevance and causality (are the main contributing factors internal or external?) The intuition that comes into play then forms higher-order change questions. Has the paradigm shifted? Is there a change taking place that is larger than the original analysis dealt with? The question of second-order change is also clarified by the outcome of the process review of each focus. If more than one focus is found to be contributing to the failure to reach strategic goals it is very likely that a second-order change is required.

Evaluation occurs within every set of actions that are tracked and reviewed. Each of the four other foci contains an internal review process, which evaluates within the respective focus. The evaluation functional focus we now address differs from previous intra-focus evaluations in that it evaluates final outcomes, i.e. it evaluates the effectiveness of the total strategic plan with its successes or failures looking for clues of possible higher-order change. Evaluation criteria are first outlined in the focus on analysis, and selected and spelled out for implementation in the focus on decision-making. They are now examined and applied in this focus. The criteria used are applicable to incremental or discontinuous outcomes depending on which choice was made. A common failure is to not do any evaluation at all. In addition to the internally developed criteria of the *determining corporate alternatives by analysing* focus, judgement is made from external comparisons to the organization as well. Evaluation leads to learning.

Criteria from outside sources

Every organization is evaluated by critical outside sources. Owners or shareholders evaluate for-profit organizations on a continuous basis. Evaluation criteria for publicly traded companies include their stock price and resulting company valuations, the level of coverage by equity and debt research analysts, the content of that coverage, as well as the market value of their publicly traded debt. This constant evaluation comes from the outside world of capital markets, including analysts, traders and the general public and is not always based solely on company performance. Market conditions, macroeconomic issues, and overall market liquidity impacting the availability of funds to invest can all affect the price of traded instruments. Nonetheless these external factors are important as they determine the ability of the company to attract capital to develop and grow as an organization. Responding to these external evaluations and making them a part of the ongoing outcome evaluation process is a part of this focus. How outsiders perceive ongoing change is necessary input for the continued evaluation of the strategic plan, as well as important input for the continuation of this plan. To look at outside input as a threat rather than an opportunity can be a mistake. One example of this is the Saint Joseph's University initiative to upgrade networks and programmes (besides promoting faculty interest) related to online learning, a clear case of viewing an opportunity where many saw threats.

New relationships among stakeholders and changes in existing ones are important aspects of evaluating corporate outcomes. Some measure of the degree of customer satisfaction and employee motivation can offer significant information to the evaluation. Customer satisfaction leads to sales and success for the organization. The level of employee satisfaction provides a key element of the climate aspect of the organization. It is important to realize that this is one step beyond the measurement of an effective plan. This is leveraging the characteristics that have made this a successful organization and that have contributed to its success through giving the organization a sense of purpose and a positive climate. A more complex set of criteria attempts to clearly identify the unstated attitudes underlying selected criteria. What climate will be produced by these outcomes? Is this the climate that is appropriate for the organization? Customers are also part of this factor in that they hold unstated opinions and feelings on the outcomes. This can be a very difficult area to get in touch with for most organizations. New people who come to work in an organization are resources for this questioning before they are crafted into the culture of the organization.

As described in the case at the end of this chapter, Subsole, a Chilean fruit company adopted the strict standard that is required for the UK market, called EurepGAP, specifically designed by the main British and Continental European supermarket chains. Subsole not only decided to adopt that GAP standard but also to find a company in Chile that could certify with international validity that their growers met the standard and that way introduced the standard in Chile. They used one of the partners of the company as the pilot who was the first grower to be certified in Chile with EurepGAP. This took the evaluation focus one step further as change from the evaluation phase impacted yet another organization in its implementation of complex accounting standards.

The process of evaluation of their own set criteria, generated by meeting the outside source criteria of EurepGAP and certified by another organization became a significant strategic advantage. The company took advantage of this opportunity to differentiate itself from the rest of the competition, having agreed from the CEO downward to adopt this strategy.

The process of evaluating corporate outcomes

The implementation process requires a clear understanding from all who have input on how information is processed. In cases of large system change, non-measurable criteria are brought into play, as alluded to above. These need to be articulated and agreed upon by everyone. The reason for this has been discussed in phases and levels of change in large systems (Chapter 7). Key process questions that have to be asked in this focus are as follows: Are the significant criteria set before starting the evaluation? Can the criteria be applied in an open and equal way for everyone in the organization? Figure 13.2 provides a schematic representation of the

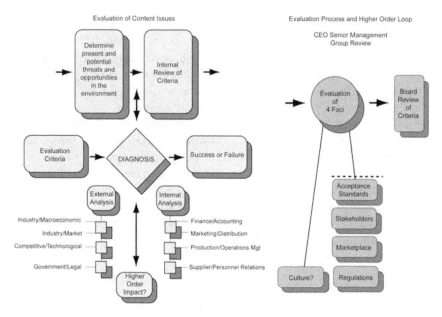

FIGURE 13.2 The process of evaluating corporate outcomes

relationship between the main components of the *determining corporate alternatives by analysing* focus and the *evaluating the corporate outcomes* focus from a process starting point. This includes revisiting corporate analysis with an evaluation focus while also examining the evaluation process at a higher order, usually incorporating input from each of the other foci.

The evaluation process involves reviewing outcomes and interpreting them. Some of the key questions that need to be asked are: Was there data contamination? Do all the affected people embrace the review process and accept the evaluation of outcome success or failure? Do we feel or intuit that the right questions were asked? Are there some larger issues that need to be addressed? A clear set of steps that will be pursued if different aspects of the strategic plan do not come into existence must be developed. These are often referred to as fall-back plans. It's easier to get agreement on these plans before they are needed than afterwards. Some sketch, even if it is rough, should be given on how outcomes will affect plans. Will certain outcomes cause second-order change? Third-order change? Will the people engaged in the change have an opportunity to belong in the new situations? A crucial characteristic of this focus, evaluating corporate outcomes, is the ability to feed information back into previous foci.

This was apparent in the early stages of Nutrisystem's transition from tele-marketing support of groups seeking to lose weight to a more individualized approach. As Nutrisystem became able to evaluate precisely the effectiveness of each of the hundreds of different advertisements through identification of web page or 800-number, understanding of each customer improved dramatically, allowing counsellors to address individual customers' needs in real time. This effective evaluation and precise use of information obtained eventually supported the company's success in changing the industry paradigm.

Roles in evaluating corporate outcomes

We now describe how evaluating corporate outcomes relates to the perspectives of the leader, of the senior management group, of the members and of the OD consultant.

The leader's role in evaluating corporate outcomes

The source of the discrepancy between expected results and those observed results is important information. If the outcomes do not match expectations from the analysis then corrections may be incremental and should not be difficult to make. The leader's role is to stay attuned and to assess the scale and sources of any discrepancy. Senior management's role is to find the source of the discrepancy and correct it without finger-pointing. Members need to find correct information and communicate it to senior management. The consultant's role is to maintain objectivity and facilitate the listening process, again avoiding finger-pointing.

NEST was founded in 1994 and has since evolved into a provider of a wide range of services (janitorial, routine cleaning and care, weather events, trade services, consulting, remodelling and retrofitting) to corporations with multi-facility maintenance and project management needs. Having developed a very unique and successful business model, the company boasts a Who's Who client list in the retail, restaurant and banking sectors, and has seen explosive growth in the years since 2008. In 2014 the company filled over 500,000 work orders for its more than 100 corporate clients.

In the CEO's mind the company's main issue was ensuring that the vision and the mission remained consistent with core values despite the expansion of service offerings and consequent accelerated growth. With the help of OD consultants, the CEO was able to unify various service- and sector-dependent versions of sales messages into a new foundation of how to pitch product offerings. Half a year into the experiment, the process was still ongoing, but the CEO had positive indications through an increase in outside deal closings and a larger average dollar amount associated with these contracts. The role of the CEO in this case encompassed the ability not only to ask the right question in the beginning and to guide the organization through the necessary changes, but also, and very importantly, to verify whether outcomes were matching objectives previously set.

If the outcomes do not match expectations and a solution requires a new critical skill to be developed by the organization, the corporate words focus needs to be revisited, perhaps resulting in the implementation of a structural change. The leader's role is to embrace the perceived need and lead the process of determining a new critical skill for the organization. Senior management's role is to look at the needs of the total organization and enable the individuals in their own functions to work through their own denying and dodging tendencies to avoid them in the face of change. Take the example of a retailer selling light fixtures and light bulbs. With increased marketplace emphasis on sustainability resulting in very long-life lighting equipment, the CEO correctly diagnosed the desirability of a third-order change leading the company to morph into a lighting services provider. In order to lead the company in that direction, support from the senior management group was needed.

The senior management group's role in evaluating corporate outcomes

When evaluating corporate outcomes, above all the senior management group needs to be focused on the objectives and outcomes of the organization as a whole. Especially when outcomes do not conform to expectations, finger-pointing is possible as senior management group members try to protect turf and avoid blame in their own functional areas. Several mechanisms are helpful in ensuring a cooperative relationship even in the face of disappointing results, such as a corporate culture that does not penalize risk-taking, an incentive structure which emphasizes results of the company as a whole, and systems which facilitate and reward open and timely communication, to name a few. The role of the senior management group, then, is to support the leader in the assessment of the situation and to identify any source of discrepancy occurring in the particular functional area under responsibility of the respective senior group member. Returning to the light fixture/light bulb retailer mentioned in the previous paragraph, the company was acquired by a larger conglomerate, and the new CEO preferred to follow the corporate-driven direction of maintaining the status quo rather than morphing the company into a lighting consulting services provider. After the acquisition, the senior management group aligned with the new CEO, with the result that a possible third-order change was not pursued.

The members' role in evaluating corporate outcomes

Member roles can run the gamut from minor adjustments in work methods to the need to look elsewhere for employment. An alternative is to search for and identify a new role within a changing and developing organization. For members who welcome and embrace challenges this may be difficult but can also be exciting. Their own career change may model the change in the organization, including the transition state on the way to a desired future.

The OD consultant's role in evaluating corporate outcomes

The key role for a consultant is to help manage the transition period during which observed results converge to those expected. If the desired future is not clearly articulated then this transition period may be difficult, so the consultant can assist in clearly articulating future goals and in helping to establish new functional groups and a new senior management group when required.

If the outcomes do not match expectations and the solution requires transitioning to a new organization, then the corporate picture needs to be revisited and a new organizational vision developed. The leader's role is to think and lead outside of the box. One solution could well be a different organization and a different leader. This type of thinking is not something done with ease. Senior management's role is to avoid panic and start a process, if possible, to generate a new organization from the ashes of the old. Members' roles may well be to look elsewhere. The OD consultant's role here is to help develop a transition process.

If outcomes cannot be measured then the decision and implementation focus needs to be revisited. The solution in this case can be as simple as a new measurement process or resetting goals so they can be measured. The leader's role in this endeavour is to ensure that the change is not a cover-up for a missed goal. Changing criteria is not recommended but changing measurement techniques to obtain the needed information is important and may be necessary to an organization. Senior management's role is not to get lost in the detail but to agree on the new techniques. Members need to buy into a new process. The OD consultant's role is to provide a bridge to the new process.

Selected interlevel dynamics issues in evaluating corporate outcomes

The task of evaluating corporate outcomes includes all four levels as individuals from all over the organization are involved in the evaluation. Teams, especially the senior management group, are involved as well. The implementation of this focus is centred on Level III, consisting of how different functional areas are involved in the evaluation process and how much time and energy is devoted to it. This is where possible win-lose behaviours are most evident and contribute in a large way to the culture of the organization. The evaluation in terms of outcome states contrasted with competitors is a Level IV analysis: 'Do the people most affected by the outcomes, customers, suppliers etc. agree with our assessment of the success or failure of the plan?'

The board's interaction with the CEO

The board in its totality acts at Level IV. It is responsible for the organization's choices as a total organization. From this point of view the board can disagree with the CEO and senior management. These disagreements, while painful, are essential for a strong organization. Sometimes divergent viewpoints are extreme and can produce a change of CEO. If the board functions as it should, it forms the conscience of the organization. Board members need the skill to confront the CEO in dialogue, when the situation requires it. This usually occurs through the board executive committee to the CEO, or through the chairman to the CEO.

The leader's interaction with the senior management group

It is important to make a distinction between the evaluations of the individual functions within the strategy and the overall success of the strategy itself. Sometimes individual functional goals are successful but the overall strategic goals are not achieved. The interlevel challenges arise in this evaluation of outcome perceptions between Level I (the leader) and Level II (the senior management group). A major point of conflict can be between the interdepartmental group (Level III), the senior management group (Level II), and the leader (Level I). Each of these will be addressed in turn.

The evaluation of the corporate outcomes most often resides with the senior management group and the CEO. This evaluation is prepared for them by the internal review team with financial criteria established by the internal audit team from within the organization with additional financial and control audit information provided by outside auditors. Sometimes key pieces of information come from customers or other unique individuals. Ultimately the board of directors evaluates this information. Another group brought into the loop is the financial analyst group representing capital market interests. Most organizations have or purchase outside analyst reports on themselves and their competitors. These documents are semi-public as investors and others can purchase them and because they can have such wide access they must in fact be considered public documents. This source of information provides knowledge to competitors as well as customers while introducing the larger system in which the organization operates into the mix.

Evaluation of both external and internal reviews provides the essence of the interlevel interaction between the senior management group and the leader. This discussion focuses on the nuances of how the data are aggregated and sliced to form information. The senior management group views the data from its interdepartmental perspective, while the leader looks at the data most often from the total organization's point of view or even from an outside point of view. Another aspect of the interaction of the leader (Levels I and IV) with the senior management group (Levels II and III) is the determination of missed criteria. Both the leader and the senior management group (Level IV) can disagree with the outside sources.

In the final analysis these are examined for range of deviations from the expected. When there are deviations it is critical to find out what went wrong. Are they due to poor outcomes, wrong strategy or the use of an incorrect model?

Level II (team level) interactions with Level III (interdepartmental level)

The Level II with Level III interlevel interaction is more often spent in evaluating the incremental deviations from goals. This questioning can be a way of testing the validity of the information. In this situation it is not uncommon for teams or groups to experience the typical finger-pointing between departments and functions. Some of this frustration can be avoided if goals are quantified in detail and agreed upon previously. As discussed in Chapter 5, denial is the first reaction to the possibility of change, then shifting to dodging, which at this point can take the form of blaming.

Returning to the Balanced Scorecard approach (Kaplan and Norton, 1996) presented in Chapter 10, the learning and growth perspective is part of the evaluations focus. In our view the learning and growth has three orders of change questions to be answered and goes beyond the Balanced Scorecard approach. It looks at the continuous adjustments to meet targets, at the discontinuous adjustments to ask what the organization wants to be, and therefore opens the possibility of self-reconfiguration to adapt and learn.

Conclusions

The continuous evaluation of strategic goals including comparing outcomes with previous expectations is often the weak link in the strategic process. Many organizations do not evaluate multiple year goals or look at the larger context. The five strategic foci enable this to occur on an ongoing basis as evaluation criteria are set early in the process and later changed as appropriate. The larger involvement of organization members also provides a gauge on progress, as goals are corporately owned, not held only by a select few, who could forget, leave their position, or even leave the organization. If ownership for change is owned by only a few it runs a serious risk of failure.

Leaders' perspectives on evaluation are whether outcomes are measurable and whether they reflect expectations and plans. Good outcomes need to be celebrated. Members' concerns are with the role of evaluation in relation to their own micro-level work and how evaluation affects their work in the longer term. OD consultants focus on whether evaluation takes place, whether it is before, during or after, whether it is celebrated and whether the evaluation brings change. The result of evaluating corporate outcomes is organizational learning and an input into a repetitive change cycle, which leads to increased profitability and integration of the strategy process of the corporate picture, the corporate words, the corporate direction, and action.

Feedback loops to other foci: Looking at the bigger picture

A higher-order evaluation process focuses on broader issues. It evaluates the contributions from each of the other foci in order to determine whether second- and third-order change is required. This process consists in reviewing contributions or lack thereof from the other four foci; examining whether the contributions of framing the corporate picture, naming the corporate words, determining corporate alternatives by analysing, and choosing and implementing corporate actions to the overall strategic plan were carried out or were attempted to be carried out. An important component of the evaluating corporate outcomes focus is the review of inter-relationships among the foci.

The basic first-order questions have been discussed above. These are the most often asked questions, some of which are even asked on a daily basis. They are the first-order feedback loop addressing the questions: Did we do what we said we would do? Higher-order questions are more complex. The second-order questions revisit the analysis and the decisions. They're less frequently asked: Have we made the appropriate choices? Were the key people who should have been involved in the decisions part of them? These questions send us back to the focus on choosing and implementing corporate actions. Other examples of second-order questions are: Did we use the appropriate analytic tools? Was the analysis broad enough and inclusive enough? These questions send us back to the focus on analysis. The least frequently asked questions are those investigating third-order change by examining effectiveness of driving forces and clarity of the corporate picture. These are the most difficult to ask: Does our major effort constitute our driving force? Do we know who we are? Is there broad understanding of what we are? Are we continuing to learn? Positive answers to these questions can include input from all four foci and probably will represent higher-order change.

These evaluation questions represent a different magnitude at each of the three orders of change. Operational issues and the resulting adjustments constitute continuous change. Organizations deal with these on a regular basis. Even adjusting the choice criteria and analysis methodology can at times be incremental. Change required to adjust driving forces or adapt a corporate picture is discontinuous change requiring much greater effort. Since these questions are not asked every day, when should they be asked? This should happen when operational goals are not met or shifting analysis methodology doesn't seem to help. In high-tech organizations existing in an environment of very fast-paced change, the timespan for asking these questions may be short. The need to morph into a new reality can occur in a very short period of time, such as a month or a few weeks, due to the volatility of the environment. The continual third-order question is, can we reassemble ourselves and still function successfully over an extended period of time on a regular and repeated basis in what we perceive to be the new environment?

Summary

The content of the fifth focus, *evaluating corporate outcomes*, is obtaining internal consensus on results, which implies an agreement not only on what worked and what did not work, but also on the orders of change necessary for the requisite course corrections. The process of this focus relates to the modus operandi of information collection, of analytical tool construction, of implementation procedures and of articulating learning so as to be able to exploit what has been learned and be adaptable to sensing new opportunities in the next coping cycle. As mentioned earlier in the book, culture is the residual, what remains as a result of actions taken and because evaluation processes tend to be important for an organization, they usually impact culture significantly. Table 13.1 outlines the task and relational issues in evaluating corporate outcomes.

Figure 13.3 provides a schematic representation of the various possible levels of change by exemplifying different questions which might be asked. Inquiries begin from corporate outcomes and lead to the sources of change. A single loop inquiry begins with corporate outcomes and investigates actions taken as well as the

TABLE 13.1 Assessment and action template for evaluating corporate outcomes

	TASK	RELATIONAL
Content	Consensus on what is successful or not Consensus on what needs to be changed	Satisfied customers Motivated workforce New relationships
Process	How information is collected How model was constructed How changes were made	How involved people are in the evaluation How honest people feel
Culture	What was evaluated and what was not questioned What new culture is forming	Protect turf, lack of openness Sense of fairness Sense of success and achievement

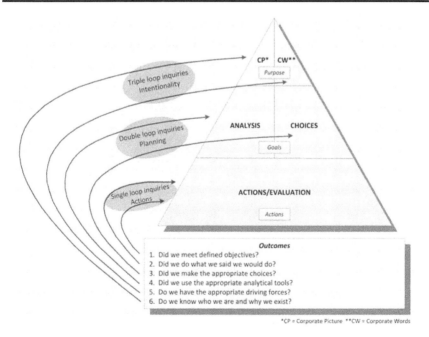

FIGURE 13.3 Cross-foci evaluation feedback questions resulting from evaluating corporate outcomes

evaluation process itself. A double loop inquiry begins with outcomes observed and questions the analysis and the selection of the preferred strategic choice. A triple loop inquiry uses outcomes to question the very framing of the corporate picture and naming of corporate words.

Reflexive engagement activity 13.1

Below you will find a blank Table 13.1. In relation to an organization with which you are familiar, fill in the boxes with what you see as the important content, process and cultural issues in task and relational terms for that organization in evaluating corporate outcomes. Discuss this with your team, or better still, copy the blank form and invite them to fill in the blanks prior to your discussion.

Reflexive engagement activity 13.2

Adopting the clinical approach reflect on the following perspectives in relation to an organization with which you are familiar, try to answer the questions.

	TASK	*RELATIONAL*
Content		
Process		
Culture		

TABLE 13.2. Reflexive activity

Leaders

Corporate leaders, whether the CEO or members of the senior management group or divisional heads may consider the following questions:

- Are the outcomes measurable and reflective of plans and expectations?
- Are they accurate?
- Is the action ensuring the organization's survival?
- Do we celebrate the outcomes?

Members

Non-executive members may pose the following questions:

- Do I agree with the evaluation?
- Do I concur with the evaluation process?
- Do I have a place in the new organization?

OD consultants

OD consultants may pose the following questions:

- Do they evaluate?
- Is evaluation leading to change?
- Do they celebrate?

Outcomes

In terms of $L=P+Q$, what P from evaluating corporate outcomes is challenged from your experience of the outcomes in your organization?

- Has the change met the challenges and opportunities that were the stimulus for change at the outset?

    a   What's your judgement about the organization's current health?

    b   What is your sense of what the external context will do next and how the organization is poised to adapt and cope?

Case: Exportadora Subsole S.A.

Exportadora Subsole S.A. is a Chilean fruit export company that specializes in the trade of fruits with North America, Europe and Asia. The company started in 1991 as an association of growers that decided to join forces to export Chilean fresh fruit.

It started mainly with table grapes and slowly opened itself to other types of fruit. Currently it ships over 10 million boxes of fruit annually such as grapes, avocados, kiwis, pomegranates, cherries, and citrus fruits to over 40 countries around the world and has an expressed commitment to agricultural systems and structures which not only are efficient but also, and most importantly, are both socially and environmentally sustainable.

Ten years after its foundation it had grown to export annually some 5,800,000 boxes with a free on board (FOB) value of 55 million US$. Subsole had faced turbulent times but had managed to overcome all of the obstacles to post a continuous annual growth. The core business operated as a trading company connecting growers, some of whom were part-owners of the company, and international fruit buyers. Its mission was (and is) to offer on-time delivery of healthy, fresh fruit to the North American, European and Asian markets.

The company was one of the few that exported fresh fruit from Chile to the UK market, which had the most complicated requirements because of very strong regulations regarding food handling and fruit growing. If a company were able to satisfy the UK market, it could satisfy virtually any other market. UK import market requirements were by and large considered the most stringent in the fruit industry.

To meet increasingly rigorous security requirements, agribusiness, especially fruit producers, needed to adapt given the product's vulnerability. Growers needed to make expensive changes to meet the strict UK standards: ignoring updated requirements meant forfeiting that important market. This challenge was significant, requiring the adoption of rigid standards of Good Agriculture Practices (GAP) that the company expected would be the way of the future.

Subsole, after a long analysis and discussion decided to adopt the strict EurepGAP farm management standard that had been created in the late 1990s by several European retail chains and suppliers, and which was widely accepted for the UK market. In doing so, Subsole was attempting to secure its leadership position and leverage its special relations with the UK market. Subsole not only decided to adopt that GAP standard but also decided to find a company in Chile that could provide internationally valid certification, thereby introducing the standard in Chile and empowering their growers to understand and meet that standard. Subsole used one of the company's partners as the pilot, namely the first grower to be certified in Chile with EurepGAP.

This product evaluation and certification process that met the EurepGAP requirements and that was certified by an outside organization became a significant strategic advantage. The company came to consider this an important factor for differentiation from the rest of the competition, and agreed from the CEO downward to adopt this strategy. To this end the company agreed to pay the growers for the changes and adaptations during the first year they were required to meet the standards. During the second and third years loans were provided to the growers for the further adaptation required to meet the standards.

Subsole therefore succeeded in setting itself apart through a distinctive external evaluation process to ensure fruit quality. Taking a threat to the industry and turning it into an advantage was a courageous decision that paid off manifold. This decision provided the competitive advantage for the company to sustain the aggressive annual growth rate they had previously achieved.

Questions for reflection and discussion

1. For Subsole and in this industry how often would the evaluation process of strategic action itself become a strategic advantage?
2. How can the evaluation focus be turned into an advantage?
3. What is the purpose of providing loans to the growers?
4. How is the process described in the case converting a threat to an advantage?

Reference

Kaplan, R. and Norton, D. (1996) *The Balanced Scorecard.* Boston, MA: Harvard Business School Press.

PART IV

Integrating and applying

As organizations engage in cycles of continuous coping and adaptation by taking in information, processing it and transforming it into outputs, they are enacting the processes of learning and change through their strategic endeavours.

Part IV draws Parts I, II and III together in a summary chapter and in an integrative case.

14

STRATEGIZING, LEARNING AND CHANGING

Understanding organizing as a normative process within organizations, herein understood as social constructions and systems of meaning, is the core foundation of this book. It is within this construction that Revans' (2011) formula $L=P+Q$ as a clinical approach is grounded. A corollary foundation is that organizations engage in cycles of continuous coping and adaptation as they take in information, process it and transform it into outputs. Accordingly the four elements of a healthy organization need to be present: a sense of identity and purpose; the capacity to adapt to changing external and internal circumstances; the capacity to perceive and test reality; and the internal integration of systems and subsystems (Schein, 1980, 2013). This cycle is enacted through different theoretical lenses which are covered in the book respectively in Part II and Part III: through organizational learning and change and through intentional strategic processes.

The five strategic foci as adaptive coping

In Chapter 8 we introduced the five strategic foci and drew on photography to describe a focus as bringing an image into clarity and so adjusting the lens to obtain the greatest clarity for that part of the picture of greatest interest. The use of focus is a technique that draws the viewer to the key points of interest in the photograph as determined by the photographer. In strategic thinking and acting a focus occurs when a portion of the whole is clarified in order to attend to it while keeping the entire strategic map in perspective. A focus is a clarified segment or part that can be attended to in perspective of the whole. Although the five strategic foci are often depicted in sequential form as shown in Figure 14.1, we also pointed out that the five strategic foci should not be viewed as linear steps but rather as an adaptive coping cycle, represented by feedback arrows in the figure.

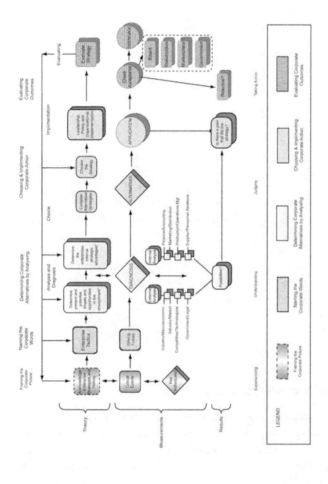

FIGURE 14.1 Representation of five strategic foci and main components with feedback loops

In Chapters 9 through 13 we described each focus in detail and illustrated their application with case examples. Table 14.1 summarizes the main questions arising from the four perspectives – leader, member, OD consultant and outcome.

The five strategic foci in strategy formation and implementation are part of a complex whole. While it is important to understand each focus it is also important to understand the relationships between the foci. The process issues that arise between the five focus points can distort the strategic outcomes.

Relationship between corporate picture and corporate words

The corporate picture deals with the key individuals and the history of the organization as it comes to affect strategy formulation and implementation. It is about the core identity of the organization. The content of this focus is the core mission and its statement of the organization, including an ethical statement, as well as the characteristics of the key players. The process aspect focuses on the construction and involvement of different people and processes and putting together and embracing the corporate mission and its statement. *Naming the corporate words* highlights those operations or functions that are the lead operations or functions over time. These driving forces give a unique and special quality to an organization, separating it from its competitors. These driving forces are central to the articulation, or lived-out mission statement of the organization.

There is a close relationship between corporate picture and corporate words that centres on the lived skills of the corporate words as an articulation of the core mission. The reverse can also be true. If an organization develops a new critical skill this can force a review and change in the core mission. If the corporate words are new to the organization it will pull at changing the core mission. A new core mission will threaten the existing corporate words by threatening the existing critical skills. This latter shift is important to anticipate as it affects the functional or Level III of an organization. A lead division losing its place because of the need and development of new skills is a major process issue.

Relationship between corporate words and corporate analysis

Naming the corporate words, as we saw above, deals with those operations or functions that had become the lead operations or functions over time. These are the driving forces and become the articulation, or lived-out mission statement of the organization. *Determining corporate alternatives by analysing* includes obtaining critical information and the preparation of these data into comprehensive scenarios or modelling of alternatives for the organization. Here, the organization analyses the information it senses from the environment. In most organizations the managers and analysts preparing the data in the corporate analysis are some of the people with the critical skills in the corporate words.

The interest in self-preservation is key to understanding this interaction. The managers in the lead of critical skill areas protect that status and may be unable to

TABLE 14.1 Summary of functional foci from four perspectives

	Corporate picture	Corporate words	Determining Corporate alternatives by analysing	Implementation	Corporate outcomes
	Intentionality	*Intentionality*	*Planning*	*Action*	*Outcome*
Leader	From where we are now, how do we get to the next level of success? How do I get others to participate to reach the next level of success?	Is the driving force appropriate? Does it enable the organization to achieve its picture?	Is the proper information being gathered? Are assessment and information intuitively correct? Are there benchmarks available? What are the benchmarks of the competition?	Is the action I wanted happening? What has slipped between the picture, words, direction and action? Is the action ensuring sustainability of the organization and true to identity? Do we do what we say we do?	Are the outcomes memorable and reflective of expectations? Do we celebrate? Do we evaluate?
Member	Do I have a role in the future of this organization? Will I fit?	Am I part of the mainstream? Do I contribute? Can I identify with the driving force?	What am I doing in this analysis? Is it relevant? Is it congruent with my understanding of the situation? What happens if I disagree?	Does my small part have a role in the bigger picture? Does anyone care about my actions?	Do we have an evaluation process? Does anyone listen or care? Does my piece fit? Is there life after evaluation?
OD consultant	Do they have a picture? Is it jointly owned?	Is there congruence between the espoused driving force and the one in action?	Is there competent data-gathering? Is it jointly owned, openly shared? Is negative feedback encouraged? Is the process critiqued and revised?	Is there a basic honesty in accessing actions? Is there a unified effort across the organization? Are there people distressed and fighting the action? Is there dysfunction?	Do they evaluate? Do they celebrate? Does evaluation happen before, during, or after? Does evaluation bring change?
Outcome	Is the stated identity perceived by the outside world?	Is the driving force congruent with the picture?	Is organizational learning the basis of what needs to be changed? Is there structured implementation and process implementation?	Is the coherent, owned, coordinated action congruent with corporate picture, words, direction?	Is there productivity and achievement? Is there organizational learning?

be totally objective in doing the analysis. Often these distortions are not at all obvious and not detected. This can be further complicated if the critical skill is the one held by the leader, for example the engineer who is CEO in an engineering company, or a CEO who came out of manufacturing in a company where that function embodies the driving force.

Relationship between corporate analysis and corporate decision and implementation

As seen above, *determining corporate alternatives by analysing* includes obtaining critical information and preparing it to provide models of the organization as well as comprehensive scenarios leading to potential alternatives. The focus *choosing and implementing corporate actions* comprises the selection of the best alternative and the structured implementation of a strategic plan of action with its concurrent implementation plans. The relationship between the two foci is as close as the alternative set and how it is formed can be a factor in the decision process. If the alternatives are pared down to one or a small number that pre-eliminates choices this has a significant effect on the outcome. Sometimes the need to keep the analysis separate from the decision process is not understood. Forming an open and comprehensive set of alternatives is the basis for making an informed decision. Not looking at enough alternatives or even possibilities reduces the chance of a best decision.

Relationship between corporate decision and corporate evaluation

Choosing and implementing corporate actions deals with the selection and structured implementation of a strategic plan of action with its concurrent implementation plans. *Evaluating corporate outcomes* deals with the acceptance of the criteria for evaluation and the appropriate review of the resulting state of the organization. The relationship here is that the outcome measured should be the outcome desired in the decision process. This relationship can fail in either of two ways: if the original criteria are not evaluated; or if new criteria not related to the original decision are generated.

New criteria for evaluation can be generated if these are more detailed, or adapted to better means of capturing the data required. Sometimes the evaluation process is difficult or cumbersome and is aborted. Monitoring of goals is a critical part of any change process and is necessary for learning. It is used to make sure that the correct end was achieved and also to make sure the new change behaviour remains in place to become the norm.

Relationship between corporate evaluation and corporate picture

Evaluating corporate outcomes deals with the acceptance of the criteria for evaluation and the appropriate review of the resulting state of the organization. The corporate picture is the core mission and its statement of the organization. The relationship is closest when the evaluation criteria are such that a new core mission or a new critical skill is part of the evaluation. In these situations the organization is in evolution and a new organization is being developed. During such an evolution the tension is the greatest. The basis for the new corporate picture is in the evaluation criteria of the corporate evaluation. This is the linkage for the ethical and social responsibility audit as part of the evaluation to be fed back into the verified corporate picture.

It should be noted that the *framing the corporate picture* and the *naming the corporate words* foci are actually transformational activities, in that, together, they set the foundation for the later activities (Figure 14.2). They are also the first two foci that must be addressed, and addressed well, when a new direction is sought. The remaining three foci, analysing, choosing, and evaluating, are collectively under-stood as incremental activities that build on the foundation and influence the direction set by the transformational activities. As incremental activities, they are no less important than the transformational activities of framing and naming, as their successful implementation and execution are essential to the near-term success and long-term survival of the organization.

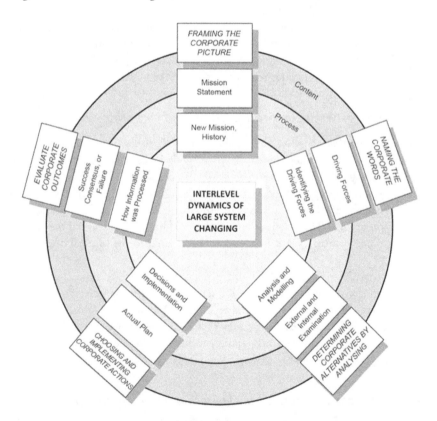

FIGURE 14.2 Interlevel dynamics of large system changing within the five strategic foci framework

Strategic foci and large system learning and change

The adaptive coping cycle as enacted through the five strategic foci exposes the organization to learning and change. In a global world where change is discontinuous, the organization seeks to frame its corporate picture, name its corporate words, determine its corporate alternatives by analysing, choose and implement corporate actions and evaluate outcomes in a first-order or single loop mode in a continuous cycle of coping and adaptation as depicted in Figure 14.3. It also seeks to engage in the adaptive coping cycle in a second-order or double loop mode as forces challenge any inadequacy of the first-order or single loop response.

The single inquiry loop takes reflection on outcomes to the actions taken and their evaluation. The outcome of such reflection is likely to be single loop learning and a first-order realignment of operational procedures and processes. The double inquiry loop goes beyond reflection on the action and questions the analysis and the choice made. Here there may be further single loop learning and first-order change as different analytic tools may be adopted or different decisions made within the existing corporate picture or words. The triple inquiry loop takes a definite double loop and second-order perspective as the fundamentals of corporate picture and corporate words are questioned and changed.

Such processes involve moving from a perceived need for change, through articulating an envisioned future, through assessing the present to determine what

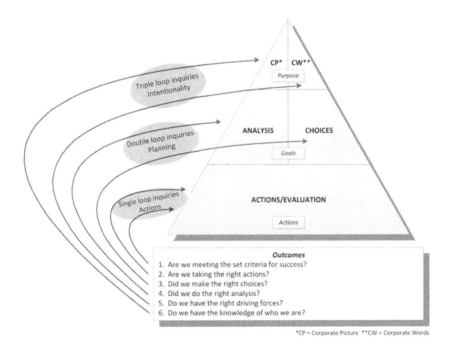

FIGURE 14.3 Cross-foci questions on corporate strategy

needs to change and getting to the envisioned future by implementing change and managing the transition. They engage interlevel dynamics in that large-scale organizational change comprises individual, team and interdepartmental group change respectively, and in that the manner in which change is introduced and implemented through the system is a complex movement from individual to team, team to team in the interdepartmental group and to the organization's external stakeholders over time in iterations where the movements are circular with each iteration being a cause and effect of another.

Each of the five strategic foci entails interlevel dynamics of learning and change. Such dynamics can be viewed from different perspectives, whether one is a senior manager, a non-executive member, an OD consultant or a student viewing the outcomes.

References

Revans, R. (2011) *ABC of Action Learning.* Farnham: Gower.

Schein, E.H. (1980) *Organizational Psychology.* 3rd edn. Englewood Cliffs, NJ: Prentice-Hall.

Schein, E.H. (2013) Notes toward a model of organizational therapy. In L. Vansina (ed.), *Humanness in Organizations.* London: Karnac, pp. 91–100.

15

INTEGRATIVE CASE

The Christian Haub era at A&P

This case is a comprehensive look at the Great Atlantic and Pacific Tea Company (A&P) during Christian Haub's leadership as CEO and later Executive Chairman of the company from 1998 to 2007. The objective of this integrative case is to illustrate the application of the phases and levels of large-scale organizational change (Chapters 3 to 7) and the five foci framework (Chapters 8 to 13) in a fast-changing environment, namely food and grocery retailing at the turn of the millennium. Although the book is structured in sequential order, the case illustrates the non-linear nature of strategic analysis, implementation, and large-scale organizational change, including the constant interplay among the five foci, such that there is no predetermined sequence in addressing each of them.

Events in the real world are messy and hindsight is 20-20: ex-post it is often possible to distinguish patterns of behaviour and decision-making that are helpful for the reflexive engagement that leads to individual learning. We have discerned three rounds of intentional large-scale organizational strategic change during Christian's tenure as CEO. We believe that the overlap and staggered nature of these three rounds are an unusually rich example of the complexities and inter-relationships among subsystems of a large organization operating in a broader environment in constant transformation. From a strategic management viewpoint the three rounds illustrate the inter-relationship among the five foci, and from a change implementation viewpoint they illustrate the flow-through of the phases of change as different members' perspectives evolve over time. Because organizations are in constant evolution both reactively adapting to the environment and proactively engaging in intentional strategic change, any retrospective synthesis such as this one involves arbitrary choices and simplifications, and different observers might well have very distinct selections. Our intention in including the case as described below is to provide an integrative example which we believe can enrich your reflexive engagement regarding your own organization.

Upon becoming CEO, Christian Haub placed his full attention on strategic planning and intentional large-scale organizational change and the case follows this trajectory. Much of the case is presented through Haub's own narrative.

History of A&P before Christian Haub became CEO

Originally founded in 1859 in New York City as a local tea and coffee retailing chain, A&P experienced dramatic growth in the beginning of the twentieth century when it introduced the concept of an economy store and then expanded throughout the country. In the inter-war period the company saw its heyday as the largest retailer in the world, with over 16,000 stores in the US in the 1930s. After World War II, as up-and-coming chains opened larger more customer-oriented stores, A&P saw an erosion in its market position and closed many of its smaller and now obsolete stores. After a series of attempts to turn the company around it was sold in the late 1970s to the Tenglemann Group, German strategic investors with extensive experience in retailing who were interested in entering the North American market. Founded in 1867, the Tengelmann Group then owned several retail chains in Europe, including its namesake, Kaiser's, Plus Stores, and OBI. During the 1980s, under this new and experienced ownership, A&P acquired several smaller chains in North America, which continued to operate under their original brand names as the A&P brand was not widely used.

By 1992, Jim Wood as CEO had led the company for 15 years, i.e. since the Tengelmann Group investment. During that span of time he impressed his style of leadership and his culture on A&P. It could be described as a command-and-control culture with little engagement of people further down the chain of command. His interaction with store-level personnel was non-existent, which led to a lack of accountability below the senior management level. Additionally, the company was living in the moment without a clear sense of a long-term strategy. It operated quarter to quarter focusing on certain financial goals without addressing long-term industry and consumer behaviour trends and consequent implications for the business. The company had concluded several acquisitions during the 1980s and early 1990s and was operating in reactive mode, dealing with the crisis of the moment. Wood was finishing his career and preparing to retire.

The decision structure at that time was very much top-down driven even though the organization was to some degree decentralized with the different divisions (the different acquired chains) in the field having some degree of autonomy in day-to-day business decisions. Any significant capital expenditure decisions or any significant personnel decisions were made in the office of the CEO. Plans basically consisted of numbers, and generally were part of a cohesive strategy, but were often not substantiated by research or insights or initiatives. This led to a company in which the headquarters office was somewhat disengaged from what was happening in the business. Headquarters were also disengaged from the employee base and from middle management. There was very little movement within management: the structure was frozen with very little opportunity for cross-fertilization between different functions. There was little or no cross-division awareness. A&P was in the supermarket business and one supermarket division was a lot like the other but, because many of these divisions came through acquisition, there never had been an attempt to merge different cultures.

Growth was achieved through acquisitions, with the purchase of Waldbaum's, Farmer Jack, Miracle Food Mart in Canada, and others: 40 to 50 per cent of the company's size came through the acquisitions made from the mid-1980s through the early 1990s. When a company was bought, the A&P structure, systems and processes were installed and the acquired company's culture was put aside and not acknowledged. This led to a pattern of acquisitions going through very difficult assimilation and performance issues at the same time. A&P basically disregarded the value of the brands it had purchased. Waldbaum's, for example, because of its heritage, was very much oriented toward the ethnic/immigrant clientele, while A&P was more typically oriented toward middle America. They both had different approaches toward going to market. When A&P tried to implement its policies at Waldbaum's, this backfired. The consumer became disenfranchised in the early to mid-1990s. This also happened to Miracle Food Mart in Canada and Farmer Jack's in Michigan. Wood had joined A&P as CEO when the company was in crisis in the late 1970s, had saved it from going out of business, and then had followed an acquisition path. Every time Wood bought a new company he went back to the suppliers and asked for additional advantages now that the company was bigger. When that acquisition period came to an end, the issue became how to integrate the many parts. How could 12 divergent brands realize their value and also be integrated? Jim Wood was at the end of his career, in his early to mid-60s, and did not have the outlook to develop a strategy for the long-term.

The command-and-control environment that had been established at the time he took over was then appropriate as the company had to be saved and this could only be done with strict controls. This same structure was not conducive to building a competitive organization in a fast-changing industry. In summary, the corporate picture of A&P in the early 1990s was that of a group of diverse retailing food chains, linked together in an attempt to run as one operating A&P system. Decisions were made by top management with little or no input from below. Because of the expansion, A&P was a significant market force.

Round 0 (1998): Haub transitioning from Wood

Christian Haub recalled his transition period to becoming CEO of A&P:

> In Spring 1998, we started the transition phase where I became co-CEO with Wood with the objective of my becoming sole CEO a year later, Spring 1999. At that point, Jim would retire from an active executive role and continue as a non-executive chairman of the board for three years. He also wanted to make sure that I was properly supported with the right group of executives during the transition phase and that led to the hiring of a few people who were more

Jim's pick than necessarily mine. But I worked with them to figure out what they were able to offer and see where they were able to take us. So at that stage, I prepared to figure out the strategy going forward, i.e. what we needed to do. It was clear in my mind that we could not keep managing the company the way we had done in the past. But I had to be fully in charge before we would really be able to make any changes considering that here I had the twenty-year serving CEO, a veteran with lots of experience, who while on active duty was willing to hear what anybody wanted to do even if he did not agree with it and was going to follow his own mind in the end anyway. So I engaged half a dozen or so of the senior executives in the company in a process of trying to assess where we were. Some of these were new people evaluating how we ranked in the industry. This was accomplished by benchmarking the most recent several years' performance and assessing our performance in relation to the rest of the industry's. They also identified what we were seeing as challenges and opportunities facing the company, including the competitive environment and the consumer's point of view. At the same time, we also engaged external consultants to help us assess the status of our people base. The questions were: what are our people thinking about the company, what are their impressions, what do they see as our challenges and opportunities, and how are they viewing A&P?

Wood brought in a senior operating executive not to replace the COO, but to strengthen that area under the COO. He also brought in an executive assistant to the CEO, a very strong person on the development side. At that time, this was a very important role as A&P believed that replacing older stores was a critical, strategic initiative going forward. The decision group looking at strategy and analysis included a CFO and a COO, both of whom had been with the company for 10 years, and a chief merchandising officer who had been in the company for over 30 years. They were all either in their early or late 50s, while Christian Haub was in his early 30s. For about three–four months, they went through internal audit and in August 1998, they came together to examine the information gathered. As Haub expected, the company was underperforming financially with respect to the industry norm. The first benchmark therefore painted a poor picture. Haub reported:

> The internal assessment from our associates was absolutely devastating in terms of a company without vision and strategy as well as a completely disengaged workforce that felt disrespected and mistreated. As I described, it was a culture where employees were just a number on the profit and loss statement, i.e. a cost that had to be held to a minimum.

Employees felt the company was run very much top-down with no voice or opportunity for feedback. It was a company with a command-and-control culture and very poor treatment of people to the degree where there was a lot of resentment toward management. People looked at their jobs only as a way to make money with no connection to the company.

When the senior management group sat down in April–May 1998, it set the criteria for the analysis. External auditors were used for the internal analysis. For the external analysis, Haub engaged investment bankers to help ensure an objective view and to obtain publicly available competitive data. These were the critical benchmarks of sales, growth, profitability, return on capital and market share. Haub feared the long-term employees might not have an objective perspective. At that time, with the exception of the CFO, there was not a lot of interest in doing the analysis. Some managers questioned why they were spending their time on this. They were saying that they had other crises to deal with and crisis management was the order of the day. Some of them objected to the work of the external consultants, but Haub took this as a good sign that progress was being made. It became clear to him that A&P had to change fundamentally and he had to start at forming an overall concept of what direction he wanted to go and what the core mission was to be. He wanted to start developing some simple concepts that people could start rallying around to jump-start the change process.

Round 1 (1998–2000): becoming a more participative and customer-centric organization

It was clear to Haub that if A&P really were to change, there would need to be a massive undertaking to get buy-in from management at all levels, including every store manager and mid-level manager. He also needed buy-in from associates in the stores because they represented 90 per cent of the employee base and were the front line in the business: selling goods and services to consumers. He wanted to get buy-in, and lead a drive for a comprehensive change programme with initiatives around developing a set of core values, looking into all of A&P's people practices, store concepts, market strategies, and supplier relationships. He was starting to challenge what some felt were the core drivers for the business.

Framing a new corporate picture

The main objective was to change consumer attitudes and to become the supermarket of choice. Haub started this by creating a new language. He created a word 'gaptitude' which he developed out of GAP (Great Atlantic and Pacific) and the new attitude that was needed in the company. It would articulate what was felt about where they were and where they wanted to go. This word initially became the symbol of the change. The word expressed a new mission and programme through a group of key values that were called the Great Actions and Priorities, which gave A&P a plan of improvement in nine areas, the nine 'As and Ps' which were developed in a conference in late August 1998. They were general and focused on customer service, improving store operations, developing new stores, putting the right merchandising approach into the business, and controlling expenses. This effort gave people a sense of direction and the opportunity to channel all of their activities.

The development of core values came out of this effort. There was a culture, but it was a culture that was undocumented and driven from the behaviour of the leadership over 15 to 20 years. Haub recalls:

> If we wanted to change the culture, we had to start by laying out how we wanted people to behave and what we believed was important to us in the company. We developed this concept by constructing a house with the foundation, pillars and roof, symbolizing the important areas and core values. We described the values in detail in terms of the examples of behaviours. Developing and introducing this into the company was a major initiative as was communicating how this was an integral part of the new direction for the organization. We started to develop a process where we brought in around 120 people every week for about three-and-a-half days. We got two thousand managers together over a three-month period.

Obtaining buy-in for a new corporate picture

The CFO and COO presented at every conference so that they would convey the same message each time. During each conference, they would go through work exercises of the core values in action and attendants would conduct self-assessments to understand their strengths and weaknesses. This helped raise engagement, buy-in, and understanding of the company's situation and the need to change. Business model changes were also considered. At that time, A&P was very much driven by getting allowances from suppliers, i.e. very much buying-oriented. Haub recalls:

> We needed a shift to become a more sales-driven organization which meant that we needed to engage our store associates a lot more because that was where we wanted to win – not at the buying desk in the office where we squeezed our suppliers for allowance dollars. We started introducing the concept of net costing where we did not measure the success of our buyers by the amount of allowance dollars that they brought in, but by the amount of sales dollars they generated, i.e. the margins they were generating. This was a big cultural shift in the company.

By being focused on buyers, A&P had prioritized middle management as opposed to store personnel. A&P was more decentralized then, with buying fragmented in many offices. The meetings led to the realization of the significant opportunities to consolidate purchasing and back-office activities. The ultimate goal was to create one centralized approach to the merchandising activity – one merchandising organization for the entire US. A&P went through several iterations to consolidate buying from six to three to one point of purchase. Some of the delay was in generating the interdepartmental-level information systems to effect the change.

1998–1999 achievements

When asked, 'what was realized by mid-1999?' Haub replied:

> The organization had a broader understanding of the challenges. The first new
> executive I brought in was a leader of human resources. I had to upgrade the
> role and get another people champion into the company (besides myself). It
> had to be somebody who could keep driving the people's side of this plan
> which dealt with implementing core values, institutionalizing the new culture,
> and seeing how to take the next step. Then we started having a fall-out, not at
> the top, but at the next level. We confronted this by having managers either
> buy in or look for other opportunities. Some did not believe in this type of
> culture because they had lived in command-and-control organizations and had
> left voluntarily or involuntarily. One of the big challenges was to turn words
> into action. If you hear the company leadership talk about new values and
> culture, but continue with the same day-to-day activities experiencing the old,
> words may lose meaning. A year later, the new values started coming into play
> because we began measuring people's performance not just based on numbers
> and results, but also on their values. We took a first pulse of the institution in
> Spring 1999 through an employee questionnaire. We got 27 per cent partici-
> pation, which is low. The feedback was still very negative. The years after
> that, 2001–02, we engaged the Gallup organization to do the Gallup
> employee engagement survey. This was a short, but very focused survey. We
> saw tremendous success with this. We enjoyed a 90 per cent participation rate
> (unheard of in the industry). Over three years, we moved from the 51st to
> the 34th percentile in our employee ranking of A&P as a company that valued
> them. We saw wide ranging improvements across the board in all geographic
> regions and across all categories of management. As a result, the employee
> engagement score remained a critical element of performance evaluation. It's
> part of each person's performance plan, individual goals and team goals all tied
> together. We made great progress in that area.

Corporate words in 1999–2000: developing critical skills in the organization

At the end of 1998, A&P introduced its first strategic restructuring. It decided to
exit certain non-core markets and close some underperforming stores. It took some
decisive action to also demonstrate internally to the organization that change was
happening. Haub was willing to take some difficult steps to change the company's
direction and to make sure that members realized the depth of the change. This
change process in developing new corporate skills centred around analysing their
entire portfolio, from a market to market perspective. No significant changes in the
managers had occurred as yet. During the first six months of 1999 the plan that had
been announced in 1998 was implemented. It was at that point that Haub began to

ask who was really on his team. He started seeing some second-tier management members dropping out and began to realize that he probably would need to make some changes. Why did the second tier drop out? Some of it was that they didn't fit and were not endorsing the new direction. Haub started getting feedback from the lower levels hearing that some managers were dismissing or ridiculing the change process.

The company started to see positive sales growth for the first time in five years and there was a sense of fresh air. People were starting to talk about it. They started to engage with the concept of 'gaptitude', i.e. having a direction and objectives and talking about their common goals. Remembering this time Haub recalls:

> We invested a lot of time and effort to communicate. Communication was a big part of the process. Whereas before there had been no communication to employees, we now were starting to institutionalise certain forms of communication on a regular basis, informing employees of the progress of the plan and change programme.

Change of this scale does not happen quickly and involves many people in the organization working together. Haub described the process they used:

> Conferences were done every six to 12 months. In the early stages, every six months, we would call people together to review progress and introduce the next set of changes or upgrade to the next level of activities. In 1999, we then said that the culture change was under way and it would take a long time. This change was something that we needed to sustain and that it was not a six or twelve months' effort. We had to get the non-believers out. We had to keep talking the talk. The first time that we let this slide, people would begin to not take it seriously. With the business challenges, we realized that this alone would not sustain our progress. We needed to start identifying the other areas that were holding us back.

He continued addressing the resources required to make the change work:

> We did a portfolio restructuring. We started to very aggressively invest in capital, into building new stores. We thought that we had to show people that we were going to grow. They would see physical evidence of the company refreshing its store base.

Evaluation follow-up

Haub had begun to wake people up to the issues. At the same time, it became clear that as a company, A&P had little concept of accountability, even though it had been made one of the core values. The emphasis in the first year and a half was on integrity, respect, and engaging employees. Once Haub realized that it was necessary to emphasize accountability, people perceived this as counteracting the culture of reliance and respect that had been previously encouraged. It seemed to some as though there were no trust. Haub relates:

> we recognized that the company was consistently missing its performance goals and there was no consequence. There were people in management positions who had not made a budget in 10 years. One could say that part of it was that we had the wrong process in place or that we didn't know how to budget, but on the other hand, we did not hold people accountable to anything.

A&P simply did not have good performance management and no measurement of goals. This was realized in 2000. A&P began to introduce a performance management system. Haub then said:

> we were structured in a way that prevented accountability. And again, that is something that is taking us a long time to correct. I think with the new structure that's evolving, we're going to have good accountability because we're flattening the organization and taking two layers of management out to ensure people have responsibility and visibility. That is where they will really have control over these things and not just keep working to show results but work to manage the business.

Round 2 (2000–2003): large-scale change process – the new IT system and accountability

In the spring of 2000 the next phase began, called the Great Renewal Programme. This was to completely overhaul all of A&P's information systems and processes. Haub announced a four-year initiative to change the majority of the information systems and to introduce new systems, new processes and a whole new support infrastructure in the company. This was named Evergreen.

Corporate analysis: the need to update IT

The organization up to this point was looking inward at core values for the first time and the senior team of managers was changing. In the latter part of 1999 to the beginning of 2000 the company started to move out of this inward look to ask what was happening in the marketplace. There were significant external threats: Wal-Mart's entry into groceries, Internet shopping, home meal replacement, alternative retail formats, and changing consumer behaviour, all of which were causing supermarkets to lose traffic: both a decrease in customers and in number of store visits per customer. A&P for the most part still continued to analyse internal barriers to furthering its potential with only some awareness of the external environment. This led to the next phase in early 2000 in which the processes, systems and organization in the supply chain were recognized as so out of date that, no matter how well the core mission of serving the customer was executed, competitors would still be ahead. MIS systems and supply and distribution information capabilities needed to be significantly upgraded to take the organization to the next level of merchandising, category management, store operations, distribution and supply chain activities.

At the foundation, this would consist of creating a common item database. A&P was still operating with no data connectivity among different divisions and could not work in a unified way with suppliers. For example, to pull information together about how much of a particular detergent was being sold at any given period was a huge effort of accessing different systems and pulling data together almost manually. Therefore, A&P was not capable of executing category management as a best practice and recognized that precise customer purchasing information was not readily available, leading to suboptimal product assortment selection and pricing decisions. The divisions were still stuck in a tactical approach to business which emphasized weekly promotion budgets, but not the granular analysis of what constituted success and failure of the day-to-day, month-to-month decisions.

Managers needed to find out what the consumers thought about their stores and how their experience compared to the competition. They needed deeper awareness of the problems consumers had when products were out of stock, or when stores had the wrong assortment, or had products perceived as priced too high. A&P was looking at benchmarks in terms of supply chain costs, which were higher than competitors in the industry. The amount of inventory that A&P divisions carried to run the business was high and inventory turns were very low. Importantly, engagement across the organization led to deeper awareness. Becoming a more customer-centric organization would require updated systems.

Building systems to support the new picture

Haub considered that by 2000 he was starting to have a real significant change at the senior management level because people had to be more accountable and the supply chain business process initiative was under way. At this point, each person who reported to Haub headed up a division. They had to run a business, which was new behaviour. But this was not without its complications. The COO, the chief merchandising officer, and the head of development left. Some replacements were promoted from within, but other replacements were new to the organization. The company went through a poor performance year as recent hires in key positions went up the learning curve. Haub discussed this time period:

> In the new management information systems initiative, we engaged IBM as our main systems integrator. We also used a change management consultant and we put a team together of 150–200 people internally to work on this initiative. It was a monstrous challenge. Basically, it took three years. And we clearly underestimated the effort necessary. Had I known then what I know

today, I might have done it differently. The cost, the distraction, the upheaval are incredible.

Haub continued to relate:

We had a four-year project outlined which was going to cost us about $350 million between people and capital investment. It was going to get us sustained ongoing benefits in improvements between $150 and $200 million annually. It was going to give us a certain set of functionalities that were also very critical. We finished it in three years, but that was mostly driven by change in the scope of the project. We reduced some of the functionality. The cost after three years was going to be about 10 per cent less than what we had originally projected, but we only received about 60 per cent of the benefits. Had we gone through the entire project it would have taken us another three years and cost us about 50 per cent more. We stopped because the costs were increasing so fast. One year and a half into the project, it was completely off the rails. It turned out that the software solution provider was a small company who did not have an SAP system for retail. We had ventured into uncharted waters looking for a new set of solutions that really did not exist. We first changed the leadership of the initiative team and within six months I changed the CIO. We put a whole new business case together. We cut back on what we thought was possible to what we could deliver in a reasonable amount of time and a reasonable cost and still preserved a majority of the potential benefits.

A&P put together a new team because all of the original functional managers, with the exception of the person responsible for distribution, had left. The new initiative was producing an information system geared toward being the best in class or the best practice in the industry around category management, around the supply chain system, and around key store operations systems like human resources management, inventory management, and ordering processes. But the key was to get the merchandising infrastructure: getting a common item database and integrated assortment, pricing and promotions systems. A&P got the foundation in a common item database, and some of the tools for managing assortment, pricing and promotion.

A&P went through another benchmark study in the spring of 2002 and had one of the best inventory turns in the industry. Haub reflects on their learning in the process:

So the areas that were left off were in the merchandising area, i.e. merchandising solutions. Store solutions were pretty much what we wanted. Distribution solutions, the warehouse management system, and the transportation management system were easier to develop and implement. We also developed a new human resource system and a new finance system.

Evaluation follow-up

The timing of the implementation of the new MIS system was different from planned. Originally, the introduction of the new systems had been envisioned on a rolling basis so as to not come all at once and overwhelm the organization. It was to have been sequenced; that did not happen. Basically, 80 per cent of the new systems hit in nine months starting in early summer 2002.

The big challenge in 2000 was significant new management at the senior level and the new MIS initiative coming off the rails and needing to be rescued. Fortunately, 2001 was a better year. Profits were up, people had learned, and the organization had settled in. Momentum from the new leadership, and the external environment was more favourable than it would be in the following year. Christian Haub, putting the results into context, stated:

> Even though we had sustained the cultural change in 2000 and in 2001 by introducing performance management systems that sustained themselves pretty well through 2002 and going forward, we did not have enough focus on the fundamentals of our business. This business was still very much based on merchandising, store execution, and the right leadership in place. There is a business to run while changes are happening, even while the company transitions from its old to a new culture. Just introducing performance management was a big thing. People had to learn it, understand it, adjust to it and deal with its consequences. Today, we have performance measures in place that can tell us whether somebody is performing well or not. The only thing we had measured before had been sales and bottom line results at store level and there had been no consequence if a manager failed to achieve them. Now we have those same budget goals, with a performance plan laid out including individual goals and objectives and employee engagement scores. We introduced 360 degree feedback programme for many middle managers and a lot more time and effort is being spent on evaluating people's performance and then tying that to compensation, promotion, stock option awards, etc. So the early period of the cultural change which had very much revolved around 'feel good' became the cold hard reality of 'this is a business and we are running this business for profitability and performance.' There still was, unfortunately, a lot of change going on, with every senior leadership team change, different personalities, ideas and directions came into play. I am still leaving out a very important aspect here. During 2000, when we introduced the new systems initiative, we started further developing our approach around strategy and developed a business model so that people could better understand how everything fit together.

Corporate words and corporate picture

Haub reflected:

In 2000, we were spending quite a bit more time on strategy and framing where we wanted to go. Let me back up to the corporate strategic framework which we looked at. Typically, companies try to pursue strategies with a focus on product leadership, operational excellence or customer intimacy. We developed our strategy around customer intimacy. This is how we were going to differentiate and drive ourselves to a leadership position. And, now, this is also at the end of the period of growth in the 1990s when consumer spending was still at an all-time high, that we recognized that we are an industry that had not done a lot around differentiating. But on the other hand, we were being more and more dominated by Wal-Mart whose operational excellence was its competitive advantage.

Out of that concept of 'this is the direction we want to go', we then developed our business model which we called 'the customer intimate business model'. This model has the customer at the core, identifies customer requirements, and then satisfies demand through execution at store level. I think we became too consultancy/theoretically driven. The gap between people at corporate and people at the store level widened. The more strategic we became, the more we lost in the translation to tactical aspects of the business. In 2000, in hindsight, we did not recognize, did not realize, and even in 2001 we didn't, that the whole paradigm of the economy and consumer was shifting because the 10 years of growth and success of sales and margin increases came to an end.

A&P had no infrastructure for measuring the external environment changes and their effect on the business. The MIS system was new, but it was internally focused and the company was not able to get to the data on the effects of an economic slowdown on customers. By recognizing that the systems needed to get to the point of measuring success on customer intimacy were years away, we knew that it clearly would be unaffordable. By the time A&P got its MIS to operationally work, the whole environment had shifted. Where at one time customers were looking for service since they had money, they now were looking for savings and discounts.

September 11, 2001 had a dramatic effect on business. With no warning people shifted into a response mode of buying for value and not for service. This apparent change was more pronounced in lower income areas, but seemed to endure for several years and pointed to real customer change. There had been a similar shift in Canada earlier. In Canada, we had been successful in developing a complementary approach. There was a certain growth of market share we could get with a discount concept while maintaining a full service supermarket. During the holidays when people wanted special food, we got a bigger spike in the supermarket part of the business. This was due to our having more specialty foods, greater selections in the deli, and a broader variety with more service than we had in the discount markets. But the average growth in the discount concept versus the supermarket business had been three/four to one for the previous seven years.

So if we wanted to have presence, i.e. market share and profitability with the key driving forces of customer orientation and customer satisfaction, we had to be able to meet our customers' economical needs as well as their service and greater product assortment needs. What does the analysis say is required to keep people satisfied? Is the right mix 75 per cent discount and 25 per cent conventional or mainstream full service? There is no single answer. We have to go through this market by market. I would say in places like northern New Jersey, we probably are going to have a higher share of full service than discount customers, but the closer we get to an area like Newark and Patterson, it's probably going to be much more the other way, more 80–20 in favour of discount.

We also need to start from the base that we have today, the markets that we are in today. If we're well positioned in Toronto and then the greater province of Ontario, my first objective has to be to create that same kind of presence in and around New York. First of all, we already have presence in markets which are underserved from a discount perspective. I think with the right approach of converting existing stores and developing new stores primarily for the discount format, we should be able to dominate this market place. From that strength, Philadelphia, then Detroit and then once we would have strong dominant presence in those markets, then see if there are new market opportunities to try that approach.

Round 3 (2003–2007): strategic repositioning

In 2002 the final stages of changing the culture towards a participative and customer-driven company and the difficult new system implementation coincided with significant contextual changes which led to a much more difficult competitive environment.

External analysis

In the aftermath of 9/11/2001 there was a period of slow economic growth and a consumer shift towards value propositions. The impact of the World Trade Center attack, especially in the New York area and in the Northeast was substantial, as the general feeling of security in the US homeland suffered a significant blow, which had behavioural repercussions throughout the population. In essence, the notions of restraint and prudence became more prevalent and consumer cost sensitivity increased noticeably. In addition, the brief recession of 2001 and the end of the dotcom bubble contributed to a measurable consumer shift towards caution and savings. In parallel, competitive movements such as Wal-Mart's trend towards groceries, the growing preference for natural foods, and competitors' new store formats led to stronger rivalry in the food retail industry. These factors contributed to make 2002 a difficult year for A&P. Haub described the thought process leading

to examine closely the two-pronged strategy where serving the high-end consumers through one retail brand and the value-conscious consumer through
another (Food Basics) had been so successful.

> It is essential for the managers of the stores and divisions in the US to have a
> strategic model that they could work against. We learned from our Canadian
> experience that there was a disconnect between our merchandising pro-
> gramme and its execution at the store level. It's not that the merchandising
> programme in itself was necessarily wrong, but there was not a connection
> between what and why. Operations has to execute in a certain way to reach
> the results that the merchandising programme is designed to achieve. That's a
> management process and a communications issue. One of our big objectives is
> to shift our business to be driven primarily by merchandising. If merchandising
> is structured correctly, then executing it at store level will be necessary to
> achieve success. But you can execute very well and still be unsuccessful if you
> do not have the correct merchandise concept approach. If you have the cor-
> rect merchandise concept and the wrong location approach, it won't work
> either. There's always a natural tension because the people in operations
> believe that they know more about merchandising then the merchandisers do.
> And the merchandisers always blame the operators for not executing correctly.
> If I want to capture this New York marketplace, I need to know where to
> have the discount and mainstream concepts and then what these concepts have
> to look like so they won't cannibalize each other, but complement each other.
> And then as this business is dynamic, how do you keep evolving, maintaining,
> and keeping it contemporary with what happens around you. The discount
> concept operated in Canada under the Food Basics name and concept.

Naming the words and determining alternatives

As the new information system was finalized and the competitive environment
worsened in the US during 2002, Haub was aware that the company's culture had
indeed become more participative and execution throughout all areas and functions
had become more customer-driven. He felt that internally A&P had made important strides during his tenure and now turned his attention to formulating the best
strategy to confront the rising marketplace challenges. In early 2003 A&P was
present in several regions of the US with divisions in the Northeast, in the South,
in the Upper Midwest and in Canada. Of these, A&P Canada had been the most
successful, having implemented the above mentioned two-pronged approach of
serving both the value-conscious customer with their Food Basics format chain and
the service-oriented customer through chains focused on responsiveness and broad
product offerings. In 2003 Eight O'Clock Coffee, a coffee manufacturer owned by
A&P was sold so the company could focus solely on food retailing. In Haub's
words 'we did not have a tradition in manufacturing and obtained a very good
price, so it was an easy decision.' During this period he also implemented in the

US a two-pronged strategy similar to A&P Canada's, tailoring stores to consumer needs with major focus on savings or niches in the higher end. Strong execution helped produce very good financial results in the US in 2003 and 2004. Meanwhile, A&P Canada continued its successful trajectory. In Haub's words:

> We had two very good years in 2003 and 2004 as we were able to target the two broad market segments with success. Now that we had the systems in place and the strategy was working we realized that geographic concentration led to much higher efficiencies and, consequently, better performance. It became apparent that being spread out in several regions was not giving us the synergies we had hoped because of customer preference differences and geographic distance. For example, despite the success enjoyed, we were not able to identify synergies between the US and Canada operations. We then conducted the analysis to understand where the largest long-term opportunities might lie. We decided to focus on the northeast of the United States for several reasons, among them the high population density, the belief that we knew the customer well, the already installed store base, and the potential for future expansion.
>
> Because the Canadian operation was substantially separated from the US and because it had a very positive reputation, we decided to put the asset on the market and obtained one of the largest multiples the industry had ever seen when we sold it in mid-2005. It was a good transaction for us as we sold at the top. That year we also divested the Detroit and the New Orleans operations, all of which allowed us to have a significant war-chest to then look for acquisitions within our target geographical area of the Northeast. The A&P Canada transaction had the additional advantage of allowing us to bring that company's CEO, who had very strong operational experience, to work with us in the US. Our operations were running well and I then focused on finding a suitable acquisition in our target area.

Choosing and implementing corporate action

At this point (late 2005 to early 2006) Haub, who with the arrival of the CEO from A&P Canada had moved to the Executive Chairman position, was comfortable that the chosen merchandising strategy was working well and that A&P was operating as a more cohesive unit with synergies across divisions. A&P now was able to focus on a more concentrated geographical area and pursued regionally the strategy which had been so successful in Canada, leading to very good operating results in 2006 and 2007. This success led to the desire to fill the remaining void by finding a way to serve the middle market segment, between the cost-conscious consumer and the discerning high service consumer. In 2006 a chain which successfully served that middle market, was identified as the ideal target. Negotiations with Pathmark ensued and terms were agreed upon in March but the transaction closed only in late 2007 due to the need for regulatory approval by the Federal

Trade Commission. The acquisition marked the end of Christian Haub's executive leadership role with A&P although he did remain involved with the board afterward.

Pathmark was two-thirds the size of A&P at the time of the acquisition and a major competitor. The acquisition was made with cash, stock and substantial added leverage as the Tengelmann Group viewed the exit from Canada as a monetizing opportunity. As a result, after the acquisition A&P was significantly leveraged. To make matters worse integration between the two companies turned out to be especially challenging for various reasons, among them the different cultures and systems integration. The impact of substantial leverage and the integration difficulties were exacerbated by the effects of the 2008 financial crisis and the Great Recession that followed. This affected cash flow from both directions because revenues fell as customers became much more value-conscious while the financing represented a significant cash drain in the form of interest payments.

Evaluation follow-up

Haub reflected on lessons learned from the experience:

> Although I firmly believe that in the absence of the Great Recession the strategy would have worked beautifully, the major take-away for me was the difficulty in integrating the two companies. My main lesson was to never again underestimate the risk of any acquisition, especially a big one. Our management team was good, and improving A&P while at the same time folding Pathmark into it with all the challenges of merging different cultures would have been possible albeit difficult in normal times, but became impossible after the collapse of Lehman Brothers and the subsequent Wall Street crash and recession. After those momentous events consumers traded down significantly, especially in the New York area, in a much deeper reaction than we had seen seven years earlier. I believe our strategy was sound as evidenced by the positive results we achieved from 2003 to 2007. In the food retail industry, with its thin margins, profitability is highly correlated with market presence and the augmented company had sufficient size and efficiency to succeed.

Update

The company performance deteriorated in the second half of 2008 mainly due to the impact of the Great Recession. The following year additional financing was obtained but operating performance still had not recovered so the new board of directors felt the need to bring in a different CEO, who was poorly chosen, and who left in the summer of 2010. The debt burden became unsustainable in the face of integration difficulties and poor operating results and in late 2010 A&P filed for bankruptcy. Eighteen months later, in early summer of 2012 new investors came in and the Tenglemann Group decided to leave the business for good. The group had been in the North American food retailing business for over 30 years and with all investments and dividend distributions over the period taken into account, had been able to exit with a positive annual return in the single digits over the period despite all the difficulties.

The first three rows of Table 15.1 provide a synthesis of the description above. The table incorporates two additional rows to include the major large system changes that occurred after Christian Haub left the chief executive role in 2007, as indicated in the last column of the table.

Discussion

The A&P case provides a rich example of the strategic foci as a mechanism for large-scale change. The case covers mostly the 10-year period between 1998 and 2007 when Christian Haub was CEO, when the company was undergoing significant change, and when the external environment was also undergoing transformation. What follows are meaningful references to each strategic focus from the case description above.

Corporate evaluation: Starting with corporate evaluation the original employee surveys were being evaluated on an annual basis in terms of core values. Haub had established a link between the employee engagement score and the amount of sales and profit growth. A&P established a strong correlation between employee engagement and individual store performance. This was based on lower shrinkage, lower accident costs, higher store profitability, and higher customer satisfaction which correlated with higher transaction sizes. The new information system helped in data analysis giving confidence regarding the chosen two-pronged strategy in the Northeast. Positive results from 2003 to 2007 corroborated this optimism.

Corporate choice and implementation: By the end of 2002, A&P was implementing the information system and was about 90 per cent finished. The functionality

TABLE 15.1 Rounds of intentional large-scale change at A&P

Round	Main objective (intentionality)	Main events	Begin	Emphasis	Haub
1	Participative and customer-driven	Culture change	1998	Internal	CEO
2	Integration and accountability	IT development	2000	Internal	CEO
3	Geographic concentration	Divestment	2003	External	CEO
4	Integrate Pathmark for middle market	Acquisition	2007	Ext/Int	*Exec Chair*
5	Reaction to effects of great recession	Bankruptcy	2010	External	*Non-Exec Chair*

of the system was being measured and benefits, both soft and hard, were being detailed as the system started up. A&P was able to reduce working capital, to reduce inventory throughout the system, and to speed up delivery from warehousing to stores, and out-of-stocks were decreasing. Haub stated:

> We interviewed the users after systems were implemented to find out how well the implementation worked. Were they trained appropriately? Did they understand how the system worked? Did they understand how they were supposed to use the system? With the feedback we identified training needs. We were also tracking the use of the system and how many category managers were using the new category management tools, how many reports were being created and things like that.

The importance of geographic focus became evident as the information system provided the ability to respond quickly to customer need shifts. As a result, Haub made a geographic market choice to focus on the Northeast, which led to the divestiture of A&P-owned retail chains in other regions. After examining several potential acquisitions the choice was made to acquire a middle-market chain, Pathmark to capture all potential consumer market segments.

Corporate Analysis: A&P was doing analysis with the help of the new system; it was now equipped to better analyse a changing environment. This analysis was different from that of previous years in that it was now also examining the external environment, the customer's world. Customer surveys were employed in the analysis and this was compared to other survey results. As a result of this improved system and consequent analytical capability better strategic decisions were made, including the choice of serving value-conscious and up-scale consumers in a concentrated geographical area, the Northeast.

Corporate words and driving forces: A&P successfully introduced a new driving force in the discount concept called 'Food Basics'. Haub stated:

> I see the driving force critical in our ability to turn around our US business as it did in Canada. In Canada, the dual concept continues to be a major driving force. And again we structured correctly around price and availability, meaning location. The other driving force that I still see in our conventional business is everything that has to do with fresh food products. I see fresh food as being the biggest product-driven differentiator for supermarkets against all other forms of retail. People come into the stores because they always find fresh fruits and vegetables, meats and cheeses and other fresh specialities.

Corporate picture. Who was A&P? What was A&P becoming? Haub's response in 2003 summarizes the corporate picture then:

> A&P was the industry pioneer of the concept of supermarket retailing, food retailing. We are the oldest food retail company and probably the most

well-known. We are the company with the most heritage – over 150 years in business. Today, A&P has lost some of the historic image. Some would say that it's an image that has gathered a lot of dust and rust and doesn't know what it wants to be. I think this is due to two reasons: size and presence. Clearly, before we had nation-wide presence, now we are regional and only a part of the system carries the A&P name. What we want to be at our core is customer-sensitive, in terms of our strategic model, customer intimacy. In today's perspective, I see that as very difficult to achieve because of the inability to measure it, and the investment necessary. In this concept there is the highest potential pay-off and the highest margin business that can be developed, but it's also very expensive to run. It takes a lot of risk to get there. And it may not be what the customer wants. Based on where we were in the late 1990s, it was probably correct, whereas today consumers are shifting to expecting the delivery of a minimum set of expectations at value: consumers want cost savings in the form of lower prices. A key driver of success will be market share because this will drive the ability to leverage cost, to leverage infrastructure, and to capture attention by offering savings to the customer. That is where the Great A&P had its notoriety. It had that kind of presence. We are seeing market share not by doing it with one concept, but by saying that there is the opportunity to capture more market share or maximize market share through multiple concepts that are complementary. It looks as though we were able to achieve that in our Canadian business with the combination of full service, fresh focused supermarkets, and low price limited-assortment-driven discount formats. And this is still going to be a business driven by how low the cost structure can be maintained.

Reflection on the change process

In Chapter 7 large-scale change in organizations was discussed with emphasis on the sequence of phases faced by different individuals and levels within the organization. When change is introduced by the leader, the subordinates going through it are one step behind, and their subordinates are one step behind them. The initial phase is denial. When most people first look at new situations they are in denial over the change required. By the time they become believers and start to move towards change, subordinates are one step behind. The second phase at the individual level is dodging, the third phase is doing, and the fourth phase is sustaining.

Change moved from Haub to the divisional level and then to the store level. The case illustrates that at A&P, when Haub was already 'doing', and at the initial stages, his managers below the senior management group were 'dodging', the store managers, one level below them, were still in denial.

TABLE 15.2 Phases and levels of change at A&P through three rounds of intentional large-scale organizational change (2000–2007)

P	Round 1 Becoming a customer-centric and more participative organization — Actions and events	P	Round 2 Accountability, the new information technology system and division integration — Actions and events	P	Round 3 Strategic repositioning: geographic focus in Northeast and two-pronged strategy — Actions and events
0	Through 1995, A&P acquired retail chains, but not as successful in integrating them into the A&P concept. Profitability slipped and Wood later retired as CEO.				
1	Christian Haub moved into the CEO role, realized the prior culture of command-and-control was not participative and did not lead to a customer-focused company.				
2	Haub took his agenda for cultural change towards participation and customer focus to the senior management group and initiated analysis. They denied and dodged.				
3	The new senior management group started work on remaking the culture, i.e. the corporate picture. Presentations to division, district and store managers.	0	Haub starts becoming aware of impediments to cross-divisional cooperation and of a pervasive lack of accountability – institutes performance reviews.		
4	Surveys indicate associate morale improves – culture becoming participative, and store level becoming responsive to customer.	1	Haub convinced that the installed information systems were weak and therefore a roadblock as store and product information not readily available.		
5	Despite accountability backlash participative culture begins to take hold – post-9/11 morale suffers but still high, customer focus also suffers.	2	Accountability-increasing efforts are met with distrust and distress by employees as perceived to be incompatible with culture – decision is made to overhaul IT system.	0	Questions asked about non-profitable stores and changing customer needs in US – 9/11 led to increased price sensitivity and competitive rivalries increasing.
6	Participative culture permeates organization despite 2001 and 2002 poor results.	3	Difficulties to develop IT system; CIO is replaced; reduce IT technical specifications; integration across divisions still very low.	1	The dual concept seeing success in Canada. Would it work in the US? Examining dual concept in US.

Round 1 Becoming a customer-centric and more participative organization		Round 2 Accountability, the new information technology system and division integration		Round 3 Strategic repositioning: geographic focus in Northeast and two-pronged strategy	
7	Culture participative and customer focus improved but not as high as desired.	4	The MIS nears completion, but modified from original: 90 per cent of cost and 60 per cent of features.	2	Sale of Eight O'Clock Coffee – decision to concentrate on food retail.
		5	IS provides better data and improves competitive knowledge and also facilitates internal data retrieval; Employees trained in its use.	3	Analysis of dual concept in US as it had worked well in Canada. Consider concentration in one geographical area – do analysis.
		6	Despite difficulties and challenges the MIS working.	4	Dual concept installed in major US markets. Developing a new concept for the NY market.
		7	MIS working.	5	Decide Northeast concentration; start divesting other areas.
				6	Seek middle market in Northeast, and remove unprofitable stores.
				7	Divested Canada, South, Detroit. Pathmark purchase. Haub leaves executive role.

Notes

Phase 0 – Ground zero: the need for change enters the organization

Phase 1 – Change awareness: the key individual denying and dodging

Phase 2 – Initiation: the key individual doing and the team denying and doing

Phase 3 – Maneuvring: the key individual, team doing and the interdepartmental group denying and dodging

Phase 4 – Integration: the key individual, team and interdepartmental group doing, organization denying dodging

Phase 5 – Achievement: the key individual sustaining, the team, interdepartmental group and organization doing

Phase 6 – Follow-through: the key individual, team sustaining, interdepartmental group and organization doing

Phase 7 – Sustaining: the key individual, team, interdepartmental group and organization sustaining

Applying levels

Table 15.2 illustrates how A&P moved through the phases and levels of change described in Chapter 7 in each of the three rounds of intentional large-scale strategic change. Each round of large-scale change is depicted in two columns for a total of three pairs. The first column in each pair represents the respective phase of change as presented in Chapter 7. The second column in each pair contains, for each phase, the description of the actions and events in the respective round. Notice that the phases of different rounds of large-scale strategic change are staggered. For example, when Haub is first considering the Round 3 change, change in each of the previous rounds is still respectively working through the organization. These temporal overlaps among different rounds of strategic change need to be recognized by the leader as the organization works through the process of change.

For each round, Haub began each change with himself (phases 0, 1 and 2, and Level I). In the beginning of each round, he worked at and succeeded in getting the individuals in the senior management group to change (phases 2 and 3). Through those individual changes, the senior management group changed (phase 2 and Level II) and began to work as a Level II team. This is followed in each round by moving into the division (or interdepartmental group) level. Haub was then addressing Level III issues (phases 3 and 4). There is a considerable difference in the amount of energy needed to change Level III as contrasted with Level I. All of the change, up to this point, was inward looking. At least two years into the change programme, Haub was still internally focused. It took an external examination on the competition's actions to move to the next level – Level IV of the organization.

The interlevel dynamics of large system change and strategy provide useful lenses for understanding and leading change in large organizations.

16

CONCLUSIONS

Throughout this book we have invited you to engage in what we have called *reflexive engagement,* by which we mean that you reflect on your own organizational situation in light of the concepts and case situations presented and see how they inform your own assessment of what is going on in your organizational setting and what action you might plan to take or have taken. We have invited you, whether you are a senior manager, a non-executive organizational member, an external OD consultant, or a student, not only to understand the concepts developed in this book, but also to engage in reflexive engagement by inquiring into what is going on around you, both inside and outside the organization, by drawing on concepts which will help you make sense of your experience, and then by engaging in action, evaluating outcomes, reflecting on learning, and developing knowledge.

We constructed reflexive engagement around Revans' learning formula, $L=P+Q$ (Revans, 2011). As we described, L stands for the learning that has occurred for you as you subject the programmed knowledge contained in these theories and frameworks on behaviour, change and strategy (P) to critical questioning insight (Q) in the light of your experience, especially those *problems* for which no single solution can possibly exist and for which there are likely to be many opinions as to what the preferred course of action might be.

Human knowing involves four activities (Coghlan, 2012). First you attend to your experience, both what is going on outside of yourself, i.e. in the organization or in the team and what is going on inside yourself, i.e. your feelings, memories and thoughts. In the context of being a manager, a non-executive organizational member, an OD consultant or a student you experience events in the organization and you experience yourself having thoughts and feelings about these events and about your thoughts about having these thoughts. Second, you ask questions about your experience. What is going on? What are you feeling? How is it that you are angry? You may receive an insight (understanding) and you follow that up by reflecting and weighing up the evidence to determine whether your insight fits the evidence or not (judgement). Third, you judge that you know, or don't know or need more time or evidence to decide. Judgements may be definite or provisional.

Human knowing is not any of these three operations on their own. All knowing involves experiencing, understanding and judging. The pattern of these three operations is invariant in that it applies to all settings of cognitional activity, whether solving a crossword clue, addressing an everyday problem or engaging in scientific research. Furthermore, being careless about these operations has consequences. If you're careless about being attentive then your understanding is flawed. If you're careless about your understanding then your judgements are untrustworthy. You can gain insight into these negative manifestations of knowing by the same threefold process of knowing: experience, understanding and judgement.

Fourth, you are not merely a knower. You also make decisions and take action. Deciding to take action is based on making a judgement of value, i.e. a judgement that something is good or worthwhile. So you may ask questions, like 'What will I do'? 'Is it worth my while?' The process of judging value and deciding is a similar process to that of knowing. You may reflect on the possible value judgements as to what is the best option and you may decide to follow through the best value judgement and you may take responsibility for consistency between your knowing and your doing.

The operations of experience, understanding, judgement and decision/action are the basis for a general empirical method, which requires you to:

- *Be attentive* to data.
- *Be intelligent* about possible explanations of that data.
- *Be reasonable* in preferring as probable or certain the explanations which provide the best account for the data.
- *Be responsible* for what you do.

The general empirical method is not grounded in a grand theory, but in the recognizable and verifiable activities of human inquiry and action.

Adopting $L=P+Q$ as the basis for reflexive engagement where you inquire critically into the operations of your organization and of your own mind may be understood as taking a 'clinical perspective' (Schein, 1987). As we have discussed and illustrated throughout the book, the clinical approach involves focusing on organizational dysfunctions and questioning problems and anomalies that are difficult to explain as to how they inhibit the organization from functioning effectively. This clinical approach gives sharpness to the learning formula, $L=P+Q$, as it refines the questioning when confronting problems, and engages that questioning with knowledge of organizational behaviour, change and strategy so as to generate your learning. As we have demonstrated, cycles of inquiry can operate at different levels of depth. A single inquiry loop looks back at actions, a double inquiry loop at goals and strategies and a triple inquiry loop at ultimate purposes and identity.

A further perspective that we have drawn on in this book is that reflexive engagement involves three practices: engaging in self-learning (first person), working collaboratively with others (second person), and being able to generalize one's learning for an impersonal audience (third person). Reflexive engagement helps you to explore your thinking, to enhance your capacity to plan and develop strategies that echo your aspirations, to reflect on the skills of your implementation, and to judge the impact of your actions.

We reminded you that organizations comprise these four levels of analysis and that as a manager, as an organizational member or as an OD consultant you are constantly working with each of these levels, making them work more effectively. This involves being able to see which one might be having difficulty at any given time, knowing how to intervene to deal with the relevant issue and being skilled at a range of interventions and styles. But experience tells us not only that these levels are discrete and separate but also that what happens at one level has an impact at each of the others. The four levels are interdependent and inter-related. Each level is systemically linked to each of the others and events at one level are both cause and effect of events at other levels. Reflexive engagement challenges you to apply the formula $L=P+Q$ to the challenges of each of the levels and to how they work together.

We considered the topics of organizational learning and change, and explored the different orders of how organizations can learn and change. The process of learning and change in a large system is full of interlevel dynamics in that large-scale organizational learning and change comprise individual, team and inter-departmental group change respectively and that how change is introduced and implemented through the system is a complex movement from individual to team, team to team in the interdepartmental group and ultimately to the organization's external stakeholders over time in iterations where the movements are circular with each iteration being a cause and effect of another. Again, reflexive engagement enables you to apply the formula, $L=P+Q$ to the challenges of how your organization learns, what its learning disabilities might be and how learning is enabled or impeded across the levels. Similarly, bringing $L=P+Q$ to how change is introduced and implemented across the levels provides insights and learning not only to how change works in your organization but first- and second-person learning about leading change.

We explored the processes by which managers, organizational members and OD consultants create a picture of who the organization is, how it is represented in that picture, how it analyses the external and internal environments, how it chooses and implements actions and how it evaluates outcomes. We presented these processes not as linear steps but as cyclical and systemic strategic actions, which involve iterations of individual and team actions and action between teams and with customers.

By means of vignettes and cases, we have provided examples of organizations that have worked through strategy, learning and change processes so that you can study them and notice how interlevel dynamics shape the process of change. We have also provided the reflexive engagement activities to challenge you to engage in reflection and discussion on understanding an organization with which you are familiar, so that you can take more informed action. We recommended that you not do this on your own nor keep your reflections private, but that you engage others in conversations of shared reflections.

In our global economy where change is frequently discontinuous there is a high demand for learning and change through strategic processes. In this book we have explored how strategy, learning and change occur through interlevel dynamics. In our experience, interlevel dynamics are integral to processes of strategy and large-scale organizational learning and change. We adopted a reflexive engagement approach with a view to enabling readers, whether managers, non-executive organizational members or OD consultants to work with and across levels in order to help organizations of any sector to learn and change effectively and successfully.

References

Coghlan, D. (2012) Understanding insight in the context of Q. *Action Learning: Research and Practice*, 9(3), 247–258.

Revans, R. (2011) *ABC of Action Learning*. Farnham: Gower.

Schein, E.H. (1987) *The Clinical Perspective in Fieldwork*. Thousand Oaks, CA: Sage.

INDEX